Rethinking Strategy for Creative Industries

Creative industry practices are increasingly manifested through hybrid models and methods and emerging sub-sectors. With ever finer dividing lines between form and content, product and service, participation and consumption, the distinctions between sectors are increasingly blurred, while new, convergent models emerge.

Reflecting this fluid context, this book provides a new perspective on strategy in the creative industries. Based on extensive original research and live empirical data derived from case studies, interviews, and observations with creative managers, it reveals strategic decision-making by analysing business manoeuvres and stages of innovation in the creative industries. Through analysing the interactive features of aesthetically driven information assets, and how new user/consumer cultures are applied, it uncovers the principles that are transforming strategy in the creative industries.

This innovative volume will be of significant interest to scholars, advanced students and practitioners in the creative industries as well as industry consultants and practitioners.

Milan Todorovic is Senior Lecturer in Creative Industries at London Metropolitan University, UK, and Visiting Professor at SAE Milan, Italy.

With **Ali Bakir**, Principal Lecturer at Buckinghamshire New University, UK, and Visiting Professor at Novi Sad University, Serbia.

Routledge Research in Creative and Cultural Industries Management

Routledge Research in Creative and Cultural Industries Management provides a forum for the publication of original research in cultural and creative industries, from a management perspective. It reflects the multiple and interdisciplinary forms of cultural and creative industries and the expanding roles which they perform in an increasing number of countries.

As the discipline expands, there is a pressing need to disseminate academic research, and this series provides a platform to publish this research, setting the agenda of cultural and creative industries from a managerial perspective, as an academic discipline.

The aim is to chart developments in contemporary cultural and creative industries thinking around the world, with a view to shaping future agendas reflecting the expanding significance of the cultural and creative industries in a globalized world.

Published titles in this series include:

1 **Arts Governance**
People, Passion, Performance
Ruth Rentschler

2 **Building Better Arts Facilities**
Lessons from a U.S. National Study
Joanna Woronkowicz, D. Carroll Joynes and Norman M. Bradburn

3 **Arts and Commerce**
The Colonization of No Man's Land
Edited by Peter Zackariasson and Elena Raviola

4 **Artistic Interventions in Organizations**
Research, theory and practice
Edited by Ulla Johannson Sköldberg, Jill Woodilla and Ariane Berthoin Antal

5 **Rethinking Strategy for Creative Industries**
Innovation and interaction
Milan Todorovic with *Ali Bakir*

Rethinking Strategy for Creative Industries

Innovation and interaction

Milan Todorovic
***with* Ali Bakir**

Routledge
Taylor & Francis Group
LONDON AND NEW YORK

First published 2016
by Routledge
2 Park Square, Milton Park, Abingdon, Oxon OX14 4RN

and by Routledge
52 Vanderbilt Avenue, New York, NY 10017

First issued in paperback 2020

Routledge is an imprint of the Taylor and Francis Group, an informa business

British Library Cataloguing in Publication Data
A catalogue record for this book is available from the British Library

Library of Congress Cataloging in Publication Data
Todorovic, Milan.
Rethinking strategy for creative industries : innovation and interaction / Milan Todorovic with Ali Bakir.
pages cm. – (Routledge research in creative and cultural industries management)
Includes bibliographical references and index.
1. Cultural industries–Management. 2. Arts–Management. 3. Mass media–Management. 4. Strategic planning. I. Title.
HD9999.C9472T63 2016
658.4′012–dc23 2015031289

ISBN 13: 978-0-367-66847-1 (pbk)
ISBN 13: 978-0-415-73059-4 (hbk)
ISBN 13: 978-1-315-85016-0 (ebk)

Typeset in Bembo
by Wearset Ltd, Boldon, Tyne and Wear

Contents

Illustrations

Figures

Table

Preface

A statement of aims

This book presents a thorough investigation of strategy in the creative industries, based on live case studies, observations, participation, reflexive accounts, media as text and interactive resources, informal conversations, and numerous in-depth interviews. The work is based on an entirely novel approach and vast original research. The innovation in this approach is that it critically adopts a variety of schools of thought in a multiplicity of areas that converge to constitute the practice, methodology and theory relevant to the field of strategy in the creative industries. These paradigms are then explored as parts of a dynamic continuum: as specific cases within intricate and complex fields of practice.

This work examines the structural relationships in varied contexts of strategy for creative industries. It also analyses the broad variety of methods in creative strategy practice. This is done by exploring the multitude of underlying paradigms of creativity, creative industries and strategy. The ambition of this work is thus to define a coherent methodology for the formulation and implementation of practical and analytical methods in this complex field.

This innovative approach requires an overall methodology that facilitates the reconciling of theoretical strands and methods. This would enable readers to identify an appropriate analytical model for any given context. Contemporary creative industry practices are frequently manifested through hybrid models and methods applied in continually emerging sub-sectors, which can be represented as convoluted plains folding into the original concept from which they have grown.

This work explores multiple cases of innovation, business concepts and models using depth approaches: investigating each layer of strategy formation, formulation, application and implementation. Key components include interaction and conceptual roundedness within given, specific industry contexts. These contexts are explored through the expert knowledge of carefully selected respondents from an array of industries, sectors, sub-sectors and emergent niches. The purposive sampling of fieldwork respondents underlines the actual interactions between different sectors, professions and industries, viewpoints and experiences, resulting in models resembling causal loop diagrams or supply/value networks frequently used in emerging business modelling literature (and practice). The set of creative industries is seen as a totality, forming a complex unity of factors and units whose interests occasionally stand in contradictory positions. If the common, broadly encompassing term 'creative industry' ('creative economy', 'creative industries') can be seen as a justifiable phrase – and it is widely adopted on all levels ranging from national (e.g. the UK's Department for Culture, Media and Sport) to global (e.g. as used by the United Nations Educational, Scientific and Cultural Organization and the United Nations Conference on Trade and Development) – then this complexity seems justified: policy makers, lobbying and pressure bodies, and business strategists alike seem to adopt the term in spite of its potential ambiguity. The policies, standpoints and strategies they adopt, represent and utilize reflect the complex and sometimes conflicting nature of such encompassing terminology, so the terminology (more on this below) is not merely a semantic matter. Indeed, as any dependable semiotician would argue, signs and practices do stand in meaningful relationships and formulating things does correspond with real, particular, specific, accountable action.

This is particularly true of the industries that deal with the notion of abstract, experiential value, inherent in age-old creative forms such as music, art and literature, as much as the abstract and experiential value of emergent, hybrid forms including video games, social media or any further emergent mutations of those forms known at the present time. As will be seen, creative industries now encompass a variety of standpoints which include the most recent – yet at present most powerful – additions, rooted in information and communication technologies (ICT). These appear to be impacting on and governing the fate and function of all but a few sectors whose *natural, physical (in a scientific sense)* characteristics *(still?)* evade such influence (as will be debated throughout the book). Creative industries and sectors, and their historic developmental components (dubbed 'linear/traditional cultural industries/sectors'), coexist in unstable equilibrium in which their *overall goals* cohere, with specific ends frequently at odds.

This research text will not settle with currently dominant definitions of 'digital' media, as such terminology may shortly become redundant due to the transformative nature of technology: digital media will give rise to new models and concepts which cannot be named at present but will inevitably arise from the key features of digital technology.[1] Thus, a novel approach is promoted: one that addresses *interactivity and fragmentation*, as well as *data accuracy in principle*, beyond the scope of *any particular technology*. In order to attain meaningful results through sustainable and replicable methods and models, this research monograph explores the ontology of communications, especially in the context of storage, distribution and coding (the latter not confined to the computing term). This rests on the thorough analysis of interactive features of aesthetically driven information assets, thus investigating applied aspects of emergent user/consumer cultures, especially their commercialization (e.g. value capture).

Contemporary observers and practitioners alike witness the ever finer dividing of lines between form and content, coding and message, product and service, participation and consumption. Distinctions between recognized sectors become blurred thanks to qualitative leaps in new, convergent creative industry contexts. These processes, alongside increased interactivity, enable practitioners and analysts to quantify cultural value and thus commercialize it in novel ways.

This book informs strategic decision-making by analysing creative business manoeuvres and stages of innovation in specific practical contexts. This is done through fieldwork combined with fundamental methodological analysis based on an ontological re-evaluation of key concepts in creative industry strategy. Fieldwork was done by consulting the carefully selected practitioners interviewed over the period of nearly eight years to date (starting late 2007), participant observation and reflective practice (including in higher creative education).

All this is done to uncover the principles that govern emerging communications models, presently known as 'new', 'digital', 'interactive' media etc. This applies to multiple contexts, ranging from those dealing with inimitable physical artefacts and artistic performances to cases where entire business models are intangible, as is the case with interactive arts, games, entertainment platforms and others. Their transformative roles affect strategy across sectors and industries and are seen to impact on entire economic models beyond 'creativity'.

Background

At the opening of this section, it is worth noting that it is fundamentally difficult to identify a real competitor of this work. It is reasonable to claim that this book is unique: the scale, scope and depth of novel, fieldwork-supported analysis, specifically aimed at redefining and formulating strategies for the (cultural and) creative industries, cannot be found in any other works identifiable at present. There are many good and relevant works in the field of strategy, but significantly because of their generic nature they seldom apply to the scope of this study without substantial work on the part of the reader. Part of the claim for the significance of this work is that this monograph contributes to knowledge in the vital understanding of strategy within creative contexts as a unique case, and beyond the scope of existing treatises in related fields.

The equivalence of strategy and innovation and creativity draws to some extent on existing works but redefines the relationship between these key notions in new and systematic ways. First, this work examines what strategy *is not*, especially in creative industry contexts. Second, it integrates the divisive notions of contest, tension, 'battle', ploy, manoeuvre, with strategic innovation and by extension, strategic creativity. Third, it does not take for granted the readings that digital/interactive technology, or models preceding it, based on copying, reproduction and reach *represent progress and innovation inherently*. (Analogue, 'ancient/antiquated' or biologically-driven, anthropomorphic forms appear most resistant to those concepts broadly reported to be undermining the notions of authenticity, authorship, creativity and economically sustainable value creation/capture models.) Fourth, this work removes terminological inaccuracies and misleading distinctions such as those between 'digital' and 'physical', or 'positivistic' and 'interpretive' – and all the strategic and analytical misconceptions these breed. (What appears to be a minor point in nuances of definition may have substantial consequences in how innovative, creative and strategic processes occur, including those of sense-making leading to decisions of long-term impact). Fifth, it understands that 'utilitarian' and 'values-based' means are specific notions of a more general set of principles, manifestations of a broad continuum of strategy in creative contexts, arguing that in strategy, *values become utilitarian*, and conversely, *utility devoid of values remains ineffective beyond temporary gains*, on the level of 'ploy' in creative contexts. (Interestingly, most of the conceptualizations suggested here are made transparent through the agency of digital/interactive media, ICT tools and evidence-based analytics they have delivered over the recent past.)

Judging, contextualizing, understanding and accurately framing the value of contemporary events, developments and processes is notoriously difficult.[2] In the history of 'now' – without recourse to any specific mindset, theory, paradigm or viewpoint – it is very difficult to stay relevant, unbiased or even accurate in mapping out the present, let alone making sense in the future, to the future or of the future. Having 'consumed' a mere 15 per cent of the current, 'new' century any of us who analyse, make sense of or predict the already overused term 'twenty-first century' in its grand and promising sense as the 'new era' need to stay cautious and methodologically sound in the best tradition of construct validity. Otherwise our thoughts, ideas and concepts will age and lose relevance more rapidly than we dare think and will look as dated, fanciful, even ridiculous as a fashion cast aside by a new overwhelming trend or any of the futurisms of the past which litter the many grand promises of multiple twentieth-century discourses that gave and assigned themselves the conceited role of the one real truth.

A validity test long adopted in science and technology is to look at the past, interpolate it to the present and extrapolate it into a future – yet even this may be proven very inaccurate, as the predictions and expectations of linear development are already proving wrong: the unexpected and truly novel developments transform things in big leaps just as the internet has already done and continues to do. Contemporary discourses of media and creativity are packed with promise that may not only fail to materialize but simply prove entirely inaccurate, a mere reflection of the present from which we as contemporary participant observers may not be able to extract any lasting value or meaningful significance that would influence future events, practices or methods. Thus, to use the crude linear comparison which was already seen as possibly flawed: the technologies, creativity and business solutions of this current stage of this current century may be as disconnected and accidental to its actualization as were the full variety of early aircraft contrasted with contemporary, standardized air travel.[3]

Such caution, however, should not stop us from postulating, suggesting and promoting a set of new, emerging and relevant developments that may lead to major leaps and improvements in any area covered by science, technology, communications, culture or art within the broad scope of what is termed 'business strategy', provided of course that we can justify the very use of the term 'progress' in any of the above contexts. To protect our reasoning, ideas, interpretations and case studies from rapid ageing and fundamental loss of relevance we need to turn to trustworthy methodologies of thought that have aided our predecessors. In a minimalist way, looking at the very foundations of things to analyse will enable us to connect matters at the core or to identify where such deep connections actually exist beneath and beyond the manifest variety of contemporary phenomena.

Therefore, in this book, the turn to a philosophical tradition, to the critique of metaphysics of reason and to transformative principles beyond the known scientific, social-scientific, aesthetic and ethical discourses is not done whimsically or pompously. Without such a move towards the deepest identifiable levels of thinking, we cannot create a sound methodology that will enable us to stay current and relevant in our thoughts in a short time-span of only a decade, in the face of the enormity of innovation and fragmentation of innovation in business, technology and their constituent social forces. Any attempt to do so without a deep rethink of what the fundament of the matter is would be confined to a historical snapshot of a quasi-futuristic discourse or an account of what may have been but was not, just as ideas and patents whose irrelevance superseded their implementation before competing concepts even developed litter the shelves of historical repositories. Without doubt, this book is a project as ambitious as is the underlying work and its professed aims. To explore each and every area of what are termed 'creative industries' would be a project worth encyclopaedic scope and label, yet due to the currency, rapidity and fragmentary nature of change it would never be up to date, and work to improve the sheer list of things that matter would never be complete.

It is therefore necessary to adopt a global perspective, one which aims to identify the causes that make something 'matter', to separate ongoing quantitative transformation from major qualitative change and to encompass all the relevant methods that may be termed 'creative industry strategy' across the changing sets of meaning representing 'industry', 'creativity' and 'strategy' in their individual and combined sense alike. The approach must be global also, because we cannot be complacent and expect innovation to happen where it 'always' did – just as we cannot afford to state that it would happen the way it 'always' did. There is 'always' or 'everywhere' with innovation.

A note on terminology

This book examines a set of complex relationships between different technologies, industries, discourses, aesthetic traditions and varied scientific, philosophical and ideological paradigms. These and other aspects form and determine the conditions, principles and models that apply to the subject matter. As a result, the terminology used in this book has to reflect and match such complexity. Therefore, this book will utilize a variety of terminological elements including those of cultural studies/social sciences (e.g. 'discourse'; 'identity'), natural sciences (e.g. 'thermodynamics'; 'inverse population'), ICT (e.g. 'meta-tools'; 'cliodynamics'), the arts (e.g. 'abstraction'; 'composition') and philosophy (e.g. 'ontology'; 'transcendental illusion'; 'social contract') alongside the established and emerging terminology of business, especially in strategy, marketing and business modelling.

The use of such hybrid, multiple paradigm terminology is necessary: it is dictated by the complexity of the subject and the intention of the author to represent and anticipate new developments for which no agreed phrasing is as yet adopted. This practice is not unusual in current treatises on areas such as business innovation. One example is the use by Graham *et al.* (2004) of the term 'virtual navigators', which encompasses a variety of digital network services from content aggregators and distributors, search engines and applications, software and hardware structures and emergent businesses behind all of the above – which 'navigate' emergent supply networks in ICT.

Respondent acknowledgements

This work consists of over 20 interviews, many hours of participant observation, numerous guest talks by industry leaders, and empirical work in creative education between 2007 and 2015. My special thanks go to interviewees and respondents from various countries and continents (most based in the UK).

List of respondents in alphabetical order, by surname[4]

Assa Ashuach, Assa Ashuach Studio, London
Aaron Bogucki, Vice President of Digital Marketing, Republic Records, Universal Music Group, New York (during fieldwork: Head of Digital, Polydor Records Ltd., London)
Tom Cardew, artist, London
Scott Cohen, co-founder and Vice President International, The Orchard
Sabine Funk, GreenEvents Europe/Sounds for Nature Foundation (during fieldwork: co-founder and Managing Director of Rheinkultur), Bonn
Montse Gallego, owner, Hundred Years Gallery, London
Tinko Georgiev, consultant, Aeye, Whiia, London
Adam Goodyer, CEO and co-founder, Concert Live, London
Peter Jones, artist, London
Dušan Kovačević, co-founder and Strategic Director, Exit Festival, Novi Sad
Cynthia Legrand, Manager, Pantone Hotel, Brussels
Jonathan Moberly, co-owner, Foundry (during fieldwork), London
Stephen O'Reilly, Global Head of Music, Gramofon Music, London
Chris Price, New Slang Media, London

Diego Serrano, founder and Chief Executive Officer, SerranoBrothers and BROOMX, Barcelona
Carl Schoenfeld, Director, Schoenfeld Films Ltd., Wallingford
Jessie Scoullar, Director, Wicksteed Works, London
Angelica Vleeming, Content and Communications Manager, Citizen M Hotel, Amsterdam

Notes

1 Many examples from the past support this approach. Moreover, careful examination of scientific and technological innovation in both neighbouring and seemingly unrelated areas seems to support the idea that radically new models emerge – e.g. mental imaging and reproduction of imagery from the actual memory of human subjects may well subvert and revolutionize any contemporary notion of 'digital' and 'media', with considerable privacy and ethical implications.
2 Reflections on the meaning of historical events, on their correlation with popular culture and social movements, and on the ideology and management of change have been addressed before in myriad contexts; what applies to counterculture should also apply to innovation (Todorovic 1999; 2003; 2008).
3 Similarly, the singular and rather misdirected stylistic brand of 'Futurism' in visual arts, as contrasted with the actual unfolding of events or innovation (not least due to its sinister bias and ideological twist).
4 Participant observation with field interviews: Propeller Island Hotel, Berlin; Michel Berger Hotel, Berlin; Be Manos Hotel, Brussels; Manhattan Hotel, Rotterdam; Aldemar Knossos Royal Hotel, Hersonissos, Crete; Birdsong Steel Pan Orchestra, Port-of-Spain, Trinidad. Keynote addresses and special guest lectures: Visiting Professors Scott Cohen and Erik Nielsen, London Guildhall Faculty of Business and Law/London Metropolitan University (Cohen and Nielsen 2015).

Introduction

The ontological discussion

This work draws from multiple perspectives and paradigms to reflect the complexity of current practices, processes and approaches forming creative industry strategy. The ontology of creative industry is the main thread of convergence connecting all these components of practice and analysis. Such ontology can be identified on the global, principal level of what 'creative industry' means in present practice and discourse. Connected to that is the analysis of what 'strategy' is taken to mean chiefly in connection to the professed paradigm shift brought about by information and communication technologies (ICT) and their impact on all aspects of production, communication and consumption across the creative media. Their actual and formal involvement in the formation of creative industries in the early twenty-first century should not obscure the fact that their origin is in science, from which stems all technological and business innovation that subverts the 'traditional' (twentieth-century) order of production, distribution and consumption in traditional cultural and emergent creative sectors. Moreover, the challenges posed and opportunities presented by ICT go into a deeper, ontological level of cultural and creative industries; the level of what something *is* is affected by some important practical and conceptual processes. For instance, intellectual property (IP) and authorship (consequently, authenticity and originality) are questioned by the deeply pervasive nature of ICT. The very definition of a work is changing and with it the formulation of its intrinsic value and the consequent understanding, analysis, exploitation and use of a work.

On the other hand, the new convergent forms such as games and social media add a sense of intrinsic value because they connect the substructure and superstructure in new ways. The intrinsic value of communications and of the distribution of content use is of a sub-structural nature, as it depends entirely on ICT. On the level of new types of work, intrinsic value is formulated through the structures of meaning that users award it in hybrid products and services (e.g. games, social media), much as as broadcast audiences and consumer subcultures used to formulate intrinsic value of cultural products by interpreting and reinterpreting cultural industry texts of the past. A substructure of linear production, mass dissemination and mass distribution of works forming the larger cultural industry text underpinned such 'traditional' cultural industry works, products and texts (e.g. television series, media brands). An older, linear type of convergence exists in forms defined in the twentieth century (e.g. film). Similarly, it is possible to identify elements of superstructure in interactively convergent and hybrid forms emerging through the substructure of ICT (processing power, speed, reach, richness, integration, interaction etc.). The convergent media and dissemination tools of the early twenty-first century are even more integrated into the production–consumption circuit than those that characterized mass production and mass communications of the twentieth century. Therefore, the first ontological thread is the one of ongoing converging transformations of culture and creativity, on deep and principal levels, through the introduction and implementation of fundamentally new rules of production, dissemination and use of culture and creativity. Such transformations affect the meaning of cultural/creative works and assets; with it, the perceived value and modes of use. These in turn affect commercialization and economic sustainability of cultural/creative works and assets.

Every form of culture production is being affected by ICT in its own unique way. This is the second aspect of analysis on the level of ontology: individual ontology of each industry, sector or experimental niche. This ontology can be explored from the general to the level of minutiae, industry by industry, especially where important nodes of production and use are connected through new means of distribution, communication and interactive (re)search. These examples are found in non-linear television narrative production and distribution (Netflix), music (Spotify), design services/practice (Assa Asshuach Studio, Serrano Brothers), fashion branding (Burberry), etc.

The impact of ontology on industry levels needs to be explored before further analysis. This is to justify the use of such a term and such an in-depth approach, examining the philosophical level of an industry and its strategy. If a strategy is understood to be a set of means matching particular ends, then these means include the interconnections between the technology that underpins creative industries and the contexts of meaning and use facilitated by such technology. The ontological level, what something *is*, is reflected in creative industry strategies in the following manner. The nature of a product or service is intrinsically connected to the practices, processes and means in production, communication dissemination and research, just as it is connected to the way in which it is being perceived and evaluated by users, audiences and consumers. Therefore, the impact of ICT, which among other things means continual transformative fragmentation of markets, services, products and tools, has its equivalent in the transformation of business practices, which need to correspond with such fragmentation imposed by technology. This fragmentary structuring will be seen to privilege large ICT organizations as well as the small, adaptive businesses based on innovation.

The *use of ontology* is the precursor to understanding the origin of knowledge and consequent applications of meaning through research and practice (epistemology and teleology). This is of importance because the notion of strategy as *matching means to ends* involves developing a systematic methodology for decision-making and its constituent application.

A note on Immanuel Kant

The work of Immanuel Kant was used for the proto-methodology for this book. This was done after careful consideration of the problem at hand. Preceding by centuries the discovery of genetics, quantum mechanics, psychoanalysis – to name but a few fundamental innovations – Kant explored the necessary thought processes required for such deep paradigm shifts. As evidenced by many innovations in all fields of knowledge, the latest being in ICT, thought processes not only reveal the nature of things, they influence them, not least through technology and its application in the 'real world'.

The concept of *synthetic a priori* was of particular interest to Kant. If something is outside of experience, how can it exist? If something does not yet exist, how can it be imagined? If something is not *a given*, a self-evident fact, how can it be formulated through thought processes alone? Common sense shows that this can be done, but methodology is not about common sense. Kant's mastery was in the ability to identify *the how, the method of critical thought* that would enable us to understand why key features of imagination can work with logic to create things that lie beyond experience, things that do not (yet) exist (other implications of this work lie far beyond a pragmatic text such as this). The human ability to innovate, evidenced frequently in the context of contemporary shifts from analogue to digital paradigms, is at the heart of applied arguments of Kant's seminal work. Imagining a set of principles such as the logical commands of software which can then turn into physical reality is *synthetic a priori in action.*

Finally, the notion of transcendental illusion, closely related to the above, may aid in the understanding of the following puzzles. If all forms of art and business tend to work together in discrete areas, forming highly varied and distinctive results, does that mean that a manager or an artist needs to re-learn management or artistic skills each time they embark on a different type of work? Does the fact that knowledge is fragmented mean that reality does not exist as a continuum? Our senses and methods of observation and measurement say 'No'. Therefore, it is logical to presume that there is a set of deeper principles, not yet understood, that allow fundamental notions (e.g. 'strategy' or 'art') to take manifold forms. It is the inability to see the totality that is therefore illusory, not the totality itself.

Literature review and meta-methods

As will be seen, strategy discourse is fragmented and somewhat contradictory, due to the variety of competing perspectives, modes of analysis and approaches. As a meta-tool, a broad interpretive methodology is adopted. Without much need to go into Kantian elaborations at such a stage, the chapter that covers varied strategy discourses utilizes a 'fusion of horizons' which may help suspend the tension between fragmented discourses. Such distinctions are often paradigmatic, for instance qualitative vs. quantitative, interpretive/critical vs. positivistic/prescriptive, or socially engaged vs. pragmatic. The guiding ontology in this book is the one posited by the notion of transcendental illusion, namely that all such manifest differences belong to the same continuum, which is imperceptible from a single, isolated viewpoint. The logic of construing what does not yet exist, or is not known to exist (Kant and Meiklejohn 2007), or is not yet understood, transcends the notion of the empirical and the positivistic and involves ideas and their formulation through the uncertainty of outcome due to the numbers of negotiations involved and the synthetic *a priori* nature of innovation. The importance of this approach is also related to the importance of innovation in contemporary creative industries that are influenced by ICT (i.e. most of them) and the understanding of business as a creative phenomenon. The equivalence between creativity and strategy is then explored in dialectic terms and scrutinized in practical detail within the context of paradigm shift from linear to interactive technologies. The depth of the problem requires appropriate levels of analysis and the fieldwork reveals the links between ontology, epistemology and teleology of creative industry practice, allowing for the mechanisms of that shift.

This is reflected in the methodology behind this longitudinal research project. Fieldwork data collection and analysis are approached on all levels, from the ontological to the pragmatic. Each respondent was carefully selected on the basis of industry position and viewpoint. The purposive selection of data and viewpoints reflected the mapping out of industry nodes, interactions, forms, sector and connections, especially in the current context of paradigm change (changes in theory, method and practice).

Questions asked ranged from highly specific (yet generic) to highly abstract. This allowed respondents to volunteer ideas, concepts and interpretations alongside examples, while negotiating and examining the terminology used by the author. The importance of such negotiations of terminology goes far beyond semantics or semiotics, as will be seen. Definition and practice are examined in dialectic terms and with practical impact in mind. The focus on what something 'is' – an industry, a method used, a production paradigm etc. – enabled in-depth conceptual discussions that revealed thought processes in decision-making alongside specific examples and in-depth analyses of actual strategies. Therefore, through the approach postulated on the ontology of the paradigm shift within a creative industry, the data collected ranged from highly abstract, to cognitive and process-related, to evidential, descriptive or reflective. Therefore, the immersive approach to conceptualization and methodology ranges from ontological creative strategy concepts to concrete examples in ways that reflect levels of thought and application in creative industry strategy practice. The links between ontology (what strategy 'is', what a creative industry 'is') and practice are thus examined from inception to implementation, interaction and innovation.

An advanced reflexive analysis involves mapping out a 'value [network[1]] of meaning', distributed across key nodes in the networks consisting of sub-sectors, sectors and industries, and defined by convergent means of production, dissemination communication and research. This is based on a purposive sample of opinions, accounts and discourses covering many of the key areas of culturally or creatively-driven sectors, including music, media, film, the arts, leisure, events, ICT, branding, design and architecture. Such a reflexive approach to data collection and analysis covers the multitude of standpoints and practitioner approaches to the ontological, epistemological, teleological and concrete levels of analysis and application.

Creative industry, multiple industries or creative/ cultural sectors

Form is content in the ontology of creative works.

The importance of definition surpasses cultural or strategic discourses. It is directly related to practice. The agency of discourse in the case of policy makers, industry bodies, critical analyses or public interest discussions shows how a form of discourse represents and reinforces the relations of power involved in the formulation of policies, strategies and models of exchange. The formulation of creative industries as those that include ICT both responds to actual need for reformulation and influences the current outcomes and future strategies affected by such reformulation. As an agent of discourse, any organization, group or individual making an impact on important formulations makes an impact that can be felt far beyond definition. A definition in creative and cultural contexts goes beyond the analysis, for in those contexts definition influences the outcome, be it in production, aesthetics, ethics, research, design, policy or market regulation. The ontology of 'culture and creativity are connected' leads to policies that group linear with interactive media, hardware developers with dance studios. Therefore, identifying the matters that connect such a disparate field of practice requires in-depth analysis of deep connections and possible contradictions between such groupings of practical specialism. Approaching them on the ontological level and then developing a more concrete structuring of how they function in relation to what is the essence of their being was the most logical way of constructing the analysis in this book. The context of paradigm shift was self-evident in most cases and its inclusion was dictated by key current issues.

The central question of reformulating creative industry strategies in the ongoing processes of large-scale paradigm change is the problem of the work. A cultural or creative work, from which numerous value propositions may be construed, is being rapidly redefined through the disruptive innovation of ICT (e.g. in the work of Christensen *et al.*). This conceptual problem of responding to the paradigm shift brought about by fundamental technological disruption is similar to but more fundamental in nature than the critically termed disappearance of the 'authority' of the object through loss of 'authenticity' (Benjamin 2008). With the development of media and cultural industries, the means of copying and reproduction depended on tactics of push-supply (Markides 2006), which were successfully controlled by integrated value chains (Graham *et al.* 2004) and made comparatively piracy-resilient through control of supply. Such control of supply was justified (see Chapter 2) through the means of the material value of the product or service – its richness compared to pirate copies – and further enhanced through established methods of push-supply media promotion, frequently the result of corporate integration in the entertainment industries.

However, the control of supply was fundamentally transformed and subverted by ICT innovation, and responses of traditional, linear cultural industries were seldom proactive. The arts and public service media followed different trajectories, which were more regulated and less centralized (as further evidenced through fieldwork). However, for different reasons and somewhat indirect causes, the arts and public media are being affected by the paradigm shift brought about by ICT and digitization.

Therefore, a necessary rethink of the ontology of creative work occurs in the context where 'creative' sectors subsume 'cultural' sectors, in new definitions that match practice and influence policy. This context includes the permeating transformation brought about by ICT, which poses a challenge to creative work itself on a level deeper than authenticity. The ontological questions posed in the environment of interactive media white noise are 'Is there a work?' and 'What is the work?'. The consequential query that can be posed is, 'if the work is, what is it?' The 'is it – what is it' question is a dual one: if a work is identifiable and discernible within the unprecedented semi-chaotic movement of masses of information, then a form of value and a form of materiality can be established concerning the work.

It is scientifically inaccurate to make binary distinctions between digital and physical. *Digital is physical (in physics!)*, and the clearer that equivalence, the more effective is the analysis of methods of creating and capturing value through the challenging environment of transforming creative industries. The conditional character of the work based on the knowledge of its existence within the incessant flow of information questions the existence of the work if it is not known or knowable, obscured by the 'white noise' of interactive communications and digital networks. This conditional character of the work, contingent on increasingly complex media environments, is to some extent about its physicality: format, form, material tangibility, data, links between tangibility and data, transience or spatiality. All of these physical features of cultural, artistic, media and other creative works are being transformed through ICT and thereby renegotiated between multiple parties, including producers, users, audiences, networks, devices, software structures and public organizations. These renegotiations of what the work is, and whether it is, in existence are superimposed on the displacement and decentralization of the notion of place, the 'where' of the work. Such heterotopia, distributing the position of the work and those connected to it across networks, is directly related to it being known or knowable. The physicality of the work is contingent on a blend of traditional and emergent assets such as spectrum, bandwidth, processing tools, content or experience.

Across the majority of creative sectors, the work is redefined through the questioning of its intrinsic value due to the displacement and disappearance of the single work within the multitude of contents, users, means of access, channels, services and fragmentary niches. Without much doubt, the development of creative industries involves two major and distinct 'genealogical' branches. Of those two, one is based on cultural industries and arts, both characterized by linear production and manufacturing, production and broadcasting technologies, fundamentally analogue in nature and less science driven (though technology-supported: not to forget that even a graphite pencil is the result of technological innovation). The other genealogy of practical knowledge, fixed in material form, is that of information and communication technologies, more closely connected to science than to art. At their core is creative work, as process; a creative work as a singular item or event, though known to exist (e.g. in design) may not form a core, ontological feature of ICT. (This is not to be mistaken for any discourses on artificial intelligence/singularity.)

A plural terming of 'creative industries' should therefore be considered broadly accurate. In the critique of the meaning and impact of terminology, the somewhat contradictory values and interests of different 'creative industries' are such that they pose fundamental challenges to formulating a coherent and homogenous strategy or policy, required at a time of paradigm change. Contradictions, variety of forms, formats, tools and methods characterize the different creative industries and their groupings as sectors (e.g. arts and culture), subsectors, operations and niches. Nevertheless, the coding, capture and dissemination of creative work as information, in the form of ICT data, is what permeates all creative industry work, including those inimitable, rich experiences that characterize live events, performing arts and physical locations. In one way, festivals, special events and theatre can benefit from synergies bestowed by ICT support and convergent experiences in the dissemination of event-related data. However, they can also be subverted by ICT-driven innovation affecting the level of demand, in principle, through the transformation of loyal audiences into more loosely, marginally connected interest groups, whose identity is construed as 'users'. The depth and scale of disruptive innovation in ICT is such that it may transform culture on a fundamental level. It is not inconceivable that such cultural transformation caused by technology may further diminish the perceived value of intellectual property works or of actual events, spatial, temporal and experiential in nature, replacing them with blended communication within controlled virtual entities and promoting a blend of experiences outside of actual, material space. Experience itself is frequently seen as a cognitive category, which is further socially construed. It is improbable that such a scale of cultural transformation would occur in one major leap, but the change of the notion of control over creative works brings with it the re-examination of the values of ownership, authorship, authenticity and originality, which traditionally constitute cultural value – intrinsic, institutional and utilitarian alike. Communications, platforms and devices form substitute services to those centred on discrete creative works, causing internal tensions within creative industries.

Digital, interactive or other: technology or a fundamental feature of culture

In the emerging pattern of creative industry strategies, the intrinsic value of user interaction may act as substitute for the intrinsic value of content. Current business models in entertainment and media aim to create synergies between the two rather than privilege one or the other. This, however, may be seen as a temporary, non-necessary alliance between different levels, plains, processes and nodes which control them in the value networks, an articulation of forces, players and discourses fixed in means and tools used for content-related dissemination in digital interactive networks (Garnham 2005; Hall 1980a, b). A non-alignment of interest was seen previously in debates on the need for IP protection prior to current measures that include content blocking and legal enforcement (Oxford Media Convention 2009). Currently, the respective interests of traditional and ICT-driven creative industries are aligned to a sufficient degree to facilitate 'co-operative competition', resulting in custom-built business models and product/service architectures supporting them to form sustainable methods of commercializing the experiential value of content and network services (which include applications, interfaces and media platforms). There is no evidence that this is sustainable, as the assets and imperatives of respective sector and industry paradigms are at odds in important aspects. While the ICT-driven creative industries benefit from the flow of information and monitoring of its use – thus including any encoded content – the traditional industries and sectors are ontologically defined by discrete units of creative work. Such discrete units take time and cost to produce and refine, far higher per unit than operations of controlling and monitoring flows of information. The latter, however, possess the economies of scale built into the networks, tools and highly trained professionals who conduct empirical work interacting with numerous networks and their users. Therefore, the underpinning technology of information dissemination and management treats any content as information, provided that it can be encoded and transferred by digital media. The only two instances in which content evades (so far) encoding and digital transfer are material, original artefacts and unrepeatable, transitory spatial events.

A definition of ICT-driven media based on technology would involve digital communications, in which transfer of content, if appropriately encoded and reproduced, may include any number of cases from text arrangements to printable industrial design items. Therefore, provided a digital encoding method is met with a reproduction method on the other end, any communication across digital media may be utilized as a unit of product distribution, either free or commercial depending on competitive context.

A definition of ICT-driven media based on research and knowledge would involve interactivity, seen here as a use-concept based on the human need for interaction. The revolutionary nature of digital communications and ICT-driven media is in the fact that the very engagement with use creates a trail of information that can be read, analysed and interacted with through the modelling of search and service methodologies developed by ICT-driven media. Interaction occurs even where use appears most passive, in search and content consumption: the very use of ICT-driven media is interactive by nature (consider the browser add-on Firefox Collusion). More than media, these ICT communication platforms and systems are interactive value exchange and monitoring structures. Papers focusing on psychological tools and research strategies of Facebook suggest that 'on Facebook, people are who they are', which serves as evidence of the network's ability to use data analysis to modify the interface to allow it to reveal character traits of users accurately. Such data is highly valuable, and the asymmetrical relationship between user (profile 'owners') and provider (social medium) is fixed in the co-habitual, symbiotic *symbolic contract*, articulated as 'service for data'.

To give a meta-summary, ICT-driven media are both digital and interactive. Consequently, practical boundaries are disappearing between disseminating information, distributing increasingly material/tangible content and using interactive networks to communicate, promote, sell, use, read, research and analyse, and engage with and influence others. The qualitative difference brought about by ICT-driven media is the first known occurrence of a potentially fully interactive system for communication which may be developed to deliver tangible material products alongside information, which is captured upon the instance of use and forms the basis for detailed analysing and engaging of users. The distinction between ideas, concepts, information and contents disappears alongside the distinctions between products and services, tools and knowledge, events and experiences.

Therefore, having developed from philosophical, scientific, literary and artistic concepts, alongside network synergies for practical use, and based on research in interaction and information transfer as content transport, emerging ICT-driven media and ICT-related sectors intrinsically represent a novel model, highly disruptive to established norms and forms of creative work. The challenges brought about by such change are deep and fundamental, calling into question both the entrepreneurial and the corporate business approaches of the past. Moreover, these qualitative shifts in technological and communicational paradigms leave an impact on the authors, owners, clients and supporters of creative work. The apparent immediacy of use of ICT-driven media challenges the intrinsic value of authentic, original, discrete and singular units of creative work, costly and time-consuming irrespective of digital production value.

There is another product of interactive, research character of ICT-driven media. *A defining component of the ICT paradigm shift is the Heisenberg-style uncertainty of interactive media and the equivalence between observation and an impact on the observed.* Heisenberg (Heisenberg and Pomerans 1971) defined the key principle of quantum mechanics by drawing the equivalence between the impulse of the electronic cloud and the position of the particle. His equations show that the dual nature of matter results in the effect of the observer on the observed. This physical feature of interactivity has further relevance for model design.

Emergent sectors and models: defining principles behind new developments

It was shown above that the impact of interactivity and reproduction richness through ICT media and devices collapses the boundaries between content, communication, distribution, promotion and research and orders them in a parallel, structurally networked manner that creates equivalence between observation (search, research) and interaction/impact (information trails, engagement with users or interactive tools). Thus functional equivalence can be drawn between the acts of observation and of influencing, affecting the observed as presented in the respective distinct traditions of radical ethnography and core principles of quantum mechanics – two seemingly illogical sources of guidance for the understanding of ICT mediation. However, a closer examination of the problem shows that the characteristics of both traditions form part of the practice of *interactive digital* communication: immersive behaviours and patterns of online use resemble the blurring of distinctions between subjective experience and fact, as in participant observation, radical ethnography or gonzo journalism. Such deep immersion is reportedly used in marketing and public relations, especially in interactive digital media. Deep immersion and subjectivity form attributes of user engagement that are of particular value to marketers and others demanding data.

On the other hand, and on a grander organizational scale, the chaotic behaviour of users can be monitored, observed, analysed, projected and influenced through the same means of software and device use that allow users to benefit from functions such as search, content use, commercial and other value exchange, communications, reflection, content creation and user-editing, self-publicity etc. By utilizing any of the above functions, the vast majority of users would interact and leave data patterns for analysis that would inform new push–pull engagement activities targeting the user. The user interacts with the medium and those behind it by performing any function of use; the person or entity controlling an ICT medium influences users by interacting with them through means designed to engage and commercialize (applications, advertising, suggestions, status updates and trending topics etc.). The scale at which such data is collected and used for more analysis and service improvements is measured in billions of rows. The sheer processing capacity required places the analysis of such data and activities on a scale close to that of meteorology (e.g. Stacey 1992; 2013). Theoretical and mathematical models for this type of analysis resemble thermodynamics. While metaphorical adoption of a quantum mechanics principle is conceptually justified to illustrate digital interactivity, the behaviour of large numbers of molecules in gases is a probability concept similar to the ones needed for the monitoring of, and responding to, patterns of use measurable in billions of actions, connections, units of transactions and communications. In summary, interactive media bridge the broadest of disciplinary gaps aptly addressed in Bloch's (2012) treatise on reconciling the paradigms of cognition (positivist) and cultural anthropology (interpretive). Radical immersive subjective actions and interpretations are analysed and utilized in numbers approaching large and complex thermodynamic systems, bridging the gap between distinctly inanimate systems in natural science and subjective immersion in the narrative of experiential, networked online cultures.

Another collapsing boundary is that between meaning and utility: the value chain of meaning. This enables the formulation and development of new processes of disruption that lead to the formation of new markets, dominant models and new strategies for emergent sectors, hybrids and niches. Challenges facing the creative industries may be resolved through the inversion of a consequentialist paradigm of justification of some opportunistic types of agency within particularly unfavourable structural settings. 'Means justify ends' is an analytical inversion of a simplified maxim incorrectly attributed to Machiavelli (1993 edition). If the same applies reversely as in the frequently misquoted, ethically problematic and logically sound proposition, then a relationship of equivalence can be drawn between means and ends, defining a coherent strategy. Chapter 2 examines this logical inversion and its consequent analytical impact, which can be used for formulating innovative and sustainable means. This book includes a discussion of a selection of cases with prominent values-based means. Such values-driven means act as components of strategies underpinning the bargaining power of creative industry organizations. Just as with the notion of changing industry definition and its strategic and policy implications, the notion of discourse will be explored in relation to the formation of emergent sectors and models. It can be argued that discourse played a very significant role in the linear creative industries (then defined as 'cultural'). Discourse was closely linked to ascertaining the intrinsic value of popular culture, best reflected in genres, styles, trends, in television film, fashion, theatre or music and corresponding market segmentation which could be further influenced by promotion and control of content delivery, both of which had their respective intrinsic and utilitarian value connected to discourse.

Why, however, would discourse matter for ICT-driven media? Discourse remains important in functional components of model design, as models are often based on ideas and metaphors, which can be used for functional solutions. As functional design adds value to ICT-driven sectors, discourse has an indirect influence on the next level of innovation and discourses it formulates. Examples include hypertext and big data (science fiction), streaming (sets and cultures) and crowd models (cooperatives and anarchic support networks). Discourse influences the ontological level of model formulation as it informs strategic aims. It will be seen how models, once fully developed, create their own discourse through branding and therefore influence the next stages of functional design.

The proliferation of fragmented discourses and theories in strategy goes beyond mainstream strategy discourse explored in Chapter 1: they relate to actual new practices and means of modelling new tools. The mapping of emergent methods is best done on structural levels and by broad strokes, identifying key trends in interactive media markets. Many novel models fail, so it is best to explore governing principles beyond their specific, context-contingent formation.

The scope and focus of this book

Turning the focus back to the ontology of the industry requires the examination of the product or service. Regarding the product of creative work, it is essential to explore its material and physical existence and then its character and rational purpose. Respondents would refer to the nature of the product in its seemingly arbitrary context. A painting consists of a set of materials, arranged in manners described as brushstrokes, technique, medium, composition, form, style, meaning. When reproduced in different form, e.g. as a digital photograph, the copy carries with it only some aspects of such arrangement, captured in the surface image, a representation of the work. A strict reading of IP legislation forbids reproduction, even in such reduced form, by copying in another medium. Therefore, the legal and policy standpoint is that the work is something other than its material nature. The very suffix 'work' implies an advanced modern context of industrial and post-industrial production and use of creativity.

Similarly, music may be encoded in notes as well as in recordings of musical performances. Moreover, with developments of digital technology, a musical piece can be encoded, saved and reproduced by software. The protection of music as a work of IP, a creative work, rests not on the form of encoding but the ability to reproduce. What is reproduced is subject to technology and skill, such as the quality of reproduction contingent on compression and hardware (e.g. format and loudspeakers), or the musical literacy and competence of those reading and performing the work encoded in traditional notation. Encoding and reproduction in any other form or medium confirms the same notion that the material nature of music is less significant than its abstract nature. Such nature may be loosely termed 'meaning', pending concrete formal and contextual analysis (not subject to a strategic ontology debate).

Examining film and television works, we find a greater dependence on technology, as these are early convergent forms dependent on formats and devices, production and reproduction characteristics. The notion of copy or signal is in this case too the notion of material and physical ability to produce and reproduce the work, which in itself is not formed out of celluloid tape nor data but consists within the medium or material in which it is encoded. It too is represented and reproduced by a set of codes, complex and advanced, presenting a hybrid of other more traditional codes and forms (drama, painting, photograph, performance). Therefore, the work, though highly dependent on the material and technological nature of devices and media, remains abstract. The copying and dissemination of a film or television programme is made similarly inexpensive and effective as is the case with music or still images. In ether case, the product contains the work, which in itself is intangible, coded and abstract in form, hence the ease of encoding, copying and dissemination.

Other noteworthy examples that do not fit this analysis will be examined as exceptions to a pattern identified by early theorists of mass culture. Those significant exceptions to copying, reproduction, encoding and dissemination form substantive investigations, indicative of possible strategic directions for creativity.

What is being protected from unsolicited use?

What is the value of the creative work as product?

The first is a policy question, which will be discussed later. It is closer to teleology debates and practical implications, though rooted in the ontology of the work. The second is an ontological question that may prove important for any business model within the scope of creative industries. In the present debate, the notion of exchange value and consequent commercialization gives way to use value and intrinsic value. The term 'purpose' may elegantly encompass both the intrinsic and the utilitarian nature of a creative product. Therefore, a new question is derived, closer to the essence of *what a creative work 'is'*:

What is the purpose of (a) creative work?

This question will be examined from the input/production and output/use end.

Purpose is not a strict ontological category: it is connected to teleology or method, and epistemology or the knowing of something. However, having concluded that the three types of creative work can be reduced to 'coding' and 'abstraction' of 'meaning' through material and intangible formats, devices and media, it is evident that little more can be extracted from a direct examination of what a creative work 'is', hence the turn to its purpose. Determining what is the purpose of a creative work and of a creative product should indirectly reveal its inner 'self'. This intrinsic level of understanding is directly reflected in the complex meaning of use: the purpose of a creative product as meaningful use. The inclusion of a 'meaning' in this analysis is the direct result of the understanding that creative works, irrespective of their material form, communicate meaning. This meaning may or may not be subject to coding, technological reproduction or dissemination: those works that may not be used thus represent a shrinking minority. As said above, works and products that form notable exceptions will be addressed separately, as they may hold some further strategic insights.

What is innate purposeful use in a creative product? Literature, drama, music, dance, art, film, all share an experiential nature which too applies to works of evidential inherent functionality such as design, architecture and crafts. It involves learning, sensory perception, cognition, interpretation, socialization, identity formation and a relationship with different concepts of pleasure. It is a work which affects those engaged with it in ways that can be described as psychological, social and symbolical. Context plays a significant role in its meaning, but its existence itself delivers a sort of meaning to those involved. It is therefore unsurprising that cultural studies frequently examine meaning on the level of definition. Reflexivity, though important in strategy, may lead to endless spirals of self-examination undermining utility, which is a core component of what strategies are. Therefore, once understood in its innate purpose, an artistic or creative work is seen to deliver a type of use that is context-dependent but involves experience of multiple facets, articulated through meaning, also subject to context-dependent reproduction. In summary, it is formed of experiences – consisting of cognitive and socio-cultural components (e.g. enjoyment, economies of culture alienation), and contextual methods of reproducing meaning. The development and implementation of such controllable contextual methods of reproducing meaning is the domain of advanced marketing strategies, involving discourses, devices, business models, performances and convergent contents. All of those stem from the innate nature of the creative product.

It will be seen that a creative product's ontologically cognitive, sociocultural and contextual nature may turn it into a node – or thread – of convergence that can articulate and generate new, more sustainable outcomes, if managed within an accurately mapped commercial and non-commercial dynamic environment. In the present text, modelling will seldom be analysed in a descriptive manner. Rather, respondent feedback, reflexive experience resources and documentary case data will address key principles of governance, structuring, value capture and exchange. The governing structure defining the anatomy and functioning of a model will be discussed in principle and irrespective of any given particulars, which may change, as will be seen from the few narrative strategy accounts from the in-depth longitudinal cooperation with industry partners and respondents. As technologies, formats and models become obsolete quite regularly, what can remain as a transferable research and design skill is the reasoning, the design approach of contemporary influencers who create *enveloping business models*.

Similarly, creative industries can be described as service industries, but such qualification needs to take into account the same set of singular features that define the product or the nature of creative work. The blurred distinctions between experiences, services and goods are inherently the feature of all creative works and as such, those correlations between constructs of value stemming from them are clearly pronounced as defining characteristic of creative (and cultural) industry work. Pine and Gilmore (1999) uncovered an existing relationship of fundamental significance to creative industries at the point at which many other sectors (food, computer retail, hospitality) began to converge with creativity through experience-driven models at the peak of the post-industrial economic boom of the late 1990s. The commoditization of cultural goods that followed soon, through the substructure of the internet, designed by creative industries (ICT) came more fundamentally than the crisis of evaluation of economic output of markets driven by experience and not production. Following a postmodern peaking of fragmented novel luxury markets in areas such as themed entertainment and retail experience branding, similarly to the post-dot-com bubble, the only sustainable models and growing businesses depended on substantive innovation, functional design strategies and product–service integration where experience as value is attained through functionality, reach, richness and reliability. This clearly privileges those business models that would not function without internal validity and external dependability, i.e. those that are designed as empirical tools rather than based on loose interpretations of value afforded by the control of supply of past linear models of *assembly-line commodification* of content. Such integrating of commodification and control of supply (information and distribution) was frequently bestowded by mergers, acquisition or other mechanisms of adoption/assimilation of innovative business models. This would be done without full conceptual integration of the ontology of such innovation. The result is that asset creators, individuals with creative skills, require a more efficient model to suit a changed substructure of ownership and control that comes from ICT and its value hierarchies based on utility. Evading commoditization in traditional creative areas requires qualitative innovation of the substantive character, equivalent in transformative value to the paradigm shift that threatens to commoditize all traditional creative goods. The strategies thus in need of developing are those that aim to redefine the position and purpose of creative works by integrating them with the principles that govern emerging ICT-driven environments. The purpose of this book is to explore the principles that govern such change and the reasoning of advanced managers and analysts that needs to be developed and implemented in changing industry environments.

Note

1 Originally labelled a '*value chain of meaning*' (Hartley 2004).

1 Understanding what strategy is

Co-authored by Ali Bakir and Milan Todorovic

Introduction

In this chapter we develop an understanding of strategy by interpreting and explaining what academics in the field of management have written on 'what strategy is'; we also support our explanation by data we obtained from creative industry practice, participant observation, reflexive analysis, the use of media both interactively and as text, and interviewing managers in varied creative industries. We feel that conducting a thorough exploration of the ontology of strategy is necessary if we are to understand how strategy is thought and implemented in creative industry business practice. Explanations of strategy that we develop in this chapter also set the scene and provide the foundation for the material in the subsequent chapters of this book.

Innovation in strategic contexts is explained separately; here we consider strategy as the chosen fundamental viewpoint. At the root of it we may have set subject focus within the realm of innovation and not strategy. Nevertheless, choosing innovation as our primary focus would have led us to explore technological and design solutions, which cannot be at the heart of this ontological analysis.

We explore strategy as a socioeconomic and organizational phenomenon whose creative features are exemplified in the industries that generate revenue by communicating and exploiting creativity and cultural value. We argue that the intrisically creative nature of strategy exists beyond the creative sectors, but we present our case here by highlighting the creative processes and features of strategic innovation in areas such as music, art, design, media, communications, film etc. By doing so we will let the reader decide if the rationalities of creative industry practice presented here may be reflected in strategies of more traditional industries.

For instance, the influence of information technology (IT) on models of production, distribution and communication has important methodological implications in this work. Yet we also argue that, though digital/IT methods represent a conceptual leap in communications and media, the essence of business models in some tangible arts remain conservative and unaffected by IT in their core features. Therefore strategy has to reflect that.

We argue for a strategic horizon based on hermenutic methodology. Depending on context and physical manifestations of production, strategy takes up varied forms according to the industry product: sometimes tangible such as works of visual arts and spatial design, sometimes highly contextual such as television formats and social web concepts. This variety of forms and development stages reflects varied rationalities more sharply than in any other field of practice. Creative industry stretegies contain many components of varied rationality, rooted in their fragmented nature; a 'five forces' approach (explained later in this chapter) may thus be justified for large organizations, and it is also justified in business analysis, *a posteriori*, even though there is no field evidence that it would inform tactical decisions when components of strategy are formulated through practice.

Similarly, we will see that some examples of 'organized anarchy' approaches (a strategic concept which we will present below) can be understood as specific cases of more general principles that govern creative industry strategy, i.e. creative models that can, in the right conditions, benefit the organization. This especially applies to industries where creative trial and error methods are key to production: in areas as varied as fashion, music, design, events, theatre and ICT, among others. In some, the product is tangible yet interpreted by users; in others, the product or the commercialized communications exchange is easily replicable and interpretation of the copy is more important than access to the original, the 'master'. In all these cases, control is distributed across actors while the focus remains on the elusive outcome of a product that communicates with its consumer. Therefore a whole array of strategic rationalities may exist in organizations of the creative industries, depending on size, organizational and creative heritage, intellectual property models, creative positions within the market, and stages of conceptual development.

Strategy depends on context, as we will claim through this book. Such claims will be supported by detailed evidence we found in extensive fieldwork covering a number of creative industry sectors. The structural nature of such contexts of strategy and its application will be explored through a systematic approach based on the paradigms introduced in the first three chapters.

The strategy conundrum

The task of developing a common understanding of 'what strategy is' is not an easy one, as the field of strategy has spawned a diversity of paradigms (Volberda and Elfring 2001) which fragmented the field (Hambrick 2004) and gave rise to a continuing debate over its value to managers (Miller and Cardinal 1994). This diversity of often conflicting paradigms is somewhat controversial, especially in the context of application, and we will address it later in the chapter.

In their review of the strategy field, Bowman, Singh and Thomas (2002) find that, although the development of models to facilitate strategy has long been sought by academics and management practitioners, there is no generally accepted definition or description of strategy tools. Two decades ago, in explaining what strategy is, Mintzberg (1987) declared after much elaboration that it was 'a minefield', and Ansoff and McDonnell (1990) concluded that it was elusive.

The mystery over 'what strategy is' remains with us today: 'We simply do not know what strategy is or how to develop a good one' (Markides 2000: vii). Yet countless studies show that to managers strategy is a tool to control business operations and improve performance – a means to achieve a desired end; in the words of an executive director:

> Strategy is, in my view, what one does to get to where one wants to be. So, if we decide to go from A to B and if B is the vision or the mission, the strategy is what we need to do to get from A to B.

It also comes as no surprise to note that this view is also echoed in academia, where, for example, Grant (2008: 17) sees strategy as 'a means by which individuals or organizations achieve their objectives'. Yet, despite this instrumental view of strategy as a means designed to achieve identified objectives, managers in practice find that defining business objectives or goals and designing the appropriate means to achieve them does not invariably result in the achievement of the desired outcomes.This has prompted academics in the field to continuously look for increasingly more elaborate theories, concepts and tools to describe, or prescribe for, a successful strategy.

This vicious circle of over-theorization of how strategy is or should be made is surprisingly coupled with a stark under-theorization of 'what strategy is'. The last serious but, as we will explain later, unsuccessful attempts at theorizing 'what strategy is' in business organizations were made over two decades ago by Mintzberg (1985) and by Ansoff (1987). Yet, in the full knowledge that 'what strategy is' is not very well understood, management academics seem to be quite at ease with churning out theoretical prescriptive and descriptive tools advising managers how to develop and formulate a successful strategy. The dilemma is that despite the over-theorization of the tools for a successful strategy, prominent writers in the field of management have criticized these tools for their irrelevance to practice as managers have not found them useful (see, for example, Partington 2000; Starkey and Madan 2001), particularly in the knowledge economy (Venkatraman and Subramaniam 2001). This is a matter of ongoing concern for Hambrick (2004), Mahoney and McGahan (2007), and other prominent academics in the field, because strategy and strategic management are projected as an applied discipline whose purpose is to describe, predict and change organizational situations.

Thus, although Bower (2008), Grant (2008) and others see positive ways forward in the study of strategy, there is a serious concern in academia that the strategy field is a 'troubled discipline' (see Jarzabkowski and Whittington 2008a).

To address this, we will explore the full spectrum of paradigms rooted in a wide array of ontological presuppositions ranging from strict instrumental rationality to an apparent lack of rational approach to strategy. These correspond to interpretations and discourses of strategy in academic writing and, we will argue, may be partially or significantly correlated to the rationalities of respective creative sectors in their strategy practice.

We suggest that it is the persistent ambiguity over 'what strategy is', particularly in the uncertain and high-velocity environment of the creative industries, that clouds our knowledge of how strategy is made; it is also what motivates us to write this book. Needless to say, as strategy academics we are also concerned that in addressing the question 'What is strategy?', we often wade through a variety of competing definitions and notions that fail to offer the student a satisfactory explanation.

In the course of this chapter, and as we develop our understanding of 'what strategy is' from reading, what Hambrick (2004) described as the fragmented strategy literature, we will by necessity link together conflicting strategy texts from various authors – their concepts and paradigm insights – into a more robust understanding of strategy. By undertaking this multi-paradigm study, we will also answer the persistent calls for linkages to be made between paradigms (Lewis and Kelemen 2002) in the strategy field. To help us with this task, we make use of Weber's (1968) two notions of rationality: instrumental rationality and substantive rationality. This is because we find that the academic literature on strategy is ontologically polarized (Tsoukas and Knudsen 2002), where a major part of it is underpinned by Weber's functional, instrumental rationality – see, for example, Chandler (1962), Andrews (1980), Ansoff (1987), and Ansoff and McDonnell (1990) – and the other part by Weber's interpretive, substantive rationality – see, for example, March and Olsen (1976), Axelrod and Cohen (1999), and Weick (2002). We explain in the following section, and develop in the course of this chapter, how our knowledge of the form of rationality underpinning a strategy is crucial to our understanding of how that strategy is formed.

Strategy and rationality

Rationality is a business organization concept that has emerged alongside strategy in the course of industrialization. In management and organization studies the term 'rationality' is always used in its instrumental form.

In economics and management a rational decision is seen as independent of emotions, personal feelings or any kind of instincts. Any rational process of evaluation or analysis is expected to be objective, logical and 'mechanical'. If these minimum requirements are not satisfied, i.e. if a person has been influenced by personal emotions, feelings, instincts or cultural moral codes and norms, then the analysis is then described as subjective, biased and irrational. In this concept of 'rationality', the individual's goals and motives are taken for granted and not made subject to criticism, ethical or otherwise. Thus rationality simply refers to the success of goal attainment, whatever those goals may be.

There is a debate over whether or not people or organizations are 'really' rational, as well as whether it makes sense to model them as such. It is quite evident from modern cognitive science and neuroscience, studying the role of emotion in mental function, that no human can satisfy this criterion.

We present the main characteristics of Weber's (1968) instrumental and substantive rationalities below and their role in explaining strategy as a social action in Figure 1.1.

Weber advanced two forms of rationality that underpin social action: instrumental rationality and substantive rationality.

1 *Instrumental rationality* is a mode of rationalization which underpins social action, where the action is seen as a means for the attainment of the actor's rationally calculated goals or end. Instrumental rationality provides the basis for operations to be calculable, e.g. the use of formal procedures (capital accounting, planning etc.) in the control of economic enterprises. In this mode of rationality, social action is seen as formal and impersonal and is determined by calculation and quantification.
2 *Substantive rationality* is a mode of rationalization which underpins social action and which is determined by human needs and values, emotions, and tradition. Weber recognizes three types of substantive rational actions:

   a Value rational action, determined by the actor's conscious belief in the value of some ethical, aesthetic, religious or other form of behaviour, independent of its prospects of success;
   b Affectual action, determined by the actor's specific affects, emotion and feeling states;
   c Traditional action, determined by the actor's ingrained habituation.

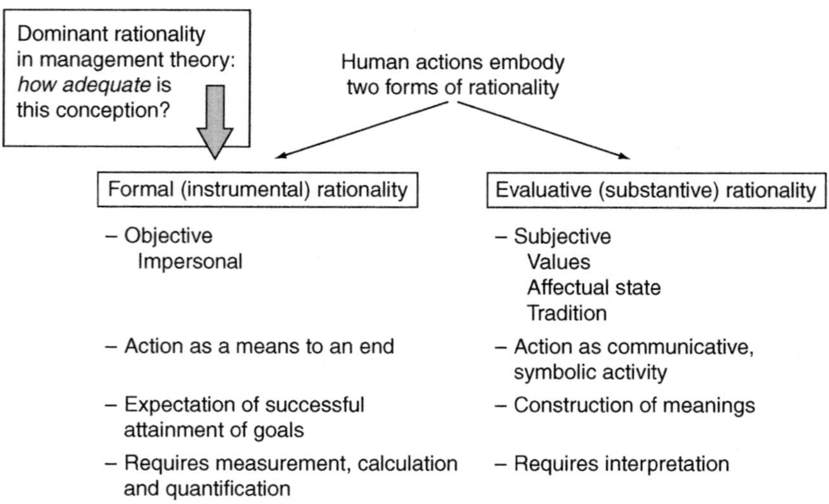

Figure 1.1 Strategy and rationality

As we show later in in this chapter, strategy in the instrumental rational approach is seen as a means to achieve a designated organizational end; it provides the basis for actions by management and other organizational members to be calculated, quantified and controlled. Financial, production and operation strategies are typically instrumental in nature. Staging events in the festivals sector of the creative industries show that in order to ensure crowd safety in these events, instrumental rational crowd control strategies are increasingly more carefully developed, where safety objectives are clearly defined and means are identified and made available to achieve those objectives. For example, complying with the Event Safety Guide and addressing the issues raised following the Roskilde tragedy, the management of Glastonbury Festival developed and put into operation a carefully calculated crowd control strategy. This instrumental strategy is covered in detail in the chapters below. Nevertheless, those same festivals and music events encompass an entirely different strategic component, that which is based on substantive rationality, as too will be argued in chapters to come. The notions of audience identity, the 'subcultural capital' of music events (Thornton 1995, after Bourdieu 1986), branding strategies and audience ethics all form part of substantive rationalities in strong contrast to crowd safety strategies.

Strategy in the substantive rational approach is subjective, which may have a number of interpretations drawn from various representations and communication activities (Barry and Elmes 1997; Tsoukas 1998; Heracleous and Barrett 2001; Worren *et al.* 2002; Ezzamel and Willmott 2008). Promotional campaigns, public relations and branding strategies are generally open to multiple interpretations.

It is a well-documented fact that early work in public relations (PR) drew significantly from the work of Freud and his theories of the id and the unconscious. It was frequently the irrational in human behaviour that was targeted in PR from its very beginnings. In terms of promotional campaigns, prime examples come from today's digital music marketing, where the notions of fan, audience and promoter are used interchangeably – if fans can be mobilized as unpaid promoters in an online artist promotion campaign, the campaign is likely to work. This is achieved with the combined use of 'apps' technology, social clustering around online networks, and (sub)cultural capital.

Perhaps the best contemporary example comes from Apple, whose followers adopt an almost religious fervour about the brand and its vision. Apple's branding strategy may thus be seen as focusing on values and emotions:

> The Apple brand personality is about lifestyle; imagination; liberty regained; innovation; passion; hopes, dreams and aspirations; and power-to-the-people through technology. The Apple brand personality is also about simplicity and the removal of complexity from people's lives; people-driven product design; and about being a really humanistic company with a heartfelt connection with its customers.
>
> (www.marketingminds.com.au/apple_branding_strategy.html, accessed 3 August 2015)

The tendency for multiple interpretations and meanings of strategy activities, we explain in the next section, originates in (a) the means that a strategy employs; (b) its sought end/goals; or (c) the means–end relationship, which may prevent the realization of these goals.

Our purpose: the aim of this chapter

The common-sense knowledge that strategy is about defining the goals – the desired end – and designing the means to achieve those goals allows us to represent the relationship between strategy, means and end in a simple formula:

$$\text{Strategy} = \text{Means} + \text{End}$$

Bearing this relationship in mind, we show that when the end is not achieved, when the goals are not attained, there are three potential problems. The first problem is that the goals/end are not very well defined or cannot be clearly defined; the second problem is that the means to achieve these goals is not properly designed or cannot be properly designed. These two problems normally arise from a third potential problem, from the difficulty of finding a clear and direct relationship between the end and the means to achieve this end; such a relationship we shall refer to as an 'ambiguous' relationship as opposed to a 'direct/clear' one.

Equally, what underpins whether this relationship is direct and clear or ambiguous is whether the strategy activity, the set of actions relating to the means and end, is objective and can be calculated and quantified, or whether it is subjective and requires understanding the meaning behind the activity. Following from Weber, as shown above, we shall refer to the objective set of action as 'rational instrumental' and the subjective one as 'rational substantive'. We thus look at the nature of the means–end relationship in strategy and the type of rationality that governs this relationship. We argue and show that both these aspects are central to our understanding of what strategy is.

In this endeavour we explore and explain the means–end relationship through an interpretive reading of what strategy is from authorial texts. Within this framework, we briefly:

- Discuss competing strategy definitions
- Discuss the two competing approaches to strategy formation

    i The instrumental rational approach and its schools of
    - sequential rationality
    - rational problem solving
    - positioning

    ii The substantive rational approach and its
    - processual schools of
        - muddling through

    - incrementality
    - organized anarchy
  - systemic schools of:
    - social action
    - complexity
  - discursive school

- Discuss the three competing strategy determining paradigms

  i capability building
  ii natural selection
  iii culture

- Develop our own framework of understanding what strategy is, and the significance of this understanding for how strategy is developed and formed in the creative industries

In the following section we present our interpretation of the writings of strategy academics – authorial texts – on what strategy is.

Three problematic dimensions of strategy

We will interpret 'what strategy is' by examining three interrelated dimensions of strategy: strategy definition, strategy formation and strategy determining conditions, which we mark as problematic (see also Bakir and Bakir 2006) as they contribute to the mystery surrounding what strategy is.

Strategy: a question of definition

Rooted in the instrumental rational approach, strategy rests on the assumption that managers take the course of action which will optimally achieve their goals. Instrumental rationality requires that objectives are well defined so that a direct and clear relationship can be established with the designed means to achieve them. It is this direct and clear relationship that allows strategy to be objectively calculated and successfully deployed and the goals attained.

A prominent early writer of this school, Chandler (1962), defines strategy as a process of determining an organization's goals and objectives by adopting defined courses of action and allocating the necessary resources for carrying them out, clearly emphasizing strategy's instrumentality and intendedness. Similarly, MacCrimmon (1993: 114) advances his first definition of strategy as a coordinated series of actions that is goal directed and involves resource deployment. He emphasizes the pivotal role of coordination between goals and actions, betweeen the various goals, and between the various actions, thus highlighting the intendedness and instrumentality of strategy.

Ansoff and McDonnell (1990) take a more or less similar position to Chandler and MacCrimmon; they define strategy as a set of decision-making rules, goals and objectives to guide organizational behavior, emphasizing its intendedness and instrumentality. However, in elaborating their definition further they assert that although strategy and objectives are distinct, they are, nevertheless, similar: that objectives interchange with strategy at different points in time and at different organizational levels (p. 4). The interchangeability of strategy and objectives points to an ambiguous rather than direct and clear relationship between strategy and its objectives; it also casts doubt on the instrumental role of strategy. As a 'decision-making rule' (a means) strategy's instrumentality is evident; however, as an 'objective' (an end) strategy is stripped of its instrumental role and hence of usefulness as a tool to managers. It is this ambiguous relationship between strategy and objectives that compels Ansoff and McDonnell to declare that strategy is an elusive phenomenon (p. 44).

It therefore becomes clear that identifying the strategy phenomenon requires further specific steps in identifying the criteria of the 'what' of strategy. MacCrimmon (1993: 114–115) recognizes that his first definition does not capture the full complexity of strategy because it does not consider the scope of its influence – its spatial dimension – nor its time influence – its temporal dimension. To solve the spatial shortcoming, MacCrimmon advances his second definition of strategy as 'a comprehensive, coordinated series of actions'; and to address the temporal dimension, he presents his third definition of strategy as 'a conditional, comprehensive, coordinated series of actions'. He attaches two properties to his third definition. The first is that strategy is conditional upon events in the environment including actions by other agents; the second is that strategy takes account of the effect of one's actions on other agents and the various interactions that may arise. MacCrimmon explains that these mutual interactions may occur over a broad area and a long time horizon.

While introducing his second and third increasingly more complex and interactive definitions of strategy, MacCrimmon nevertheless retains, through the notion of 'coordination' in these definitions, the intendedness of strategy. However, as he widens the spatial scope and temporal dimension in his second and third definitions, the instrumentality of strategy is progressively undermined by the increasing ambiguity of its relationship with its objectives.

Acknowledging the difficulty with understanding strategy, Mintzberg (1987) advances five interrelated strategy definitions: 'plan', 'ploy', 'pattern', 'position' and 'perspective' (also in Mintzberg *et al.* 2003: 3–9), where strategy gradually moves from an instrumental rational tool to a substantive rational one. He suggests that his interrelated definitions 'explicitly' acknowledge strategy's multiple meanings and 'help people maneuver through this difficult field' (Mintzberg *et al.*, p. 3).

As a 'plan' or 'ploy', the link of strategy to its objectives is direct and clear, emphasizing its intendedness and instrumentality in the pursuance of those objectives. As a 'position', strategy is again a means of placing an organization in an environment (Porter 1985, 1991), and again posseses the characteristics of intendedness and instrumentality. However, Mintzberg argues that a position may be identified and targeted through a plan or it may emerge through a 'pattern of behavior'. Thus, while strategy as an intended position points to its strong instrumental role and clear and direct relationship to its objectives, strategy as an emerging position dismisses this role and points to an ambiguous rather than clear and direct relationship with its objectives. Mintzberg further underscores this ambiguous relationship by his 'perspective' notion of strategy, orienting metaphors (Chaffee 1985), which exists inside the organization's collective mind. In this 'perspective' view, where every strategy is 'a figment of someone's imagination' (Mintzberg *et al.* 2003: 8), Mintzberg still acknowledges the intendedness of strategy but dispenses with any direct or clear link with its objective, thus firmly dismissing its instrumental role.

We also note that Mintzberg's reference to the emergence of unintended outcomes – 'unintended position' and 'emergent pattern' – as 'emergent strategy' undermines the intended utility of strategy. This distinction is important for our understanding of strategy, which we shall return to in the course of this chapter.

Hax and Majluf (1988: 102) find no irreconcilable contradictions between the various definitions of strategy. On the contrary, they suggest that new insights are revealed by integrating all the definitions into a single 'more comprehensive' and all-encompassing one. Strategy, they state, is 'a coherent, unifying and integrative pattern of decisions', which

> determines … the organizational purpose …: its long-term objectives, action programmes, and resource allocation priorities; … selects the businesses the organization is in …; attempts to achieve a long-term sustainable advantage in … its businesses by responding … to the opportunities and threats in the firm's environment, and the strengths and weaknesses of the organization …; engages all the hierarchical levels of the firm …; and defines the nature of the … contributions it intends to make to its stakeholders.
>
> (p. 102)

Here, the complexity of strategy is acknowledged but at the expense of clarity of application.

In this view, strategy's intendedness is apparent in its portrayal as patterns of decisions to achieve organizational objectives. However, its instrumental role is undermined by the great multiplicity of objectives which are insufficiently defined and which often compete or conflict as they derive from complex interactive environments. In these environments, where substantive rational considerations (e.g. values, beliefs, emotions, interests, traditions) prevail, it will not be possible to find a direct and clearly defined means–end relationship which will allow the deployment of a 'coherent, unifying and integrative' strategy. In a similar vein in the latest edition of their text book, Johnson, Scholes and Whittington (2008: 3) define strategy as 'the *direction* and *scope* of an organization over the *long term*, which achieves *advantage* in a changing *environment* through its configuration of *resources and competences* with the aim of fulfilling *stakeholder* expectations' (italics are original).

We again find in this definition acknowledgement of the intendedness and instrumentality of strategy to achieve its goals. However, there is also recognition on the part of Johnson *et al.* that the instrumentality of strategy is progressively undermined as the relationship between strategy and objectives becomes more ambiguous with widening spatial 'scope' and temporal, 'long term' dimension and with a 'changing environment'. It is this ambiguity that prompts some writers from the substantive rational school to dismiss altogether strategy's rational instrumental role (Cohen *et al.* 1972; Stacey 1996) and with it the role of managers.

It is also disappointing to note that despite the promising title – *What is Strategy, and does it Matter?* – of his illuminating book, Whittington (2001) does not provide an answer to the first part of the question he poses, and which we argue is central to our understanding. Instead, he answers 'two fundamental questions: What is strategy for; and how is strategy done' (p. 2). We acknowledge that the answer to the latter constitutes an essential part of our understanding of strategy; however, the lack of an answer to 'what strategy is' makes an understanding of how it is 'done' difficult to obtain. Thus, although prominent authors, including Whittington and others from the strategy-as-practice school, recognize the mystery surrounding the definition of strategy, they nevertheless, surprisingly, take its meaning for granted and focus entirely on studying how it is formed.

From the complex system perspective, Stacey (1996) views strategy as a game managers play, inside and outside the organization, interacting with each other in 'a circular process' of moves which provokes responses that feed back into counter responses, and so on, 'from day to day' (1996: 2–3); he focuses on the system's self-organizing feedback processes and the dynamics they generate. In subsequent writings, Stacey (2007) incorporates insights from psychoanalysis, defining strategy as 'complex responsive processes' focusing on 'how intention emerges in local interaction taking the form of ordinary conversation between people' (p. 450). The later Stacey remains focused on interactions where outcomes emerge from a complex interplay of intended actions and responses, and where, through this interplay, instrumental rational calculation gives way to substantive rational interpretation. However, Stacey's new formulation of strategy somewhat counters the effects of his previously radical approach to the lack of managers' actual influence over intended outcomes.

Similarly, in an empirical study of leisure and cultural organizations, Bakir and Bakir (2006) find that managers view strategy as a purposeful, complex, fluid and interconnected process that gives rise to intended and unintended outcomes. The 'purposefulness' of strategy in Bakir and Bakir's findings indicates that managers understand strategy as intentional and instrumental in achieving their desired organizational objectives. We also note an implicit recognition on Bakir and Bakir's part that the instrumentality of strategy diminishes as the ambiguity arising from 'fluid' interactions within and outside these organizations increases, resulting in 'unintended outcomes' and the deployment of new 'intended' strategies, which may be different from the original strategy. We argue that it is this ambiguity between strategy and its goals, caused by the interplay of subjective interpretive actions, that is at the root of the difficulty with formulating an instrumental rational strategy; it is also the source of goal shifting and the emergence of unintended outcomes, erroneously referred to in the strategy literature as 'emergent' strategies.

In dialogue with the text

We are exploring justifications for strategic thinking in contexts in which it exists. By doing so we seek to understand the effectiveness of proclaimed plans and emergent patterns in relation to the match between intended action and resultant effects, arguing that their contextual relevance comes from intrinsic factors in the modes of production, consumption and distribution characterizing an idustry or sector.

Therefore, in those instances in which there is a relation of equivalance between distribution, consumption and promotion, content identity determines the model of value creation, which is central to business modelling. This we examine through the analysis of various theoretical models, considering their relevance in practice through respective sections dealing with them. If we explore and interpret strategy as an abstract notion in business, and its ontology as the most abstract aspect of strategy, then the principles we identified through the act of interpretation will serve us well in exploring the most specific and applied notion of strategy in the field, the processes and cases of business model development. Following the logic that if strategy exists it must be at the heart of effective application, we posit that the dialogue with authorial texts should at least direct our search for the ontology of strategy.

In our act of interpreting strategy definition above, we entered into a dialogue with what strategy authors have written – authorial text – where we questioned both the instrumental rational and substantive rational premises of the text. We found that although authorial texts from the instrumental rational persuasion emphasize the intendedness and instrumentality of strategy in achieving organizational objectives – 'authorial intention' – they nevertheless are unable to convince us that the necessary conditions for this instrumentality to work (i.e. a direct and clear means–end relationship) is always obtainable.

We have also found that although emphasizing the emergent nature of strategy, authorial texts from the substantive rational school are unable to dismiss the intendedness and utility of strategy as a means, albeit an interpretive subjective one, to achieve defined but continuously shifting objectives. Our dialogue with authorial texts further reveals that the role of strategy as an instrumental rational tool diminishes in favour of its role as an interpretive one as the means–end ambiguity increases. What emerged as a source of problems with strategy definition is two-fold:

a the ambiguity of the means–end relationship which causes goals to shift, and
b the fact that more than instrumental rational calculation is required to understand strategy.

We will use this interpretation in developing our understanding of strategy later in this chapter. Next, we turn to the associated problem of strategy formation.

Strategy, a question of formation

The 'sequential rationality' school, though still prevalent in current strategic management textbooks, is now much disfavoured in academic research; we show our version of how this school describes strategy formation in Figure 1.2. In this approach, strategy is viewed as 'a process of deliberate calculation and analysis, designed to maximize long-term advantage' (Whittington 2001: 3). A prerequisite for this analysis is the assumption that there exists a direct and clear means–end relationship. The largest body of this literature represents frameworks and models of the process. Early proponents of 'sequential rationality' (Chandler 1962; Andrews 1980) view the strategy process as consisting of two sequential sub-processes: formulation followed by implementation, concerned with identifying the desired objectives and designing a suitable means which then becomes instrumental in achieving those objectives.

Although the use of instrumental rational strategy tools has been associated with traditional strategic planning (Mintzberg 1994), a number of recent studies (e.g. Grant 2008) show that these tools are still widely used within strategy development, where coordinated implementation actions are visible across the entire organization. These planning activities, Whittington (2003) points out, are often overlooked as the mundane, means–end practices of strategy; this, he argues, neglects the way these practices socially structure strategy outcomes.

It is widely accepted that linearity and planning cannot cope with complex environments (Campbell and Alexander 1997) such as those found in the creative industries, where a direct means–end relationship is unobtainable. Acknowledging this ambiguous means–end relationship, researchers from the instrumental 'rational problem solving' school argue that integrated views of formulation and implementation in the form of structured decision processes (e.g. 'devil's advocacy', 'dialectical inquiry', 'scenario planning') and other aids are more beneficial in helping to develop and analyse alternative strategies (Kaplan and Norton 1993; Armstrong 1995; Malhotra 2000; Nemeth *et al.* 2001).

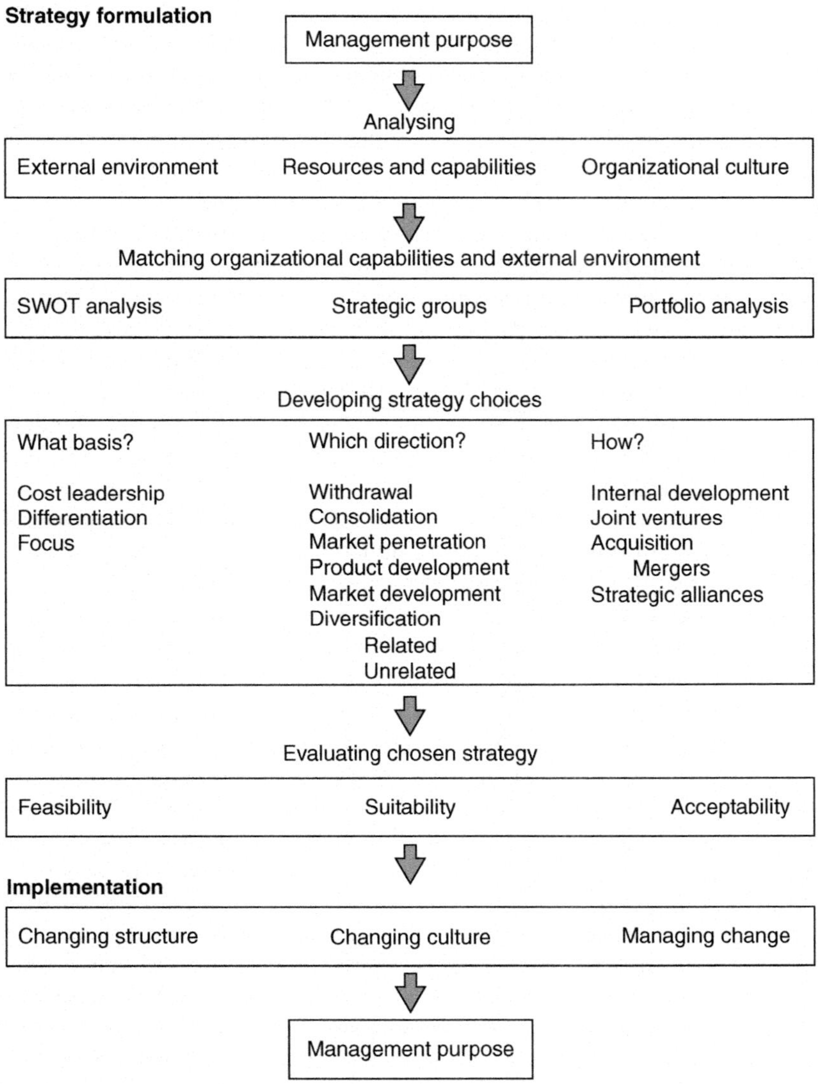

Figure 1.2 The instrumental rational approach to strategy formation

By 'linearity' we refer to a clear, direct and proportional relationship between cause and effect. A linear game presents a player with a fixed sequence of challenges; a nonlinear game allows greater player freedom and challenges that can be completed in a number of different ways. (These too will be explored in creative industry strategy contexts later in the book.)

In rapidly changing environments, Malhotra posits, there is an imperative need for the consideration of Kantian and Hegelian inquiring systems, such as dialectical inquiry based on dialogue – 'a free flow of meaning between people' – that can provide multiple, diverse and contradictory interpretations (p. 9). The 'dialectical inquiry' requires the researcher to identify and explore competing models emerging from respondents' anecdotes, narratives and a variety of assertions (Berniker and McNabb 2006). What underlies dialectical inquiry is the use of substantive rational, subjective insights to aid the design of intended instrumental strategies. The same way of thinking is also employed by the 'devil's advocacy' approach (Skemp 1976).

Scenario planning blends the known and the unknown into a number of consistent views of the future that span a wide range of possibilities. The technique can also include anticipatory thinking elements that are difficult to formalize, such as subjective interpretations of facts, shifts in values, or new regulations or inventions. It is a group process, which encourages knowledge exchange and development of deeper understanding of central issues important to the future of the organization (Schwartz 1991; van der Heijden 1996; Ringland 1998). The scenario planning approach is widely used in the creative industries, for example in advertising.

It is now clear that we have entered the realm of authorial pragmatism. The shortcomings of linearity and planning have also allowed the 'positioning' school to take hold, underpinned by microeconomic deductive, analytic, and predictive methods (Hirsch *et al.* 1987). From this perspective, an industry is attractive if an organization operating within it can find a stable and defensible position by erecting barriers to entry and through collusion with other organizations, thus minimizing competition and gaining sustainable advantage (Porter 1985). Market positioning tools have proliferated and are widely advocated in strategy textbooks and courses; primary amongst these are Porter's five forces and generic strategy frameworks. The five forces model looks at market agents' interactions and interrelationships, leading to an assessment of the attractiveness of the industry. Implicitly recognizing the ambiguous means–end relationship in strategy, Porter's five forces framework employs a combination of instrumental rational tools (e.g. market size and growth rate, market share, profitability margins) and rational substantive and interpretive tools (e.g. relationships with suppliers and purchasers, retaliation moves, erecting entry barriers). The same argument applies to other market positioning models such as portfolio matrix analysis, strategic grouping and market segmentation (O'Brien and Dyson 2007). We shall explore positioning tools along with other strategy tools in detail later in this book.

In the processual schools, strategy emerges from a pragmatic process of bodging, learning and compromise (Mintzberg 1994), and adaptation (Whittington 2001). Early writers from these schools (e.g. Lindblom 1959; Simon 1960) find that where organizations are characterized by uncertainty and information overload, managers tend to seek solutions that are characteristically fragmented, 'incremental' (Quinn 1981), intuitive and compromising, rather than instrumental ones.

The 'muddling through' process of decision-making is seen as an example of politically motivated behavior that arises from the absence of clear organizational goals (Lindblom 1959; Cyert and March 1963). Mintzberg and Waters (1985) posit that realized strategies develop on a continuum from full intention by management to pure emergence. We read from the above text that what gives rise to Mintzberg and Waters' 'emergent' notion of strategy is this process of bodging and compromise that characterizes uncertain, fast-moving environments, particularly prevelant in the creative industries, where the outcome of one intended decision dictates the next decision and a pattern of outcomes thus emerges, causing shifts from the original goals.

Changes in tastes and fashions in the consumption of creative products may be very hard to predict or influence. Some examples in music, fashion, film etc. show the unpredicted emergence of outcomes and consequently entirely new strategies that subsequently come into effect. In some cases, markedly the ones concerning unintended consequences of technological change, an industry may itself generate causes of emergent and even undesired changes to some of its key sectors, as will be shown later in the book. On the other hand, the very nature of creative processes in production, dialectically intertwined with the social connotations governing processes of consumption, arguably adds to the uncertainty and slippage in audience tastes, aesthetic/creative trends and corresponding strategies.

Similarly, Cohen *et al.* (1972) argue that independent individual assumptions about organizational intention may result in a behaviour that resembles the 'garbage can' model of choice, where strategy emerges from 'organized anarchy'. They find that ambiguity characterizes each aspect of a decision process, cause and effect relationships are difficult to identify, and participation is fluid.

Concerned with the every day micro-activities of strategizing, a new stream of literature, 'strategy-as-practice' (e.g. Whittington 2001; Johnson *et al.* 2008), has emerged within the processual school, focusing on how individuals think, speak, politicize and routinely interact within groups and shape strategy outcomes. These micro-phenomena, writers from the systemic 'social action' school emphasize, need to be understood within their social context, where strategists draw upon socially defined modes of acting that make their actions meaningful to others (Balogun *et al.* 2007; Chia and Mackay 2007). Although Foucauldian writers tend to conceptualize the construction of the micro-activities of strategy through narrative, language and discourse (Knights and Morgan 1991; 1995; Barry and Elmes 1997; Shaw *et al.* 1998; Heracleous and Barrett 2001; Ezzamel and Willmott 2008), increasingly, however, these activities are being viewed as a form of bricolage (Schön 1983; de Certeau 1984).

As a bricoloeur, the strategy practitioner is seen to do the work of strategy innovatively by using the tools at hand – which might have been designed with an instrumental rational purpose – in a subjective, social, interpretive way (Munro 1995; Tsoukas 1998; Worren *et al.* 2002). This is frequently the case in marketing, where active re-interpretation of communication tools is essential. Similarly, the audience's micro activities tend to have a substantial cumulative effect on the public relations strategies of a creative industry product. Strategy as bricolage is most evident in contemporary digital media marketing, as stated in an earlier elaboration of the substantive rationality behind promotional practices. The strategist engages in direct dialogue with the audience member/user/fan – all of these terms may be used interchangeably, depending on context; by doing so, the strategist utilizes the bricolage practice of interactive audiences, who in turn adopt interactive tools for communication and entertainment, the design of which reflects the communications patchwork of bricolage. The attention to the minutiae is of the essence here; such strategies may generate significant emergent and undesired consequences, but in contemporary interactive media no public relations activity can survive without such subjective audience engagement, as will be elaborated in depth later in the book.

Pushing the concept of the subjectivity of strategic activity to its limits, proponents of the 'complex ecosystem' school (e.g. Stacey 1996; Axelrod and Cohen 1999; Kelly and Allison 1999) view organizations as complex adaptive feedback systems where unpredictable patterns and new orientations emerge from a process of self-organization. Stacey views this process as one of political interactions and learning which allows new strategic directions to emerge. He argues that the focus of strategy should be on controlling, promoting change, constructive contention and dialogue, and dealing with ambiguity (p. 485) – all of which are consciously intended activities, mainly of the interpretive and communicative form, whose purpose is to move the self-organized processes in the direction of the originally intended strategy and goals. More recently, Stacey (2007) has moved away from the self-organizing feedback system proposition of strategy; nevertheless, he remains focused on interactions in his current perspective of strategy as 'complex responsive processes'.

Thus the views of writers from the various substantive rational schools of strategy as complex, contextually situated, interpretive and communicative social activities acknowledge an ambiguous rather than linear means–end relationship. There is also recognition on the part of these writers that although strategy formation may not follow instrumental rational models, it is nevertheless a process of consciously intended, interpretive activities, which gives rise to a persistent shifting of goals – what Johnson *et al.* (2008) call: 'strategic shift' – and emergent outcomes. This recognition is significant, as we contend that the use of the term 'emergent strategy' is misleading. Our reading of authorial text from the rational substantive schools on strategy formation points to a process of intended actions brought about by 'complex, socially embedded, and reflective being[s]' (Jarzabkowski and Whittington 2008b: 283), where substantive rational activities driven by subjective ideologies, values, traditions, emotions and interests operate within a social context, causing continuous shifts away from the original goals.

Interpretive horizon summary 1: on strategy formation

In this sub-section, through a dialogue with authorial texts, we have shown that the text on strategy formation is fragmented and, therefore, problematic, shaped by a number of competing and conflicting paradigms (Hambrick 2004). As interpreters, our conversation with the text shows that where the means–end relationship is direct, strategy formation is best understood by the instrumental rational strategy schools, and where the relationship is ambiguous, it is best understood by the substantive rational schools. As with the previous sub-section we have attempted to confront our prejudices and widen our interpretive horizon by incorporating authorial text from conflicting strategy formation schools. We have thus arrived through a fusion of horizons at an understanding that strategy formation is dictated by the nature of the means–end relationship and the type of rationality that governs this relationship. This understanding will feed into our definition of strategy later in this chapter. However, understanding what strategy is and how it is formed is closely linked with the determining conditions which affect its deployment; this we elaborate next.

Strategy: a question of determining conditions

Jarzabkowski and Wilson (2006) recognize that strategy development is complicated by a host of intervening and external uncontrollable variables which blur the link between strategy and its objectives. They categorize these variables into two contextual conditions:

a 'environmental velocity' – a characteristic of the market; and
b 'knowledge intensity' – a characteristic of firm behaviour.

Clearly, these variables which impinge on the process of strategizing are brought about by organizational and market agents through instrumental calculation and subjective interpretation within a specific social context (see Tsoukas 1998) and structure.

Writers from the substantive rational schools stress that psychological, social and cultural factors within organizations have significant influences in the process of strategy. Some writers consider managers' character – personality, disposition and temperament (Ghemawat 1991; Porter 1991), creative foresight (McMaster 1996), intuitive capacities (Hurst *et al.* 1989; Weick 2002), and shared values and beliefs, i.e. ideology (Mintzberg *et al.* 2003) – as key determining conditions of strategy.

Authors who emphasize the importance of the role of managers ascribe a dominant role for organizational capability-building in strategy development. These writers come from the traditional resource-based (e.g. Wernerfelt 1984; Barney 2001) and core competences paradigms (Prahalad and Hamel 1990), and more recently from dynamic capabilities theory (Teece *et al.*

1997), all drawing from similar conceptual fundamentals (Lengnick-Hall and Wolff 1999). They argue that the resource structure and configuration of an organization form the foundation of its strategy (Grant 1991; Barney 2001). However, capability-building theory, Jarzabkowski and Wilson (2006) point out, is conceptually ambiguously expressed in terms of what constitutes a resource or competence (Priem and Butler 2001). Hence, such knowledge, they argue, lends itself less to concrete strategy tools and more to a framework of general concepts. Nevertheless, the competitive conditions within the knowledge economy have prompted some authors to suggest that knowledge capacity of an organization has become the key source of competitive advantage (Grant 1996; Nahapiet and Ghoshal 1998).

In contrast to the capability-building paradigm, advocates of the 'evolutionary' paradigm consider the external environment as an *a priori* determining condition in strategy. They argue that the environment has a dominant influence on most organizations and that strategy development occurs as a response to changes in the environment. Whittington (2001: 4) observes that for these advocates (e.g. Williamson 1991), because the future is 'far too volatile and unpredictable to plan for, the best strategy is to concentrate on maximizing chances of survival'; thus evolutionists see strategy emerging through natural selection, where market forces rather than managers make the important choices. In this view, as we have pointed above, the instrumental role of strategy is undermined together with that of the manager. The latter is viewed as mere adaptation to uncontrollable forces of the market.

Stressing the dominant influence of the external environment, Johnson *et al.* (2008) find that within the processes of strategy development, variations occur in the type of organizational processes, structures and systems which may be relevant to the environmental pressures the organization faces. Porter (1985 1991) argues that the environment influences both the initial conditions of a firm and the choices available to its management. Accordingly, he advances a number of widely used strategy tools – e.g. generic strategies, five forces industry structure – to help firms develop competitive advantage and successful strategy.

However, in high-velocity environments characterized by ambiguous industry structure, changing market players, rapid innovations, short product lifecycles, new technologies and unpredictable change (Eisenhardt and Martin 2000), existing strategy tools were found inadequate (D'Aveni 1994; Eisenhardt and Sull 2001); a new conceptualization, that of hypercompetitive or high-velocity strategy, was born.

As with capability-building tools, Jarzabkowski and Wilson (2006) find that the tools arising from high velocity environment research are imprecisely expressed; for example, D'Aveni's (1995: 48) 7S framework is not 'generic strategies or a recipe for success'; rather it represents 'key approaches … to carry the firm in many different directions'. Similarly, Eisenhardt and Sull (2001) call for strategizing by simple rules in order to retain sufficient flexibility to make rapid decisions. Jarzabkowski and Wilson also state that these tools are primarily oriented towards enhancing speed in decision-making, facilitating experimentation, and designing flexible organizations to aid in rapid reconfiguration of resources (e.g. Bowman and Hurry 1993; Eisenhardt and Brown 1999; Miller and Waller 2003). They further point out that high-velocity theory indicates some interdependence between environmental velocity and the knowledge capacity of the organization, and they stress that these conditions are the primary factors that challenge the relevance of existing strategy theory to practice.

The evolutionary and capability-building paradigms respectively find either the environment or the organization's capability to be instrumental for a successful strategy. However, authors from these schools increasingly acknowledge, as we have seen above, that in high-velocity environments it is difficult to identify clearly defined objectives for which successful strategies may be designed. This is particularly so in the creative industries, where strategizing is driven less by instrumental rational calculation and more by substantive rational and subjective interpretation.

Interpretive horizon summary 2: on strategy conditions

This brief exposure reveals that authorial texts recognize three sets of complex and competing strategy determining conditions: organizational capability-building; forces in the external environment; and the social and cultural context of strategy, including the individual and group psychology of strategy agents. Although Jarzabkowski and Wilson (2006) view these conditions as interdependent, different authors have nevertheless conferred a prominent position on the strategy determinant that they subscribe to. However, by entering into a dialogue with authorial text, we find that no authorial text entirely dismisses influences from the other views. Nevertheless, by advancing their own view, they fail to consider that in the interactive context within which strategy is developed where all the determining conditions operate the dominance of one condition over the others can only be temporary. We have attempted in this subsection to expand our own horizon by incorporating the horizons of different authorial texts in order to accomplish a fusion of horizons. What emerges is that while any of the three sets of conditions may occupy an *a priori* position, such a position is more precarious than permanent, particularly in the high-velocity environments of the creative industries where ambiguity reigns. This understanding will also inform our interpretation of what strategy is in the next section.

Conclusion: what is strategy?

We find through our interpretive reading of authorial texts on 'what strategy is' that the necessity of coordination between actions and goals, whether achieved through objective analysis as in the instrumental rational authorial texts or subjectively through interpretive activities as in the substantive rational ones, confers on strategy an intended character. Our interpretation also shows that instrumental rational strategies are only obtainable in non-interactive organizational situations. In these situations, where the direct means–end relationship is not undermined by the complexity of interactions, intended strategies can be objectively formulated and then become instrumental in the achievement of the designated goals.

However, as the spatial domain and temporal dimension of strategy widen so that strategy becomes progressively more complex due to interactions with agents inside and outside the organization, the means–end relationship becomes more ambiguous and strategy increasingly less instrumental. Our reading of authorial texts shows that in complex, interactive, high-velocity environments, the intended role of strategy is still retained while its instrumental objective role is superseded by a substantive rational social one, requiring subjective interpretive and communicative actions; the latter result in persistent shifts of goals from the originally designed one and in emergent outcomes.

Thus our reading of authorial text from various schools and paradigms reveals that strategy can be viewed as a series of intended, partly instrumental and partly interpretive activities that is goal-directed and requires resource deployment. However, the extent to which the goals are achievable depends on the nature of the means–end relationship. When this relationship is direct and clear, characteristic of non-interactive environments, the goals can generally be achieved through instrumental rational calculation in the form of 'planning', 'positioning' and 'rational decision-making'. In these environments there is little room for subjective cultural interpretation, and the determinant strategy paradigms that operate in an interlinked way are the organization's capability-building and the organization's cultural context, including the individual and group psychology of organizational agents; the expected outcomes are generally those that were originally intended.

When, on the other hand, the means–end relationship is ambiguous, characteristic of interactive environments prevailing in the creative industries, instrumental rational strategies give way to substantive rational ones which are focused on subjective interpretation and communication. Here, strategy formation can be viewed as processual – 'muddling through/incrementality', 'organized anarchy' and 'strategy-as-practice'; systemic – 'social action' and 'complexity'; and discursive. The interlinked paradigms that operate as strategy determinants in these environments are 'capability-building', 'natural selection' and 'the social and cultural context, including the individual and group psychology of organizational and market agents'. In these complex environments, the goals persistently shift, as a result of interactions, from those originally designed, and the outcomes are predominantly emergent. We show this, our understanding of strategy, in Table 1.1.

In this chapter, we have developed a dynamic understanding of 'what strategy is'. We offered a novel contribution to knowledge in pointing out that the treatment of the means–end relationship and its underpinning

Table 1.1 A hermeneutic multi-paradigm understanding of strategy

Strategy: A series of intended, partly instrumental and partly interpretive actions which is goal-directed and requires resource deployment	
Instrumental intended series of actions ←	Strategy continuum → Interpretive intended series of actions

Non-interactive environment
Clear and direct means–end relationship
Requires calculation
Strategy formation
Instrumental rational schools
• Sequential planning
• Rational decision-making aids
• Positioning
	Interactive environment
	Ambiguous means–end relationship
	Requires interpretation
	Strategy formation
	Substantive rational schools
	• Processual
	  • Muddling through
	  • Incrementality and evolution
	  • Organized anarchy
	  • Strategy-as-practice
	• Systemic
	  • Social action
	  • Complexity
	• Discursive

Strategy determinant paradigm • Capability-building • Individual and group psychology of organizational strategy agents	Strategy determinant paradigm • Forces in the external environment/natural selection • Capability-building • Cultural context, including individual and group psychology of organizational and market agents
Expected outcome • The intended outcomes, with few or no emergent ones	Expected outcome • Some or none of the intended outcomes, and persistent shifts of goals and emergent outcomes

rationality is central to our understanding of strategy; this treatment has not been attempted before. By offering a robust understanding of strategy through interpreting a wide range of authorial text we hope that we have removed much of the confusion that surrounds the strategy phenomenon. Furthermore, in developing an understanding of strategy which draws upon opposing paradigms from the breadth of the strategy literature, we have reinforced the view that any one strategy paradigm provides only a very partial knowledge of strategy, particularly in the complex high-velocity environments of the creative industries, while also contributing towards our understanding of some aspects of strategy. Thus we have offered an example of multi-paradigm theory-building as we have linked and juxtaposed conflicting paradigm insights into a novel understanding. We have demonstrated that a multi-paradigm inquiry has proven useful in understanding a complex organizational concept, particularly as we have strived to respect contrasting approaches by juxtaposing the partial understandings they offer through a fusion of horizons.

Our understanding of strategy has also a significant implication for managers. We noted earlier that managers find the academic tools of strategy wanting. In highlighting the inadequacy of the various strategy schools and paradigms to capture the totality of strategy, we add to the strategy discourse by offering explanations as to why strategies may or may not work. We point out that in the instrumental rational approach of strategy, managers are seen to use the available means in pursuit of designated ends. However, in some of the substantive rational approaches, particularly the evolutionary approach and 'self-organization', managers' agency is reduced to mere response and adaptation; hence the notion of 'emergent' or 'unintended' strategy. Thus managers who are empowered with a privileged agency in the instrumental rational approach are seen largely as mere bearers of 'emerging patterns' in these substantive approaches. Our understanding of strategy allows us to recognize and reinstate managers' agency through the notion of 'intendedness' of strategy; and by offering an understanding which portrays strategy as intended, instrumental and interpretive, we alert managers to the problems inherent in instrumental rational calculation and in some of the substantive rational approaches.

In the next section we give a brief description of the methodology which we have used to read authorial text on 'what strategy is' so that you can have a view on how we interpreted the literature.

Interpreting the literature on 'what strategy is': our hermeneutic methodology

In our interpretive reading of the literature on 'what strategy is', we followed Schwandt (1994) and Prasad and Prasad (2002) in viewing interpretive research as a broad philosophy of social construction whose goal is to gain understanding rather than to capture a pre-existing reality. To this end, we used hermeneutics, not as 'a narrowly defined method but as a broad epistemology and philosophy of understanding' (Prasad 2002: 23), to interpret authorial text on 'what strategy is'.

We drew insights from Gadamer's (1975, 1989) philosophical hermeneutics and Ricoeur's (1981) concepts concerning the 'exploration of the act of interpretation' and 'critique'.

The concept of 'hermeneutic circle' is used by the classical hermeneutic writers, Schleiermacher (1985) and Dilthey (1976), to imply that 'the part can only be understood from the whole and the whole from the inner harmony of its parts' (Palmer 1969: 77).

Prasad (2002) points to an important methodological consideration which follows from this concept that emphasizes the significance of the context for the purpose of interpreting a text. He sees the necessity not only to define the context but to do so at different levels of comprehensiveness. He thus advises organizational researchers to begin the process of interpretation at a lower level of context and gradually move up to higher-level contexts: from the 'parts' to the 'whole' with increasing comprehensiveness (p. 24). In this work, we depart from Prasad's linear, 'part/whole' treatment of the text because we feel that it would not reveal the complexity of what strategy is. Instead, we apply the hermeneutic 'part/whole' dialectic to the interplay of texts between the different levels of our hermeneutic circle (see Figure 1.3). The 'whole', the totality, that we are trying to understand in this chapter, is 'what strategy is'. The context of the first level, which is central to our understanding, is the 'form of rationality' that underpins this understanding and the means–end relationship in strategy. This also governs the various strategy schools and paradigms – the second-level context. Emanating from the totality, moving down the schools of thought and strategy paradigms, a set of lower-order formulations – derivatives of specific conceptualization closest to the context of concrete enquiry – make the context of the third level of the hermeneutic circle. These formulations consist of strategy models, frameworks, tools and practices, such as planning models, market positioning frameworks, problem-solving tools and social practices associated with strategizing.

In the interplay of textual contexts from different levels – the 'parts' – of the hermeneutic circle we hope to arrive at a robust understanding of 'what strategy is' – the 'whole'. For this understanding to emerge, we follow Palmer's (1969: 87) admonition to go beyond logic and analysis and into the realm of intuition. By doing so, we acknowledge that our pre-understanding of strategy and the way we constructed the contexts and levels of our hermeneutic circle display our 'value-laden dimension' (Prasad 2002: 24).

Central to Gadamer's hermeneutic philosophy is the concept of 'pre-understanding' of the interpreter, embedded in the tradition or historical-social background of the interpreter and the horizon within which the interpreter understands the text. Gadamer (1989: 269) points out that the act of interpretation occurs within a circular movement between the interpreter's prior understanding, or prejudice, of the 'whole' and an examination of its

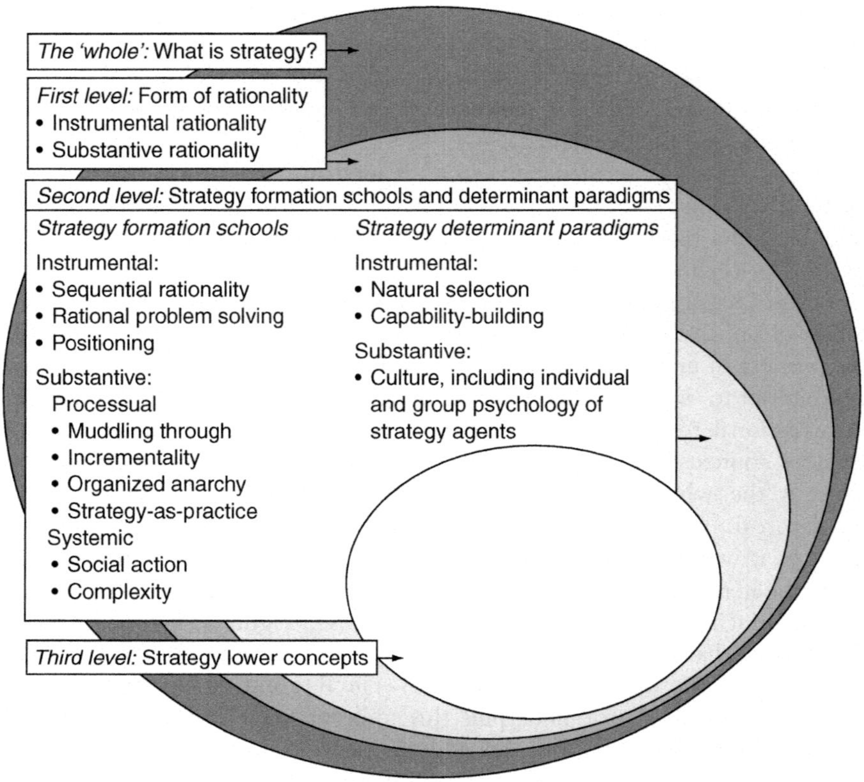

Figure 1.3 The 'whole' and the 'parts' of a hermeneutic circle of strategy

'parts'. It is our prejudices which constitute our own 'historical being' (Gadamer 1975: 245) and define the limits and potentialities of our horizon of understanding (Gadamer 1989: 302).

Gadamer (1975: 263) draws a distinction between 'productive prejudices' that enhance understanding and 'unproductive prejudices' that hinder understanding and lead to misunderstanding; he asserts that in the process of understanding, unproductive prejudices must be eliminated to allow the fusion of the horizon of the interpreter and that of the text (p. 266). Similarly, Ricouer's (1981) concept of 'distanciation' encourages interpreters to distance themselves from their own prejudices and preconceived understandings and from their reading of the text. Conscious of our prejudices, seen in our own hermeneutic horizon as strategy academics where our knowledge of the 'whole' is shaped by our reading of the strategy text, and of our unproductive prejudices displayed in: (a) our subscription to the view of strategy as a troubled discipline, and (b) our experience as practitioners[1] of the low value of the strategy text, we endeavoured to suspend our unproductive prejudices, allowing our productive ones to facilitate our understanding. We attempted to do this by refusing to privilege or reject any authorial strategy paradigm or concept – our productive prejudices. Instead we endeavoured to expand our own horizon of prejudices by entering into a conversation with the text; we also showed openness for tradition by calling upon and questioning conflicting authorial texts from divergent strategy schools, paradigms and concepts to arrive at authentic understanding. We, in a sense, displayed a measure of methodological self-reflexiveness and 'critique of prejudice' (Ricoeur 1990). Critical self-reflexivity was also present in our remaining conscious of the potential that exposure to the literature might impact upon our views while drawing concepts and questions, and checking the appropriateness of our explanation of the meaning emerging from our conversation with authorial text.

Gadamer's (1989) philosophical hermeneutics and Ricouer's concept of 'appropriation' reject 'authorial intention' – the author's intentional view of interpretation – of the early classical hermeneutic writers. They urge the interpreter to derive meaning from the text, independently of 'authorial intention' and the historical, social and cultural factors of its creation. For Gadamer and Ricouer, understanding means to understand the author's text with reference to our own horizon of experience – the meaning of a past text is defined in terms of the questions put to it from the present. Textual interpretation is, therefore, not only a reproductive exercise but also a productive one: a moving forward, exploring, challenging, shaping and altering the horizons and prejudices of the interpreter (Langdridge 2004). By adopting this mode of textual interpretation, we tried to challenge and expand our prejudices and preconceptions and move our own horizon to develop a new understanding (Geanellos 2000) of 'what strategy is'.

Gadamer (1975, 1989) points to a further limitation of classical hermeneutics, its reliance on the notion of the dichotomy of subject (interpreter) and object (text), which he finds philosophically unacceptable. He considers interpretation not as a 'mere acquisition of the mind', not as 'something produced by remaining outside the text', but as participation in the tradition of the text (Prasad 2002: 19). Such participation, Gadamer (1975: 331) elaborates, implies that interpretation or understanding is a 'dialogue' where the meaning of the text emerges through a conversation between the interpreter and the text; to Ricouer, this dialogue is a dialectic between distanciation and appropriation (Geanellos 2000).

As interpreters, we followed Gadamer and Ricouer by refusing to confine meaning to authorial intentions; instead we allowed meaning to emerge from our conversation – 'hermeneutic dialogue' – with authorial strategy text, attempting to bring about a 'fusion of horizons' (Gadamer 1989: 306). The systematic approach to text was key in our interpretive reading of strategy; starting from the most general order of significance, i.e. the 'ontological' level, moving on to the specific schools of thought within the two key paradigms of rationality and ordering them in a dialectic fashion. The point of data saturation was reached upon recognizing that the intricate nuances between different paradigms and schools of thought were seen in their dialectic complexity, and then fusing the horizons of the somewhat opposed modes of rationality in third-level strategic concepts. Thus we formulated our hermeneutic circle through the order of significance: the totality level/ontology; the higher level/epistemology; the medium level/teleology; the lower level/concrete emanations, multiplicity of contrasting and somewhat contradicting applications, models and tools.

Note

1 Ali Bakir occupied senior managerial roles with engineering consultancy firms and educational roles with senior managerial responsibilities in the public sector; he hardly used strategic management tools, and from his observations, nor did his management colleagues. Also as management consultant, he offered these tools to clients, who did not find them very useful. Milan Todorovic has been a creative industry practitioner since 1992, and has in this context observed the failure of existing strategy literature to account for the complex cultural phenomena that act both as the evidence and recognized cause of strategic decisions in this fluctuating field of practice.

2 Methodology, tools and analytics

Introduction: towards an integrated methodology

This chapter is dedicated to methodology of creative industry strategy. Some key elements of findings will be presented below. These are discussed as part of the contribution to the understanding of links between the specific ontology of what a particular industry is, and the way in which such ontology formulates the general approaches to knowledge further defined through methods applied in practice (epistemology to teleology). One of the key tenets of this book is that a specific strategy can be logically derived from the in-depth understanding of the core features of a creative work epitomizing the specific industry or sector ('vertical mode') and the segment or niche ('horizontal mode') under analysis. Examining the combination of abstract and contextually-specific features of a strategy is done context by context, each classified across a variety of methods and approaches.

Utilitarian value approaches

'Value as utility' is intrinsic in nature.

It can be read as *analytic a priori*:

> *Value is useful.*
> *All use is of value.*
> *Usefulness can be evaluated.*
> *Evaluation can be useful.*
> *Usefulness is evaluated.*
> *Evaluation is useful.*

There is no evidence that any of the above statements contradict one another or require further elaboration. They are axiomatic, not subject to proof. However, the nature of relationships within those statements is worth exploring in detail. *How* is value made *useful*, *how* is use *evaluated*, may be understood through observation, interpretation or speculation. Whether a particular value is of use, or a particular utility proven valuable, is subject to method of measurement and comparative context, a system of reference.

Therefore, any business model, any strategy, any product or service *centred on utility* may be subjected to measurement and requirements of evidence of causality. In times of industrial revolution, paradigm change and the transformation of systems of reference, entire value models may be subverted and notions of standard practice may become obsolete. This occurs where the entire foundation of 'what constitutes value' and 'what is use'/'purpose' are redefined on a fundamental level, the substructure of any fixed form. In such cases, concepts of causality will change relative to the conceptual shift. Even if the value of utility cannot be disputed on a fundamental level, its efficiency could, which would result in large-scale renegotiations of bargaining power. In addition to the role of public speech and personal identity, re-representations of bargaining power relations constitute causes on the scale of redefining the *social contract* (as loosely termed and derived from the work of Rousseau). The material, measurable impact of methodological shifts relates to qualitative changes of the positions, roles and codes in society. To what extent these relationships are causal cannot be postulated without actual data (*synthetic a posteriori*). This book presents such ambiguous relationships as dialectic in principle – before conclusive evidence of test validity/reliability for a class of cases, e.g. in software.

Causality-driven processes and operations

A respondent from the ICT sector declares his interest in causality by identifying the logic behind the software built to make decisions in the absence of human intervention – part of his and his company's mission is 'causality'. Alongside transparency, and the understanding of the totality of all data that is available within the context of an observed phenomenon in a given context, this respondent believes that evidence of causality in relation to one's own actions can create a new sense of responsibility and nurture it culturally through ICT tools and media. He has no doubt that causal processes can be identified, analysed and proven, and that what online tools and data analytics contribute is centred on *revealing the facts that were always there*. He remains unconcerned about the issue of devaluing of content as its multiplicity and ubiquity indicate that the means of capturing value by commercial exchange exist; they are there, yet remain hidden, undiscovered at present. The conviction that digital tools can resolve the matter of matching art with audiences is underpinned by a discourse that is influenced by the disciplines of mechanics, mathematical logic and ecology alike. Complementing this discourse is the respondent's reflection on disruptive innovation and of the inevitability of change, which would involve a form of artificial intelligence to make sense of data sets that humans cannot process.

This element of *innovation as strategy*, placed within the ontological level of formulating an ICT service, acts as a complement to traditional business model planning. The process, controllable variables, clear identification of cost and value, evaluation of revenue streams and decision-making: all are components of mainstream operational modelling. Moreover, this respondent's positivistic approach is confirmed in his observation that statistically, the output of content must mean that more of that would be available to users and in a selective manner, given the right ICT tools. This discourse is not isolated, as its assumptions are methodologically sound and they are based on logical models akin to the tools developed by the respondent's company. However, this causative discourse is complemented by the multidisciplinary nature of some leading works in theory and practice citing chaos theory and thermodynamics in management and data analysis, as well as cognition/culture intersections. Both of these supersede the current ability of ICT to develop abstract decision-making.

There is further evidence that a classical *means-to-ends* school of thought is successfully and continuously integrated into practice in creative industries, sectors and even emerging enterprises. A leading content distributor uses SWOT analysis (strengths, weaknesses, opportunities, threats) for its marketing planning, reporting and effectiveness monitoring; meetings are held to promote shared values in approaches to planning; revenue streams are evaluated against operational costs; networking and outsourcing is planned in terms of effectiveness and cost incentives etc. (Jarzabkowski 2010). On the other hand, a respondent ponders if a politically-motivated decision on collaborative projects in a public medium was behind the illogical and ill-conceived policy shift towards major market cooperation for documentary shows. Contrasting the logic of business rationality is the comment made by an entertainment media professional on continued investment in loss leaders. On the other hand, where rationality itself is not being disputed and its innovative form endorsed, the crude means-to-ends measurements are criticized by those respondents who believe innovation brings value by creation and not acquisition.

Respondents from major entertainment sectors are cautious to note that value structure online should be analysed and transformed in a complex way, but with the necessary in-depth understanding of what a particular component of a model does, some of those components not being entirely rational, as 'experiences'. An innovator and entrepreneur states that his design studio 'cooks' the ingredients, working with high-end technology through empirical means that involve substantive operational and processual planning. A highly logical structure of value operations is tested against *interpretive* results of *user experience*.

Causality therefore should not be considered in a narrow sense of the term. Respondent accounts and salient cases in strategy practice indicate that working in field environments involves a combination of planning of value structures, detailed performance analysis and conceptual development which requires imagination; an interaction between the rationally construed and culturally conditioned/historic practices; a complex interplay of *value and values* etc. The number and scope of human and human–machine interactions is such that empirical models can be drawn to represent behaviour in terms of thermodynamic systems as drawn by Stacey in his pioneering work. A new equivalence needs to be drawn here: the correlation between a discourse of scientific rationality and actual natural phenomena (notwithstanding any matters that may make human behaviour unpredictable or non-deterministic). The subject of science *seldom behaves scientifically* at times of transformation of entire systems reference: as *synthetic a priori*, fundamentally altered substructure (technology, ownership, discourse, method, business- or social-logic) forces changes in language which would be used to describe changing or emerging phenomena. It brings out the surprise with the newly discovered – or revealed – relationships between components of a system; it is not predictive by definition. Even where measurable targets are set by institutional funding models and their policy impact can be accounted for, this does not guarantee that the formulation of such targets is rational from the causal-utilitarian perspective.

Semiotics and symbolic action

Semiotic analysis in cultural and creative sectors is frequently confined to audience studies, fan cultures or media text analyses, i.e. the matters relating to social reception of a media text. Less frequently explored is the strategic relevance of organizational semiotics in creative industries, i.e. the effect of symbolic value on structures of planning and practice in creative sectors (Bilton, Negus and Hesmondhalgh produced notable work in this area).

However, as claimed by respondents, digital media and their constituent ICT substructures create the means for transparency and *reveal 'what was always there'*, and the emergent digital media organizations possess the means to represent their value through an advanced use of symbols that represent their actual utilitarian brand value, based on reliable services and intrinsically defined signs of superior performance. The combination of representational and abstract signification is at the heart of such persuasive branding tools.

This study covers interviews with several decision-makers in the fields of media, marketing and communications within the creative sectors, as well as those who design such tools used by creative professionals concerned with targeting and analytics. Moreover, two respondent sources and corresponding design strategy cases are of particular interest as these entrepreneurs use their own in-house ICT solutions to formulate subtle matters of branding and representation which are fully integrated with their project operations and modelling (Serrano Brothers, Assa Ashuach Studio).

Possibly the best example of such conceptually rounded symbolism falling outside the fieldwork conducted for this book is the complex message read into the branded application 'Map of the Internet', covered elsewhere in this book. The free application written for tablet computers and smartphones epitomizes the kind of expertise required of a web-support and hosting service. The elegance of application design is not merely visual, though this is a visual tool; it is conceptual and functional in nature. Its limited functionality is inherent in the popular format: in principle, a user of the Map of the Internet can focus on any important node in an 'ISP universe' presented on the screen. However, the limitations of format and of the very material of tangible application media used (tablet devices) indicate that this is a mere branding tool showing, in principle, how aware and data-focused the company is and how well it applies its knowledge of networks: a visual representation of network expertise.

Symbolic action in strategy

Organizations can enact their own internal symbolism, which is meaningful in their identity and loyalty constructs. Symbolic action is ritualistic, as in cases described by Jarzabkowski *et al.* (2010) detailing the meaning of symbolic enactment of reinsurance rituals with special designate underwriters' pens, used for traditional signing and counter-signing of important documents. Questioning the actual value of such established business rituals as contrasted with modern, high-efficiency methods of processing is a highly relevant subject in many ways surpassing this particular study. Yet it is indicative of the importance of 'ways things are done' and ingrained practices reflecting organizational culture which may hold some lasting relevance and significance, or in a number of cases be obsolete and an obstacle to progress, innovation and efficiency. The ritualistic nature of 'standard [contractual] deals' is one such example – the 'proper' way of doing things may prevent an organization from evolving and staying competitive and relevant. Licensing innovation, data processing and development of disruptive business models is thus frequently left to 'outsiders' that subsequently or consequently capture the market by enveloping the opponent with a radically altered proposition (as will be seen below in this chapter). The historical and developmental features of a widely adopted industry strategy can be read into by examining the symbolic value of widely adopted contractual or licensing models across entertainment industries, this including (sometimes obsolete) terminology fixed by a set of (past) practical considerations (especially in music and media sectors).

Examples of *bricolage* are found in strategic marketing practice (interview data) in ways resembling the discursive character of organizational experimentation.

Below are some interview extracts from the areas of high-end digital music marketing and advanced integrated/blended experience architecture. These provide valuable insight into improvisation, bricolage, creative editing as features of organizational design and inherently symbolic practice it entails.

> You have to understand how technology works, how the platform works, how it really, really works, and how it connects within the system, how it connects with the end user … and when you do, do it well, and then go like, I wonder, if I mashed that up … or I wonder if I

> took that API and I did this, for example ... we're building a game on Spotify at the moment ...
>
> You understand how Spotify works, it's cool, it's social, it's exciting, it's quick ... it's cloud ... you kinda go ... the problem is the discovery's there but it's not driven by certain things, and then it's social but it's not fun with friends so ... how do we create something that is fun with friends and is new – well, let's make a game!
>
> (A. Bogucki interview 2013, hereafter AB 2013)

Consulted on a similar matter of functionality management, Diego Serrano reflects

> It's brand new, the concept [hotel room experience]. Which scenario you wish to wake up with. Select the earthquake – the bed shakes. 'My City' is another scenario. We can install new experience through the internet connection we have in a hotel and we can connect to our server to install the new experience. For instance, we will have this kind of room in Brazil so for the World Cup we can install any experience we like, to make it immersive like this [shows]. Because it is interesting for your guest. And that is the point. We are thinking, planning, working always with the guest in mind.
>
> (D. Serrano interview 2014)

Contrasting and comparing the two respondents' reflections on organizing for innovation, the following observations can be noted:

> [Use of interaction].... It really depends on the creator, the artist, producers, the writer ... it really depends on their openness for collaboration, for manipulation, or any sort of engagement that would allow to alter, is one way of putting it, or allow the consumer, the person that's consuming that bit of creative art or whatever it is, to become either part of it, or ... across creative industries ... with mobile technology becoming part of our everyday lives, the opportunity for artists to engage in such things are infinite, but ... in the music industry it would alter what these artists are, and that would change the whole perception of it, it's understandable that artists are protective of their identity.
>
> (AB 2013)

Bogucki also reflects on any number of techniques for generating ideas, including brainstorming – stating that it is good that the current climate characterized by change facilitates such rethinking of tools, techniques and models. However, the hierarchical nature of major corporation operations dictates appropriate structuring; such meetings facilitate innovation but the norm remains fixed, due to organizational imperatives in highly competitive environments. By contrast, Diego Serrano observes, while presenting a meeting area specifically designed by the studio for use with partners and collaborators:

> A multi-use space. Space for the partners, for the architects to meet and creatives for partnerships because we are here in Barcelona. Did you know about the area.... Technological innovation area.... We want the people collaborating with us. Collaborative community of creatives more than a normal studio.... It's been a hard time and you have to find a way to collaborate. People working online, sending messages and cooperating.... It's a big challenge – all start-ups need some funding, the other part is people.
>
> (DS 2014)

This is an example of cooperative competition, which was postulated in the works on transforming supply models especially in the wake of ICT business culture (Graham *et al.* 2004). Cooperative symbolism generates its own value structures – or cooperative structures reflect a change in the evaluation of symbols as carriers of meaning. A design studio or independent TV producer may operate that way; not so for the major record company sector, as commented by a key respondent in that area – conceding, however:

> And there is the big media which is threatened by individuals with a powerful voice created by themselves. There is a lot of bloggers out there. 'Perez Hilton'.... They're 'themselves, inc.'.... YouTube channels, kids ... all these young people who are creating verticals for themselves who are happy to cooperate with each other. The cooperative competition exist there on YouTube.
>
> (AB 2013)

Symbolic action represents and reveals structures of meaning that connote the sets of beliefs, ethics and values an organization upholds. In their previous guise as participating members of audiences, subcultures, countercultures, consumer segments as genre and style groups and scenes, people adhered to less dynamic structures of meaning and socio-cultural identity and their identification with a given discourse was marked by comparative loyalty to their 'home' audience/style segment. Identification ran long-term and when it withered, it did so in a way that was ideologically charged. Meaningful and sustainable symbolic practice seems to be shifting from audiences and individual creators (now users and creative workers) to organizations and their brands and business model interfaces.

The current terming of 'traditional media' and 'culture industries' played a transformative role in the formation of markets for mass culture characterized by linear modes of production, dissemination and distribution within a comparatively small, discrete number of market segments in various forms and sectors. The drivers of trends were frequently connected to youth scenes and genres, with corresponding market sectors and segments, which would lead to adoption across mainstream media and consumer markets. These included fashion, music, events, media, design, and to a lesser degree theatre, performing arts and visual arts (unless subversive or connected to discourses of fashion trends or hedonic leisure). These market genres and forms frequently displayed mutually exclusive discursive relationships based on inherent contradictions of binary opposition of meaning and connotative expression. Their corresponding conceptualizations were frequently at odds on aesthetic, ethical and ideological (expressed or implied) grounds. Binary, dialectic tensions of theses and antitheses in linear cultures of a discrete number of linear mass discourses in leisure created a sense of membership and adherence to sets of meaning known as genre, style or scene. The terms 'independent' in the context of film and music, 'street fashion' or 'underground press' represented powerful narratives reflected in organizational, economic and subcultural structures driven by artists, producers, audiences and entrepreneurs.

Such conceptualizations were at the core of phenomena such as scenes, subcultures (subculture as demographic) and audience segments. These conceptualizations ranged from overt and conscious representations of ideological discourse (hippies, punks) to implied meaning enacted through leisure practices (disco, acid house). The transitory nature of audience segments (post-Maffesoli 1996 and Bennett 2001) appeared as a new feature of the latter stages of the centralizing scarcity control of linear 'culture industries', preceding the dominance of networked, ICT-driven 'creative industries'. The transitory nature of audience allegiance and the disappearance of most of the fixed, oppositional movements, subcultures, genres and scenes marked the decline of long-term ideological adherence of their members to any major discourse. This happened in the latter stages of media fragmentation, as centralized broadcast media started to adopt digital multiplicity of channels and niches, and the corresponding fragmentation of digital production into a stylistic multiplicity of niche genres. Epitomized in Kellner's (1997) statement that 'difference sells', this was the final fragmentation of centralized linear media and centralized linear culture industries expressed by means of diversity targeting in culture consumption trends. The relative hegemony of old electronic media is of near monolithic proportions when a case is observed, reflecting the high relative focus of mass culture over digital mass-custom fragmentation: the Google crash over searches related to Michael Jackson in June 2009. Following such symbolical representations of paradigm shifts, audience discourses seem more fleeting and transitory than ever, through the levelling illusion of online networks over major discourses, and over art forms which become 'content' in the potentially infinite fragmentation of audience attention across content niches.

In contemporary online interactive environments, the most successful virtual navigators (Graham *et al.* 2004), even the most meaningful of audience discourses, are marked by a shift from audiences to users, which is equivalent to the shift from linear culture industries to distributed creative sectors. The power of *virtual navigators* as mediators lay in their ability to enable focus by facilitating discursive distribution of user communication and their ability to treat meshes of communication, content and user preferences as data, irrespective of the dense, *thick descriptions* of interpretations of 'meaning' and treating the most profound of discourses as content. The resulting diminishing of value not only affects the creative works through distribution and free use; it also levels the value of all discourses and events, which too are *content-laden forms of data.* This is not to say that users may not follow or participate in the creation of symbolic action: they do, and it ranges from fan-generated content to pledge and peer-support models of crowdfunding. Enactment of singular, authentic user-driven discourses seldom occurs on such a scale as to formulate transformative symbolic practice. Notions of neutrality, perfect competition and user empowerment, uncritically adopted in early public discourse, gave way to the examination of emerging structural hierarchies in online media distribution and communication. In such circumstances, creative organizations and entrepreneurs emerge as the symbolic actors and this informs their strategy.

The discursive power of business models is reflected in branding (which also counts for the more static business models before the online ICT paradigm shift). This is of particular interest when examining the connections between functional solutions in value structures, experience-orientated project planning, and links between aesthetics, values and utility. This will be examined in more detail in Chapter 5. Start-up organizations are particularly important in formulating the utility of such symbolic action that leads to evidential outcomes in business innovation. Here, symbolic action is part of a product–service continuum. It is a component of an integrated operational structure, co-causally connected with function, performance, user targeting, user research, experience design and implementation. Such an integrated structure characterized by innovation, reach and use value has to demonstrate its utility before a symbolic meaning may be formulated for, with or by users. It will be seen how respondents across varied creative and cultural industries' sectors reflect on symbolic practice in their fields.

Representation and abstraction

Worringer (1908) wrote on the creative shift that marked visual arts of the 1900s, revealing a tension between the paradigms of visual art.

Why this example?

Representation and abstraction stand in *binary* opposition of the kind that can be found in *linear* modes of culture production that defined twentieth-century media and mass-culture. Taken as a literary or visual tool, representation aims to blend the symbolical form of art media with the manifest material nature of the object. Abstraction, on the other hand, aims at extracting the deep meaning and presents it in reductionist form. This can be seen as an equivalence of methods for organizational learning such as case studies (representation) and political economy models of analysis (abstraction) in culture production and creativity. Moreover, representation may form symbolic texts on processes encoded in such as brand image, which consists of many more concepts and stimuli than the term 'image' would imply. Rather, it forms a network of associations, texts and media discourses, organizational cultures and experiences related to the brand, thus clearly of strategic significance. As such, brand or company 'image' is an abstract notion based on a metaphor rooted in visual representation. A further, structural elaboration connecting the study of *plastic anatomy* and business models is examined in Chapter 5.

Another abstract notion, that of pattern: one of the very few visual illustrations used in this book, and the only diagram imported from external sources, is the screenshot of a Peer1 Hosting application, Map of the Internet. This application is a prime case of evidence-based, value-driven PR that is contextually rounded: a hosting services firm designs an elegant, conceptually accurate and effective visual model of the internet. Beyond the evident branding implications of this software application (part of their business model), which is also discussed in Chapter 5, lies a more fundamental exploration of the two models of design employed here: the *geographical* and *structural view* of the internet map. These two clearly show the validity of an 'artistic' approach to rational components of management, as well as the evidence-driven functional design as an aspect of business aesthetics (the latter eloquently discussed by a designer respondent).

While the geographical, representational aspect of the map says little more than was already known about the spatial distribution of economic power, technological assets and nodes of influence, the other aspect of network *physicality* is made far clearer in the structural representation of the map, which reveals an operational hierarchy, irrespective of particular geography or history of the internet. Rather, it represents it as an entity in principle: a generic network phenomenon that possesses a particular form, the outlines of which would vary little irrespective of a different history of control or ownership, as the diagram thus conceived represents the hierarchical structure inherent in the model itself. The structure of the internet is thus far better represented to those who need to understand its functioning by abstract (structural) than representational (geographical) means. However, as is accounted for in several interviews dealing specifically with digital networks and data analytics in management and marketing, fully functioning analytical diagrams that are used as tools for management, planning and design would create clear and accurate representations of detailed correlations between the respective spatial and structural views of networks. One reason why both representational and structural correlations matter: operational analysis of functions performed in environments that are tangible, spatial, material and corpuscular, i.e. those of measurable value and quantifiable impact.

Abstraction can in turn be presented in the form of chains, networks, meshes, business model tools and high-level interpretations of matrices and detailed performance analyses. Paraphrasing a designer/product designer respondent, the copying of what was already done as a functional solution elsewhere is closely connected to the market capture approach behind horizontal, vertical and diagonal acquisition. On the other hand, he sees his rationally construed design role on the side of the abstract, where concept development and contextual planning precede any concrete representation of an 'aesthetic' or 'form' in a visual sense. Functionality comes before visual form. Thus, the form of a design solution, or the economy of business modelling in operation/service design, may have 'aesthetic value' of a 'beautiful' solution. Such abstract approaches relate to the root concept of the unknown and unknowable character of innovation before a solution is postulated on the basis of a imaginary problem that is the result of conceptual extrapolation of the known environment (empirical in nature).

An artistic analogy with *plastic anatomy* was seen to offer an approach: understanding anatomy means understanding replicable structures, but every individual is uniquely built. An imaginary x-ray was used by generations of classically trained art students, who would build the anatomical structure into the description of visible surfaces of the human subject in their art-studies. Such a coherent and rigorous method is artistic in nature but not fancifully 'creative' (as will be seen, some respondents are not at ease with connotations of 'creative'). A rigour inherent in classical art training combines the understanding of technique and form that corresponds with the creative skills required for work and practice in the more recently emerging sectors including audiovisual production, product design and software development. Artistic work and creative production share a combination of analytical rigour and the understanding of opportunities and limitations of technologies and techniques used. Conceptually rounded approaches to value creation and value capture are similar, in that they combine analytical tools and creative methods within a thoroughly researched business context.

Reflexivity, identity and creative enterprise

Reflexivity in strategy is contingent on its purpose and application, its methodological consistency and evidential value. Its effectiveness is contrasted with the infinitely repetitive spiral of questions, frameworks and conceptual analyses in cases where processes of reflexivity in research strategy and analysis of knowledge concepts are not tied to a definitive goal.

Strategy, positioning and manoeuvre

Elsewhere, this book explores creativity as a feature of strategy and the converse correspondence of the strategic character of creativity. This work acknowledges the contributions of other authors and builds on them by examining the ontology of relationships between strategy and creativity and its inherent logic, especially those aspects of it that govern innovation.

Manoeuvre and positioning are therefore perceived as creative categories, as the cognition of innovation characterizes some defining moments in subverting all future actions of the opponent by anticipating deep-level change in a market in which the newcomer has little room for positioning. The well known contest of Apple vs. Sony that 'removed the Walkman brand from the market pretty well' (MIDEM 2013) and by extension enveloped entire 'traditional', 'content', linear/culture industries is contrasted and complemented by a longitudinal case study based on a novel type of business model that has made a cumulative impact on events and entertainment experiences across Britain and Europe. The first part of the nearly decade-long research feed concerns one of the very first data-driven business models in events, merchandising and experience management that has metaphorically 'legalized' live 'bootlegging' by providing evidential means to redefine its specific contextual position within a *high competitive rivalry environment.* The reference to Porter's Five Forces (1985) and supply chain (1985) analysis is intentional. The former was used to explore innovation leaps as causes of qualitative transformation of the market configuration, secured through multiple facets consisting of quantitative data, sales and royalty impacts, and privileged, fresh access to audience data through tactics labelled in this text 'content for contact' trade-offs. The latter is used to explore various revenue stream configurations; the validity of the 'chain' concept is confirmed *through its reconfiguration as network, or as a specific case of a general notion.* If it were incorrect to formulate value structure as a chain, then the conceptualization of value/supply networks would be even more far-fetched. Since its validity is evidenced through existing business models, the network further validates the chain as its proto-paradigm, a discrete cause within the continuum of functional configurations. It will be seen that in both cases the creative innovation *within the product/service concept* acted as a destructive and subversive force from the point of view of its established competitors and their set business model logics.

Positioning and manoeuvre are explored by social pragmatists (e.g. Bernays, Gramsci, Mintzberg, Machiavelli) and methodologists (Hall, Foucault). The metaphorical poetic style of Sun Tzu also hints at turning abstract notions into the logic of value contest, risk evaluation and gaming foresight. The notion that *strategy is art – not science* (though logical) is rooted in its generic aims, which include contest, overpowering the opponent, domination and control.

Means justify ends

Pragmatism and application are among the key drivers in this research, in spite of its abstract and conceptual form. The aim of analysis is to achieve the breadth and depth required by the scale and nature of the problem; focusing on technical matters would not allow for such results. The relationship between means and ends and the utilitarian nature of strategy is queried across sectors. An emergent result of this is the examination of the equivalence between means and ends, found to be an important inherent feature of creative industry strategy. Whether this notion can be extended to strategy *as such*, subject to new research, will be examined alongside the relationships between creativity and strategy in the concluding sections of this book. The phrase 'ends justify means' is misattributed to Machiavelli. His discourse in *The Prince* is far more ambiguous. Moreover, the origins of such a maxim (never identical to the phrase thus cited) can be traced to Ovid and Sophocles. Machiavelli was inspired by the Ancients (Rome and Greece), just as many of his contemporaries were, and it is not surprising that he explored the classics in the context of the turbulent political landscape of Renaissance Italy. His pragmatism and thorough critique of the actual mismatch between the morality codes of the classics earned him undue vilification. His contribution, however, was not limited to the misattributed quote on methods of seizing practical gain through opportunity (a far more nuanced version of the ultimate consequentialist maxim does exist in his work). He debated the interaction between Fortuna and Virtu, concepts imported from Roman thought and dissected in fine detail. Their modern counterparts are structure and agency, the two tenets of many social science methodologies, not least the interaction between the entities of the economy and management. A careful reading of his work may indicate that this amounted to a refined precursor of today's ubiquitous SWOT analysis. Observing the pragmatism and consequentialism of such concepts leads to the investigation of strategy as utility and the questioning of 'values-based' approaches as purely altruistic. After all, a strategy without application is not a strategy. Therefore, values may act as tools, means which are just as utilitarian as are management techniques, research tools and marketing gimmicks.

In this research, abstract questions were placed alongside generic ones. Both were aimed at connecting the abstract nature of strategy formulation and conceptual planning with the concrete, subject- and practice-specific character of its implementation. The two notions that deserve added attention here are 'crisis of content' and 'gatekeeping'. Both terms are highly charged, and the respondents' varying comments on the two are indicative of their position and discursive stance as well as the operational practices in their respective sectors. For example, an ICT developer/manager seeks an understanding of the term 'gatekeeper' in the sense of subtly influencing data use by accurately understanding information about user behaviour. In this respect, the notion of gatekeeping is seen in a neutral manner, due to the changing notion of gatekeeping in digital interactions, whereby those who are capable of understanding the flow and use of data become capable of understanding the effective commercialization of content and emerging methods of value capture. This case represents the gatekeeper's metaphorical gate as the one that monitors and manages flow of use. A respondent from entertainment media rejects the term outright, considering it rigid and inappropriate to the type of responsibility of a media professional. He discusses the paradigm shift as the movement of media management professionals' focus from editorial to curatorial roles. The difference in wording and formulation is meaningfully reflected in practice and operations: editorial filtering (i.e. gatekeeping) practice is a far more linear practice of formulating playlists and other content promotion tactics, a process directly controlled by producers in a centralized manner characterizing one-to-many communications of broadcasting. Contrasted to that is the curatorial role of subtle content management by directing media content delivery and communications based on the ability of digital media models such as streaming, to learn from audience use and taste preferences, trending content and online chatter. The process is seen as even farther removed from the restrictive notion of gatekeeping, and curation is described as a light-touch, audience-conscious, data-led, research-informed, technologically-aided process of managing existing patterns of content use in interactive online media. This redefinition of gatekeeping, editing and filtering is qualitatively different from the one defining the linear media and traditional cultural sectors. It is closer to ICT-driven services referred to above, and while it does advocate specialist expertise and *values-based* decision-making, it is a more neutral and light-touch, pull-supply model of media content management. Similar findings are reflected across the digital media, including bundling and curatorial services of higher rank than streamers (Shuffler). Contrasted to this is the candid and contextually appropriate response of a major music label's digital marketing manager: 'we are the gatekeepers'. The tools and methods of industry practice are further unfolded in his reflection on the means of control and filtering adopted by high-level corporate strategies in music. In this context can be seen his reading of types of innovation, effective digital project management, planning tools and stages of implementation. It will be seen that terms such as 'crisis of content' elicited varied debates with respondents, frequently closely reflecting their operational position, market sector and segment, alignment of interest and clients both direct and indirect.

A connection between abstract and generic questions and means utilized in practice is revealed in each such case, including the opposite end of the spectrum of creative work, where respondents' formulation of strategy involves concepts as varied as those of social engagement, cultural and artistic development or reflection. An artist respondent rejects the notion of financial utility and sees it as a means to a non-commercial ends. Another visual artist respondent examines funding policies in public arts that have led to the rise of conceptual art within the context, or as a function of early neo-liberal policies. Their gaze, aim and focus are different, so there appears to be an inversion of means and ends when contrasted with managers of media and content management organizations, from small IT businesses to corporations. The means-to-ends relationship does remain utilitarian even in such cases: the interest of the artists *and gallery owner* interviewed for this book differ radically from those managing content-driven services such as music media – still, they employ practical, business means to attain less fixed, abstractly driven ends. Both of those key strategic components are as clearly formulated as their circumstances allow, and it will be seen that their utility is of a different ontological character but that the utilitarian nature of such planning remains.

Other respondents, such as the two managing directors of European festivals, also indicate a values-driven approach to management of means. Correlated to this are responses of art venue managers and gallery owners, visual artists and designers, architects and some hotel managers, as will be seen later in the text. The Exit festival and Rheinkultur are positioned at two very distant ends of events discourse in music and public support for culture and heritage. Both of these large-scale annual festival events significantly depend on public support of varied types. The means they employ turn into realized strategies that define them. Therefore, ascertaining the link between the abstract notion of strategy (ontology) and the best modes of implementation within the concrete (case) requires addressing teleological questions on contextual equivalence between means and ends common to all sectors examined. Those questions were posed within a broad context of possible scenarios involving functional, abstract and socially-driven strategy tools.

A seemingly inverse logic of the title is based on the dialectics of relations of equivalence: postulating the equivalence between strategic means and ends. This enquiry is particular to the context of creativity and culture.

The inversion of a *consequentialist* argument is for the purpose of testing the relationship of equivalence between ends and means. If it is proven that the value of the procedure tools and processes deployed in strategy does represent a form of utility that is coherent with desired types of outcome, then the outcome is proven to be directly or indirectly contingent on methods, tools and processes. The direct evidence of utility may not always be available, just as predicting the outcome of an innovation is unknowable in actual and definitive form. The impact of processes and procedures may not be causally defined in a generalizable sense. However, strategic implementation may come from noteworthy cases centred on the coherence between the in-depth understanding of core competencies and the selection of (intrinsic) *values-based* tools and processes deployed in the place of, or in addition to, utilitarian ones. Such coherence aids the decision-makers working on strategy deployment in order to develop and enact a shared sense of perspective, first within the organization and subsequently with its partners, competitors, clients and stakeholders.

In creative industries, form *is* content. The function of a fully developed creative work is matched by its unique aesthetics, as some respondents have discussed.

If 'the ends' of any given business strategy may be defined on the highest level of abstraction as mundane and generic expectations of every organization driven by commercial imperatives, then 'ends' in business can be abstracted to maintaining or increasing revenue, profit, market position, share, range, market capture, control etc. If the minimum end for any organization is a continuation of its operational existence, then such existence rests on sustaining its ability to operate in markets or other public environments (as the necessary cause). Such generic ends therefore range broadly, covering all aims from survival or continued operation, to organizational autonomy or operational independence, to *meta-goals* of revenue generation, profit-making leading to segment, sector or market position, market capture and market control. Irrespective of level of expectation and degree of interest, any fundamental organizational ends remain generic and mundane, shaped by material forces and evidenced through the relationship between costs and *measurable* returns. Therefore, the exploration of principal, ontological strategic 'ends' is insufficient for an in-depth re-examination of strategies for creative industries. On the ontological level, any organization aims to survive, operate and capture value.

If the focus of examination turns to means for attaining such essential ends, this is where subject-specific variety of creative and cultural concepts adds to the meaning of utility of strategy. The ontological level of analysis of an organization's adopted means reveals its purpose, thus defining its sector, segment, niche or niches, innovation methods and implementation modes. Irrespective of form, strategy means are ontologically utilitarian, as they serve a purpose; otherwise they would not be contemplated, planned or deployed. Therefore, the values-based methods that centre on meaning, such as those in social-cause-driven events and arts venues, are utilitarian in the same sense as are the tools of content use analysis of media or commercially-driven, evidence-based analyses of the experiential value of virtual interior architecture that is used for the purpose of securing hospitality and events commissions. Organizational autonomy and operational independence are the aims of socially-driven enterprises mentioned above: whereas revenue and profit may contribute to such ends, these are not ends in themselves. Revenue and profit generation may not be the ultimate ends of commercially-driven creative organizations, as the notion of market share or market control rests on a more fundamental level of result than profit, which can be seen as the *meta-means* contributing to market control. The evidential use value of output, ranging from socially- to commercially-driven organizations, may not be quantifiable and commercial intrinsically, in itself. Values of meaning and constructs of societal impact are notoriously difficult to examine in quantitative terms, which adds to the complexity of cultural policy. In visual and conceptual arts, the evidence of cultural value is connected to the policy-defined target-based testing done by peer-reviewers and funding body committees. On the other hand, it may not be possible to directly quantify the functionality of an application, design solution, industrial product, environment, service or device. The same applies to the use-value of deeply abstract, fundamental cultural and creative forms of music, dance, drama, prose or poetry, which do attain substantive commercial potential in cases of the alignment of interest between content owners, creators, media, distributors and linked sectors, connected to the 'value chains of meaning' (Hartley 2004).

Examples of this range from values-driven strategic means to those highly pragmatic and result-driven analytics models. Values-driven means include those formulated and deployed by public-supported festivals such as Exit and Rheinkultur: policy, political discourse, educational concepts, the promotion of inherent ideology or societal value, heritage, community experience/engagement. The utilitarian and technically driven software tools include ICT heuristics, referred to by a software developer, or wireless networking models (as in the case of Concert Live) used for major promoters' venue- and festival-centred merchandising. These varied means allow those organizations who create and implement them to claim evidence of value that justifies such organizations' continued operation, market position and autonomy.

Similar examples can be drawn across the creative industries. Listing the possible means in use, irrespective of their 'intrinsic'/'substantive' or 'utilitarian'/'instrumental' nature may include a number of abstract notions reflected in specific methods of strategy practice. Means include: democratic, egalitarian, non-hierarchical organizational models and PR representations of democratic, egalitarian, non-hierarchical models employed by hierarchical organizations for market positioning; charitable, creative, experiential models; leisure-oriented cultural representations; integrated blended experiences of ICT and events; mass-custom product and service applications; performance- and event-driven models; artefact-, place- and space-driven marketing; data analysis etc. Ends include more mundane notions such as profit; (discursive) dominance of a brand; capturing a market, sector or segment; competitive advantage across integrated processes/sectors; presence across emerging sub-sectors or niches etc. More specifically, means include communications practice; cooperative competition; editing, filtering and distributing content and information, and targeting a public; participant coordination; lifestyle destination marketing; product, interface and service design; campaign design; software development etc. The more specifically developed the means, the greater the bargaining power of those who represent the industry, sector or profession in question.

Anticipating and enveloping the other – a short note on creative destruction

The iTunes/iPod case takes centre place in the well-documented and detailed accounts of an ongoing narrative – that of the expansion of the world's most powerful brand, Apple. It will be argued that such creative destruction can be found in the history of combat, the first recorded evidence of such refined ruses found in the accounts of Carthaginian general Hannibal Barca and his destruction of Roman and allied armies at the Battle of Cannae. Learning from such cases *a posteriori* is not a guarantee or prerequisite of future success. Drawing parallels between business and military strategy is nothing new; some may even consider it vulgar. Nevertheless, with all the data available in the public domain – non-disclosure agreement details are not that relevant – the depth, scope, scale and term of the iPod/iTunes strategic move reveals a thought process and deep insight surpassing any number of cases in creative industry strategy or business strategy as a whole. Nearly 15 years after the event it is apparent that Apple not only captured an entirely new market, previously the preserve of some highly established technology and entertainment companies, but is also part of a broad, deep and long-term drive for global domination affecting all the traditional creative industries now dwarfed by a single corporate entity; moreover, it redefines the respective roles and position of creative content and the device-operations continuum at the heart of the rise of ICT. The ability to anticipate and pre-empt any moves of competitors by several major steps had as much to do with understanding and subverting the mental framing of their self-identity as it did with innovation in technology and distribution models.

Strategy and the self: organizing the unconscious

Bloch's work on reconciling the respective paradigms of cognition and culture does not delve into the terminology of psychoanalysis, save for one example when exploring the Western culture of creating representational self-narratives (narrative as a contingent term in Bloch's 2012 treatise). One such representational phenomenon is, he claims, psychoanalysis. The anthropological terms adopted in relation to types of representation and re-representation of the Self (a term also contingent in the cited work) are analogous to other traditions of classification by type of preferred interaction with the environment. Moreover, the purposefully selected 'blob', as visualization of the fuzzily stratified levels of Self (cognitive, hybrid, social), shares some generic structural and representational features with the iceberg metaphor and the self-actualization pyramid concept. The underlying direct experience of Self as existence, devoid of meaning but defined by a few core cognitive processes, serves as the foundation of all higher reflective, representational and cultural interactions accounted for in this structural evaluation of deep integration of cognition and culture. Here, the barriers between internal and external environments are formulated as semi-permeable membranes, showing that the Self of an individual subject is not merely made up of a generic cognitive structure with appended superstructures of cultural connotations ('there is no such thing as a generic person'). Rather, every subject is seen as a unique Self, shaped by culture and defined by those key cognitive principles that are known as generic features of personality. Many of those semi-permeable interactions (some of them used to explain corporate culture) occur in non-rational manner below the threshold of *consciousness*.

Note

1 Adam Goodyer, owner of Concert Live, devised a version of Porter's Five Forces specifically for the purpose of presenting the core of his original business model to students of Music and Media Management at London Metropolitan University. In it, he explained how ICT, legal innovation and chart criteria formed the tools by which this model successfully penetrated the highly competitive music events markets.

3 Emergent strategic configurations of power

Seemingly contrasting processes of fragmentation and concentration can be evidenced across the industries and sectors concerned with cultural and creative experiences, products and services. The two concurrent processes stand in contrast and complement one another, forming a functional dialectic relationship. Such tendencies were clearly identified in the 1990s at the peak of the linear media age (Kellner 1997; Du Gay 1997). Capturing the market meant offering a diverse set of products and services, primarily in the mass media of the time. Such diversity was defined by liberalizing market regulation and a 'postmodern' fragmentation of discourse through an endorsement of the variety of lifestyles, tastes, even ideologies which seemed to empower the audiences and consumers through celebration of cultural, stylistic and market diversity (Garnham 2005). Nonetheless, as Kellner (1997) and Du Gay (1997) argued, this happened under the auspices of media corporations that had a global reach. Part of the strategies securing such global reach was to penetrate, capture and control various markets by adapting to local cultures and influencing them through various communications and product development methods; Levinson (1995, in Du Gay 1997: 56–9) documents this by exploring the varying respective methods that MTV and subsidiaries of News Corporation adopted in capturing global audiences. Indeed, as Kellner argued, these processes were not confined to geographical notions of market control but employed the more subtle methods of encompassing the full variety of legitimate audience discourses epitomized in the neatly construed observation that 'difference sells' (1997: 16).

However, such diversification of form, content, format and style can be found across industries, sectors, segments, niches and mutating business models significantly beyond the realm of media, entertainment and the arts. There are many more implications than originally thought of Pine and Gilmore's (1999) observation that the internet is the most powerful commoditizer known to date (the distinction between commodification and commoditization needs to be drawn, as the two relate to distinct notions and processes affecting creativity and culture). In a very early study of the impact of online technologies on music (and consequently other cultural forms), the author of this piece stated that downloading an ironing board is not (yet) possible, clearly implying that music was the first of all the industries to suffer the adverse effects of online commoditization of creative works (Todorovic 1999). Implied in this statement was that it is only a matter of time until the measurable and tangible material impact of the internet on many other industries becomes a feasible proposition that would subvert relations of power established since the Industrial Revolution. Now, with ironing boards and many other material goods 'downloadable', the richness and reach of online information (Graham *et al.* 2004) poses truly philosophical, fundamental challenges to the material nature of many forms of production, distribution and consumption well beyond the confines of entertainment and media sectors first affected by the emergence and nascent popularity of the Web. One of the key relations of equivalence explored in this book is that of information, distribution and promotion across 'aggregate states' (as understood in physics or chemistry). The blurring of boundaries between the once distinct forms of material existence and practice would surpass the wildest expectations of theorists and visionaries of the early twentieth century and run closer to the realm of science fiction (teleportation being an obvious if still far-fetched analogy).

The richness and reach of information (Graham *et al.* 2004) emanates products, services and experiences in tangible and material form through increasingly effective and complex tools of reproduction. Coupled with fragmentation understood as a fundamental feature of internet-based channels and environments, it spreads across areas beyond music, text and linear media and starts to affect events, artefacts and industries traditionally engrossed in the production, manufacture and consumption of material, utilitarian goods. This subverts the order of things established since the nineteenth century beyond the scope of 'culture', 'entertainment', 'information' or 'authorship', as information *becomes* material form. The potential to both empower and weaken any corporations, enterprises and individuals involved is unprecedented. Therefore, talking of a paradigm shift is not, this time, far-fetched; the shift perceived, noted and analysed is truly on the scale of scientific revolution whose nature and scope equals that of the industrial revolution and whose depth invokes Kantian and Cartesian metaphysical implications.

It is necessary to explore fragmentation further, in all of its material, spatial and temporal implications, in order to make sense of ongoing processes of *concentration*, the 'other direction' of the proposed dialectic. The following argument will take a cultural turn towards the areas beyond the web, internet or any constituent digital media channels, models, tools or devices. Fragmentations of discourse, culture, identity practice and power will be explored as a function of space, time and material form much in the same way as Foucault and other post-structuralist writers conceived methodologies of the minutiae of displacement.

Fragmentation of discourses, forms and standpoints and a concentration of strict regulatory policies that favour *marketization* of culture results in such cases as those of Rheinkultur in Bonn or Foundry in London's East End, or – as widely reported in relation to music and media genres – fragmentation of audience and fan lifestyle and taste, markets and modes of culturally construed leisure, coupled with concentration of use of dominant, 'push-supplied' digital business models (e.g. media content streaming services, music discovery models or applications). The cases of Foundry, Rheinkultur, Exit, Hundred Years Gallery etc. are analysed from fieldwork, and the latter phenomenon – the digital fragmentation of audience cultures – from fieldwork and documentary data. The context of independence is challenged in some areas by restrictive regulatory measures and in others by liberalizing regulation. Dependent on context, emergent regulatory frameworks appear to support a concentration of power which is then distributed across acquired value structures or developed independently and then co-opted into the existing market structure. Such markets have been in continued flux ever since the realization of the potential of 'free' came through Napster and early peer-to-peer models. The search (based on social preference, which will prove pivotal later), as well as the reach ability, were the two chief innovations on the ontological level. Any content, however complex, that can be encoded as information and reproduced on the receiving end would consequently become inherently vulnerable to copying. The experiential value, which could be labelled inherent, is lost through the ubiquity of the product (commoditization not commodification).

The emphasis on IP protection does not remove the issue of concern over (lack of) *fundamental innovation* in sectors affected, the sort of innovation that would rethink and redefine the core form of the product. The relevance of this can be seen in areas where product innovation happened on the ontological level: smartphone-based computer games that create global merchandising opportunities before being co-opted into a major film brand. The vertical or diagonal relations that such models attain are less important than their inherent value in the ability to utilize technology, narrative and design in a coherent way. Gallery art and festivals both undergo renewed stratification in what appears to be a differently redefined market, less directly affected by the internet at present yet with significantly transformed value capture tactics. The interpretation of regulation seems to favour major market forces, on the basis of policies beyond the intricate needs of independent and autonomous organizations attempting to retain their market position and continue a values-related strategy. The heterotopia and displacement of these tangible events spaces is intentional, and though instrumental in the formation of a market or the cultural value of a place, it, the counterculture should *move on*. On the opposite, virtual end, the improvisatory displacement of content and ideas is both fragmented and ubiquitous – and therefore ineffectual without the support of mass-communications, push models or more sophisticated methods of online promotion which would use far more advanced ICT tools.

A strategic nexus: ascent/descent of power

Early twenty-first-century IT-driven models in communications are being described under a number of headings: new media, digital media, interactive-, user-generated or user-driven communications, '*freemium*', user-customized, etc. Such plurality is not merely semantic or descriptive (sometimes involving branding); it also represents the flux in *strategic conditions* at the present time. This includes market stratification, segmentation and fragmentation, but also the contest for prevalence and dominance or improved position *between* multiple stakeholders, key corporate bodies and manifold cross-sector interest alliances. The cases of leading search, analytics and communications companies seems to prove that loose-network and temporary alliance models may merely represent the current/ongoing/temporary state of affairs during the nascent phases of formation of new sub-sectors in ICT-driven media. The normative paradigm of growth through acquisition and assimilation of knowledge, operations and functions is rapid and effective, while the newly termed notion of start-up requires further authentication as a viable future model (*with a name that indicates transience*).

Looking at power distribution in the context of advancing internet communications, changes of practice, value processes and business-led innovation do seem to occur simultaneously in large organizations and small enterprises. This is in spite of the fact that tangible fixed-technology – and other assets – micro-enterprises can, inherently, compete with large bodies due to the abstract nature of ICT-driven assets which frequently owe more value to human skills than physical infrastructure. This appears to be the qualitative change that fundamentally transforms the nature of mediated communications and content management. This implicitly affects all the organizations involved in interactive communications, their operations and markets, and redefines the role of users, citizens and the consumer public. It may be far-fetched to talk of qualitative leaps in user empowerment, as market forces do tend to be better concentrated than any consumer initiative; furthermore, attaining advantage over competition, consumers and regulators is a significant and recognized reason why organized market forces innovate. This constant feature of market behaviour means that consumer empowerment is of limited effect; still, the shift from consumer to user is in itself a form of empowerment as users have a greater impact on a medium, product or service than consumers traditionally did in the previous 'linear' paradigm.

Consumers-as-users form clusters and networks defined along the lines of preference for particular media and contexts. Education does play some role in the use of media: channels, applications and portals, for example, are exceptionally user-friendly so the main determining factors for user stratification and differentiation are those defined by user preferences, which are in turn reflected in their social and cultural conditioning and psychological profiles; both of these represent key commercialized data sources for portals and networks.

Surveillance in a Foucauldian panopticon sense of the word is the key to these processes, and the extension of personality into a network is what tools such as 'bots' search for. Apps, add-ons and analytics extensions such as Firefox Collusion and Map of the Internet show clearly the distributed, fragmented, trickled-down structure of internet communications, removing any illusion of equivalence, let alone end-user empowerment. It is thus impossible not to emphasize the key role of physical, tangible infrastructure including cables, the electromagnetic spectrum and hardware e.g. servers. The distinction between so-called physical and digital is an inaccurate one. Rather, correct terming would be the dialectics of tangible and interactive/digital; similarly, digital and physical is a poorly termed dichotomy – the CD was the first broadly commercially available digital retrieval format and the true dichotomy is again between tangible and online format. Since all media formats can be digitized, from patents and blueprints to films and games, the abstract nature of information is being made equivalent with a literal, digital meaning of information as a set of commands and data. Being able to monitor user behaviour so as to understand their motives and methods of content use becomes as important as the content itself. The content informs market research tools and applications of the demographic and *psychographic rooting*, or subcultural leanings and interests of users online. Also, their behavioural patterns inform market researchers of the preferred way of unmediated user behaviour, enabling commercial organizations and other powerful stakeholders to refine their understanding of user-friendly tools for sales, marketing and publicity practices aimed at networked users/consumers.

The key factor and a frequently used phrase is that of engagement. Engagement is considered the key stage in monetization, i.e. commercialization, of user/consumer preferences, tastes, and social and cultural identity. The closer the network and tools can read their users' behaviours, the more likely it is that engagement will be seen to completion and commercialization. The accuracy of data thus obtained justifies the investment in such online research tools, cloaked under the name of social networks or apps. One of the key questions posed by industry experts to trainee teams in social media marketing is: how did they use the geographical analytics and other data? The other relates to point of sale engagement – a virtual point of sale with evidence-based results beyond publicity, communication, audience interest or fan engagement. It appears that traditional content industries relating to *primary modes of production – metaphorically speaking* – in the arts, are still doing a significant amount of digital marketing innovation through trial and error, and that the culture of organizations such as digital media networks and app-based business models is slowly being assimilated into the knowledge base that informs practice through showcases, conferences and, more recently, joint ventures, investment and subsidiary acquisition.

The descent of power is well recognized in practice through such concepts as those used in broadcast or marketing terminology, so-called push strategies and distribution models of all the primary, traditional creative and cultural sectors. The stratification of commercial players, strategies and policy making was also recognized in grand strategy theories of economistic and processual orientation; analysing strategies as power contestations between strata and consensus-coercion dichotomies is not unheard of in critical treatises on corporate strategy. Emergent stratification, defined by the prevalence and reach of ICT and interactive methods, formulates a different descent of power. The consensus on payment shifts, but the focus on content remains. Coercion is not as effective as previously, with models of supply based on linear control of content. Therefore, the emergent models of commercial – and other – strategies, based on the descent of power through consensus built between key suppliers of content and communication, take a different, more distributed and user-orientated form. What was lost in value adding processes dependent on control of content use, specific to twentieth-century mass-culture models, is counterbalanced by the unprecedented accuracy of user behaviour research and the potential for modification and refinement of product or service offers. The illusion of user empowerment is there because more subtle methods are used to entice value exchange in the form of commercialization of tangential interest – beyond content use. Also, those possessing the means to create far-reaching and rich interfaces for business communications with users are the ones that can best utilize and adapt their offering to users less wiling to pay for ownership of a copy of temporal content (media of any sort). By implication, it is clear that such assets and knowledge-based practice are seldom at the full disposal of traditionally defined, linear creative sectors. The shift of power from creative content producers to ICT and interactive media organizations is therefore mapped out as a result of a fundamentally improved function of research in ICT-driven models.

Research is the precursor of accurate targeting. Consequently, successful commercializations in unstable, interactive market approaches, superseding advertising, linear distribution and push product strategies, need to be based on research capacity. Research is the necessary cause of successful commercialization of reproduced, copy-based content value. Performance is as original, singular, as is experience. Any medium is a copy. The distribution of luxury models is infinitesimal. It narrows as it goes to the top and increases in number and variety with degrees of market exchange value, by consensus of commercialization. In a similar way, the end of the asymptote of a life cycle or product/revenue distribution is infinitesimal in size while the variety of product niches increases in number, reversely reciprocal to the revenue per niche. The changes to the market through short-lived innovations resemble the ascent of power, in such cases unsuccessful, as they fail to attract (1) early adopters, (2) peers, (3) potential collaborators or business clients, or (4) strategic investors in higher strata. In those cases, they remain unarticulated with higher reaches of power ascent and wither in a similar, albeit faster, way, as subcultures and scenes of media narratives that are left without direct investment, whether organizational, financial or societal, sometimes referred to as cultural capital.

Advertising and utilization of user networks for amplifying the signal of an online marketing campaign are being made possible through the same forms of power ascent that define online phenomena in user-generated content, talent scouting and clandestine media content promotions. As audiences become more literate, campaigns of early web interaction are no longer feasible so new methods of exciting audiences, or influencing the influencers, are being invented. Frequently those are not sustainable, as they act as gimmicks and perceptual hooks of limited shelf life. Little more can be learnt from singular case studies of user-generated blips in the white noise of the internet or community/peer-supported campaigns backed in fact by large media organizations. This is due to their singularity; the only patterns and replicable processes that can be identified are those of innovation in audience excitation, engagement and recruitment for marketing campaign amplification. Such methods resemble activism, and contemporary users, audiences and entrepreneurs mid-2010s elect to broadcast, narrowcast, update, curate and reveal their reflective selves invariably linked to any of the increasingly fragmented facets of popular culture, content and knowledge.

Looser licensing models emerge as a result of pragmatic renegotiations of power relations between traditional primary nonlinear content industries and the sectors and emergent enterprises dealing in data, information, analytics and various communications services. This is partly due to recognition of the facts on the ground, where policies of coercion cannot be effectively enforced without dabbling in the nature of the social contract (Rousseau) – for which it is not a sufficient cause. This is also due to the passively communicated interest of users through their expressed lack of interest in unit-by-unit payment for the vast majority of fixed, mass-manufactured copies of cultural goods. The commercialization processes based on scarcity of supply, coercion and effective control of information flows are thus undermined and are likely to represent a sector-driven market segment for culture consumption, not the all-permeating business philosophy of the recent past, defined by the exclusive marketing of media content distributed through a discrete number of channels. Even at the time of peaking of satellite television, the discrete number of hours spent did not change in spite of the unprecedented distribution of channels; this resulted in the fragmentation of licensing income.

Those who benefit most from such an asymptotic function would be those who (1) control the flow of content and licensing income and (2) own or produce or otherwise control the ownership of content (asymptotic function = a more accurate and technically relevant term for the so-called long tail). The emergent state of affairs follows the changes brought about by the leakage of content, infinitesimal fragmentation of channels, communication modes and platforms. In such a state of affairs, in the concrete strategic layout of configurations on the field, or strata and actors, the balance between content holders/producers and those who control the flow is tipped in favour of the latter. Though it is fair to accept the market potential of the asymptotic segment of product/distribution (type/revenue) ratios in niches and singular events along the tail of the sales distribution function, the only organizations set to benefit from this are those who control the flow of information regarding content, and therefore the flow of content itself. The other outcome of the infinitesimal fragmentation of media channels, platforms etc.

is saturation with the metaphorical white noise of myriad media channels. The number of suppliers greatly increases, leaving room only for the established ones in *traditionally linear, primary content creation* and management, and upstart start-ups whose probable fortunes cannot be ascertained so as to allow for a conclusive speculation that the returns would come.

Many such start-up businesses fail: though content is being created and often distributed free of charge in the hope of later stages of value capture, it does not benefit the producer. The only benefit flows to those businesses that control the network or acquire the right to use the content at a later stage. Thus the asymptotic long tail privileges the new business models and emergent dominant forces managing or curate the content flow insofar as the business model remains agile and the flow curators maintain their control of demand for information. This threatens traditional medium-sized businesses and leaves room for negotiations rather than competition between UGC-upstarts, start-ups, established players in interactive media and those highly integrated organizations who maintain the control of large content portfolios.

Strategy innovations are most rapidly generated in the intersection of descent and ascent of power in content and communication structures. There is a notable impact of this on truly traditional creative industries outside of the media and communications sectors, be it 'traditional' (twentieth-century models) or emergent (digital) ones. Interaction is a feature of human behaviour through communications, preceding any interactive media at the focus of many ambitious treatises. Interaction exists in those contexts most traditionally associated with the arts and culture, crafts and design, and any sort of events, culturally conditioned service sectors and areas covering a spectrum of activity as broadly conceived as the distinction between design and cultural tourism. Therefore, it is logical to assume that the growing power of near-instant communications would internally transform those sectors adjacent to creativity (some authors speak of the limitation of the speed of light). On the other hand, a balanced and reflective approach to the state of affairs in flux shows that labour divisions change, skills sets are modified in response to demand, while both collaborative *production* and publicity practices of more traditional art and culture practitioners demand more frequent editing, promotion and regular networking, but not far more than that.

It is not the aim of this analysis to privilege the terms of media and interactivity in its narrower sense over the other creative sectors dealing with artefacts. It remains clear that there is an inherent interactivity in creative work and management. It should also be made clear that what is being sought in this work are the core principles of what the strategy *is* in its full context, as they should inform the practice and methodology of any number of creative sectors. Therefore, in both artefacts and events – and thus singular-value-driven markets – the logic of interaction is both more abstract and more traditional than what is being subsumed under the term 'interactivity'. The economic argument for artefacts is rather reflexively presented in a curious case of a leading book in PR. Edward Bernays's capital volume *The Engineering of Consent* has not been reprinted since

1969; the book cannot be legally downloaded irrespective of charge, and its actual market value as a physical artefact ranges from $345 to over $1,600. This proves that the scarcity rules of 'old-fashioned' media economics and scarcity of supply very much apply in the 'age of free culture'. Reflecting on this finding is of significant value to the very notion of the supposed boundlessness of the 'brave new world' of the internet.

Capillary power and new models of creative industry practice

Early internet research posed some relevant questions. Just as was the case with every new medium or format before, the visibility of the internet – as it was behaving as an iceberg (in psychoanalysis) or blob in recent anthropological work (Bloch 2012) – so its core functions were explored by researchers who had no prior knowledge of such a model of functioning. One social researcher postulated the problem of space and locality through a work subtitled 'Is there a "there" there?' The spatial illusion based on concept and context, not material space, is the precursor of a potential distribution of power through online networks, allowing free agents such as artists and new models to proliferate. In contrast to some positively intoned projections of the time (Anderson 2009; Graham *et al.* 2004), direct links between creator and user/audience member that can be commercially maintained proved an exception rather than the norm. Capillary distribution of power through niche discourse has not created a major wave of growth in customer intelligence. It has only dispersed existing segments, genres and niches which are more fluid and difficult to sustain commercially. The long tail did not return value *thus far – a quality/quantity question* – on the distribution of potentially infinite content to those who produce it.

Capillary power is a concept derived from Foucault (Todorovic 2008) and its importance is beyond the academic. Policy is influenced by Foucauldian thinking and this can be seen in the way various cultural targets are defined across Europe. Pockets of power, resistance and autonomy are equivalent to the micro-organizational nature of 'heterotopia' which fragmented discourses occupy. Targeting such minute niches of discourse, and the communities and groups connected to them, appears to be one of the modes of formulating effective impact on the part of cultural policy makers. Inherent in this is an implicit but effective promotion of a market-driven context, since such minute fragments depend on external support or commercial engagement.

The proclaimed end of history did not survive the peak of the age of linear media (Fukuyama 1989) or of the grand narrative (Lyotard 1984). A discreet multiplicity of channels, however significant in number and influence under the auspices of a relatively small number of highly integrated companies, created the illusion that the future of creative popular cultures lay in endless irreverent reinterpretation of highly coded cultural goods and references as the plateau had been achieved. This was true for a number of forms, while the impact, breadth and reach of interactive communications was underestimated by many in industry and academia alike. The example of record company behaviour in the wake of the internet shows this rather clearly: what is being replicated to this day is the dominance of asset owners who reproduce the status quo in the digital context, thus not evolving in tune with the times, making losses where gains could be made – save for a few notable exceptions.

Power is currently being distributed across emergent models of communication, use of content and sales of content flow over time. Innovation is evident in ways in which it previously existed in the interim in areas such as advertising or music. Many forms in those two industries remain static and fixed in genre classification. On the other hand, boundaries of creative entertainment, cultural change and media/service strategies are moving in areas for which there were few if any definitions or descriptors in *linear, primary content production*. Wherever there is an app – the new buzzword for creative content engagement tactical tool – there is a structure behind it representing a potential business model, whether or not a commercial end is envisaged in the business plan behind it. Functioning, sustainable, successful apps are based on operational structures which are creative in their own right, therefore enhancing user/audience/consumer experience through a convergence of functional and aesthetic design (found in fieldwork).

Capillary power was not conceived as static or immutable (Foucault, Todorovic) as the ascent of power from the ground up is itself an agent of change which disappears once it has achieved its purpose or become visible. This is true of effective public relations and of technological or socio-cultural disruptions. The disciplining component of the ruling strata in creative sectors does exist in the form of criticism and monitoring of illicit use of content-driven online communications. The disciplining, however, appears delayed at present: partly due to the lack of consensus among varied stakeholders as to what rights can be enacted top-down to police content use online. The current state of flux in digitally defined creative sectors may only be a specific case resembling stages of consolidation, rapid innovation and format wars of linear creative industries a century before.

Qualitative changes have occurred in the wake of developments advancing the web and digital media, enhancing the disruptive reach of new phenomena and the unpredictability of any such future change. A relationship of equivalence was drawn in practice between knowledge and other, more fixed industry assets, and this was the salient and evident result. Start-ups and online pop culture phenomena are both targeted for investment and purchase as the new sectors grow vertically and not horizontally, as was the case in the advanced linear age. Therefore the most lucrative acquisitions – and commissions from the *emergent virtual navigators* – are those where innovation creates an infinitesimal new vertical and is immediately acquired as investment or copied with reverse engineering of its purpose and function, once other means are used for limiting its impact (from patent suits to excessive use of supplier power and *collusion* between threatened key players).

Capillary power of users can be harnessed to business benefit. Examples of fan clubs, audience voting in reality TV and demand structures of crowd-funding services are the visible examples in entertainment and media. The permeating nature and reach of rich user experience extends to the boundaries of creative industries and beyond, in the cases of booking and travel services based on points, reviews, recommendations and reward mechanisms. Strategic harnessing of capillary power of users can provide the impulse for the growth of orders. Ascending in miniscule ways on an individual level, the impact of reviews, opinions and recommendations from users grows in magnitude with the increase of flows of orders and communications resembling moderated blogs and social networks. The trust and loyalty of consumers grows for responsive services that allow such user moderation to the effect of attracting new orders as the peer-reviewed model appears transparent, fair, self-reflective and therefore able to learn. The trust thus built is the currency of the service provider that can be commercialized (monetized) through investment, retail, subscription, advertising, fund-raising or stock trade. The first global online book retailer enabled such change, growing its power through core competencies in order and stock flow management as well as the perceived user empowerment through seamless, open and responsive service with robust search competencies at the core of its original model (Amazon being an example well covered). Therefore, the descending power of large-scale operational and organizational practices in emergent nonlinear models is also a capillary one, as it meets the capillary demand of interactive users of such services.

Articulation of forces and models

Stuart Hall's analytical concept of articulation, originally confined to cultural and media studies, was later explored as a functional aspect of strategy in a programmatic critical management studies (CMS) paper by Levy *et al.* (2001). The non-necessary alliance of different social and economic forces, using culture as a field of linkage and media as means of formulation and dissemination, is frequently perceived as a purely social/cultural phenomenon, while Hall proposed reconciling the disciplinary dialectics of 'ethnographic' and 'economistic' approaches to a complex phenomenon such as a movement or media discourse. As was the case with other academic authors, the critical or analytical approach adopted on purpose does not preclude potential pragmatic application. Adorno's understanding of branding (a remark on Rolls Royce), or of what would much later become known as 'diagonal integration' and 'licensed use of content across verticals' (product circuits), and indeed of the decentralized, virtual and elusive nature of internet content fragmentation, were not put to practical use. Alongside the lack of fieldwork insights, and the *a priori* negative judgment of the 'culture industry' paradox, this absence of interest in application forms a significant aspect of his critical writing. However, should the reader chose to ignore the negative connotations ascribed in such works, the analysis of key functions and mechanisms reveals an abstract notion of strategy akin to that of classic authors and thorough analysis of key forces shaping the market.

A similar analogy is drawn to the work of Foucault, apt to explain the minute innovation in capillary models; contrasted with competition and functional barriers of entry such as licensing or operational costs (e.g. bandwidth), it shows that emergent start-up models can be only as strong as the weakest link in the cost of supply, or as the infrastructure/substructure value restrictions allow. The articulation of forces and models is therefore seen as a joining of people, organizations and the means they have developed to formulate sustainable models of revenue generation or methods of adaptation that would re-represent the content or brand, the meta-representation of a meeting of creative and organizational cultures that enhances business models and niche media texts.

Following systematic and detailed fieldwork, it has been found that all but a few contemporary business models operate in a media vacuum. The terming of media here is without consequence to the centralized models known in the past. Since content is at the heart of the vast majority of creative industries, especially in emerging sectors, and content may be infinitely replicable at comparatively low cost (even design goods), then the conclusion is that there is a new equivalence that defines creative strategy. This is the qualitatively new equivalence between communication and production; or marketing and design; or information and tangible form.

This shows that an entirely new mode of reasoning has to be developed, as such new realities show in terms of methodology. In addition to the qualitatively new equivalences between qualitative and quantitative, interpretive and positivistic, fluid and controlling, voluntary and ordered, the whole process of research in commercial interactive contexts becomes equivalent to action, implementation and management.

- communication ↔ production
- marketing ↔ design
- information ↔ tangible
- qualitative ↔ quantitative
- interpretive ↔ positivistic
- fluid ↔ controlling
- voluntary ↔ ordered
- research ↔ action

This way strategy is practiced in those organizations where aims are high and peak performance and high-risk thinking are informed by high conceptualization and evidence-based research. Here, articulation is used as a different terming that encompasses a number of processes. These include all levels of formulation, social-economic strategy formations acting as agents, branding and identity, user identity, user subcultures, scenes, networks and cults, and their relations. Where such relations are commercial, the changes in practice can be traced as a re-articulation of forces. New models of supply and value relations emerge as a result of re-articulation of position and interest redefining alliances in social, economic, managerial and market formations.

Therefore, emergent links established in new configurations affected by interactive media tend to turn production, sales, marketing and communication into parts of a research- and feedback-driven, semi-open supply–value configuration. The term 'chain' should be understood in conditional terms, as linearity now plays a limited role in particular due to the equivalence/ dichotomy of communication and production. The production circuit is partly outsourced to the user.

The promotion too is outsourced to the audience. Once media stopped fighting the perceived threat from social networks (Lucasfilm is a classic example), they harnessed them to amplify the signal of promotion through various types of social networking, social network sites being just some of them. The potential threat to such models of hybrid new-old media promotion is in the possible disenfranchisement of a collective of audiences who may passively or actively withhold their free labour in the commercialization of cultural and creative goods. So far, such voices have not been overtly raised and it appears that any change may be subtle, in the form of migration to ever-emerging new media, platforms and modes of communication, not an outright rejection of what may to some appear as exploitation, the ethically problematic taking advantage of audiences. Audiences and users by and large appear more than complicit in these roles, and this may raise questions on the validity of user empowerment discourses. In any case, the current inclusion of audiences, users, consumers and semi-active micro-opinion leaders seems fully voluntary and unchallenged. Most users switch roles through their use of interactive media, and they can act as one or all of the above categories at any given time. A micro-opinion leader would stir a response on social media pages while acting as an audience member of a television show and user of a licensing model to consume it online free of charge. Such a person performs multiple roles at once, becoming a point of convergence for a number of different commercial interests, media types, content models and other users.

The sustainability of this type of approach may not depend on the perception of alienation of the value created through social grouping of users and interactive audience communications. The perception of empowerment in seamless entertainment and consumption seems to take hold. The new configuration is a consensual one. It is an articulation of the present agreement between different strata, from users to corporate bodies. This agreement is changing the nature of use of cultural and creative goods. It recognizes the pragmatic imperatives of an emergent paradigmatic relationship where use and purchase are forced to blend and fuse due to the leakage of content, so that controlling the flows of information becomes more important for persuasion and commercialization than an overwhelming control of content or blanket promotion. This is the direct consequence of the change in communication, production and sales methods from one-to-many or few-to-many to the *so-called many-to-many* methods.

In the latter, it is understood that there is no real equality among the many that communicate or trade in this way. Nevertheless, the equivalence exists – a single consumer can disrupt a product campaign with one short text, and the reach of that event can be global. The re-articulation of respective positions of forces and practices does not happen voluntarily. However, the disruptive innovation brought to the media in the early 2000s forced the change through. New discourses emerge; users' voices and irregular habits are recognized and respected as part of the trade-off for maintaining control of the commercialization of culture. The most active of users tend to be among the most loyal of audiences, and some of them may take the sense of ownership in campaigns they help amplify. Their participation is more than willing, just as is the ease of sharing the most intimate of thoughts and most sensitive of biographical entries with strangers on social media. The sense of ownership felt by core audiences and the most agile of users resembles subcultures and scenes that defined music and media of the late twentieth century. Consensus on new rules of use through sharing and posting draws to the fore many of the previously invisible facets of culture.

Such facets of culture expressed through interactive media can be mapped and commercialized. In a manner which is very different from the previous subcultural formations, these groups are willing participants in the process of commercialization, owing to a number of factors, one of which is the sense of influence as online visibility articulates their voices which are part consumer, part user, part critic, part curator or editor. Minute articulations contribute to the desired outcome on all sides: consumers become curators while businesses attain media amplification and detailed market data.

Stratification of content media and industry players

Stratification is a historical fact of creative industries which is fixed in material and discursive form: the former in the ownership of assets and the latter in the structure of agreements and organizational practices. Developments, both intended and realized, that can be loosely termed 'strategy' can be seen in a number of forms and aspects of creative industries, especially the ones now termed 'traditional' (mainly twentieth-century sectors): brand names, organizational structures (Hanlon 2004; Negus 1999), standardized agreements, licensing and investment models, organizational culture/ingrained practices, business models adopted through integration by merger and acquisition (an approach criticized by a lead designer in this research), outsourcing (result of staff cuts referred to by another respondent) etc. Self-evidentially, the developmental strategic changes of the past – whether intended or not – are fixed in various material forms and verified through agreements of ownership and control. The history of linear creative industries is ingrained in their structures, which are highly stratified and concentrated across the creative sectors, forms and formats. The greatest turnover in visual arts appears in secondary markets where value creation is speculative through the trading in established creative names and artefacts. On the opposite end of the spectrum are community arts frequently sponsored or funded (depending on the economic model and tax incentives) with particular aims in mind – targets set by public arts and culture policy bodies which work closely with the high-end curatorial organizations to set such policies for new value creation. This practice has been reported and scrutinized by a number of respondents who work as alternative, fringe or socially engaged visual artists, curators and gallery owners. Market concentration has combined with stratification and with a network of public and private organizations which formulate policy on the basis of negotiated interests within a liberalizing framework for art and culture. Tools of funding and investment, mergers etc. are used in other areas as disparate as design and events and the functioning of an industry, its sectors and players within a distinct policy framework reflects the processes of market capture, corporate discourses and structural dominance. These processes are credited among the strengths characterizing creative industries. However, such set practices and broad-ranging agreements, formal or not, may pose as obstacles to innovation and weaken their business models and overall position. As Markides suggests, not all business model innovation is based on technological innovation. Moreover, the test of growth of the market is the test of creation and capture of new value, which validates a business model. Business models, seen as 'logics of business', are subject to internal construct validity and external reliability, as any other empirical projects would be. Some noteworthy business models in content and communications management (e.g. Twitter) remain speculative and dependent on investor confidence more than on market performance and actual new value capture (C. Price interview). As such, they do qualify as innovative but the generation and capture of new value remains elusive at least in the long run. However, the innovation that generates new value and expands markets occurs at the core of new business models, the specific type which is based on the understanding of what the sector, its product, service and experience are about in their essence.

Therefore, Twitter is a research and communications tool for ICT as much as it is a media platform; Spotify is a content management platform that utilizes a combination of user preference data and content structures and patterns, a software tool; these are software models that appear to serve the purpose of content management and communications. Similarly, innovation occurs on the level of new areas of practice, in new forms and sub-sectors, which emerge from traditional creative forms: a case of tablet and smartphone games, which attain iconic status and capture new value across verticals, enhancing the brand in a diagonally related sector/segment node – *Angry Birds* and *Star Wars* for example. A case of corporate investment in new products, brands and business models shows that sources of innovation which lead to new value capture operate on the level of fundamental product innovation.

In music, film and broadcast media, this would mean risky investment in entirely new genres – this is if one supposes that talent shows and different variations of reality television are not a fundamental shift from known genres of entertainment. Discussing the format of *X Factor* as a sublimation of a gladiator game, an artist respondent commented that the original gladiator contexts did not probe into a contestant's Self, which talent show formats do. Reduced to a logically economic narrative, many reality formats resemble games with asymmetrical audience interactivity. The innovation bringing the format itself is superseded by numerous combinations of contestant/audience identity, game context and media content in reality TV, but the market itself is not transforming. A case of fragmentation appears across media-driven entertainment sectors, and the established businesses in those sectors are increasingly risk-averse.

This threatens to undermine assets and strengths, as the core of innovation is within the form itself – each new entertainment format model grows at the expense of established ones. Audience shift from content and content media to networked communications, distributed platforms and micro-content replace focus on consumption and retail, without generating substantive value to content owners. In the words of Pine and Gilmore (1999), the commoditization (not commodification) of such content signals a shift from content to other value. That value, however, rests with new players that innovate on the level of fundament of their own medium, where their 'means' are best defined (see Chapter 2). Another analogy to Chapter 2: Apple and iPod enveloping the Sony Walkman – as a relative newcomer to music, Apple was effectively able to allow losing in an area outside its core competencies and treat the iPod/iTunes experience/service project as a test. To Sony and others in the linear, traditional entertainment industries, this would be equivalent to experimenting with core competencies and risking both the rational, operational assets and the internal/external goodwill regarding a known brand and the possible implications of the 'New Coke' type of failure. What for Sony would be the risky and costly process of redefining a core brand name, for Apple was a diversification experiment based on their core competences in computing. Further asset-defined extensions applied: capture of legal download markets and consequent influence over the use of content across content media organizations, affecting long term plans across the highly stratified, integrated and highly standardized 'traditional', linear creative industries established under the twentieth-century market models of mass-culture. YouTube performed a similar role for audiovisual content, and the growing influence of Netflix in televisual video streaming was met by ISP responses which temporarily favour the traditional content media. Reportedly, the plotline innovation in a leading Netflix brand with own production credits stems from networked and research core competences, resulting in collaborative audience-research-led *strategic scripting* of a series. This is done in coordination with a non-linear release of the whole series at bulk, pre-empting any issues of content leakage, free access and sharing that affect the traditional content formats such as those delivered by established networks. In this case too, the innovation is disruptive, and it does increase the value of revenue streams for on-demand, subscription-based digital delivery models at the expense of other forms of entertainment.

In conclusion, business models based on stratified ownership of content are challenged, and risky *formal* innovation is frequently employed by 'outsiders'. Those new players in the creative field do not carry the burden of legacy and patterns of emergent strategy inherited from the past. This enables them to act as free agents in an established field, unlike those whose organizational assets, content control and knowledge, operations, practices and distribution methods face a fundamental threat: are their means justified?

Ownership and control vs. open utility and participation

Creative industries dealing in music, drama, film, art or hand-made objects are in this book labelled *linear*, *primary*, or *traditional*. This is a relative terming of what their scope or method of activity is, and the delineation rests on the distinction made by the advent of interactive digital tools. It is being argued in this book that interactivity precedes any current or emerging interactive media; and that it is the interactivity of human culture that gives rise to the growing demand for, and increasing impact of, such media. It has further been argued that interactive tools surpass the definition of media so as to include practices that blend communication and production and fuse user participation into the commercial circuit. At this stage, such case studies have seldom been analysed in great depth. The theoretical and methodological framework takes precedence in setting the scene for analysis. The minutiae of functioning of such new commercial circuits will be examined in more detail later in the text.

The linear, traditional, primary processes of creative businesses have been known to depend on restrictive approaches to intellectual property. Such restrictive approaches are embodied in law, licensing methods adopted across industries, and ingrained practices of marketing and distribution. Often these have given rise to terminology that seems both restrictive and outdated. Such practices and discourses have long been criticized by authors from a number of different – sometimes conflicting – standpoints: from those whose work rests on critical theory and political economy, to present-day futurists who proclaim the advent of a brave new connected world where there is no room for defensive approaches to authorship and ownership of ideas fixed in material form. For now, any such ideological presuppositions will be set aside. It is more important at this stage to note that many such critics of linear creative industry practice agree on a few salient points. These have included the short-termist nature of dominant linear approaches and their negative long-term impact on creativity and development of new forms; the disempowerment of authors, performers and audiences in favour of the centralized and concentrated power of corporations; inefficiency and choking of innovation; lack of genuine interest in any of the arts that these organizations manage; and the limited impact of any measures designed to control user behaviour through well-known means such as message repetition, product scarcity or legal coercion. Elements of these can be found even in the most directly diametrically opposed ideologies of culture production. As early as the 1930s a most prominent critic predicted 'improvisatory displacements of things' that would remove the control of the product from the grip of the culture industry, as it was then termed.

'Culture industry', as a critical term, was coined to represent the paradox of the industrialization of culture, something seemingly alien to the very notion of culture itself. Its current ready adoption and use in varied form shows that the paradox is lost to the later readers or users of such terminology. Termed as they were at the outset, the culture industries had not changed in principle from the 1930s to the late 1990s. The one-to-many control of production and dissemination was their hallmark.

Now the redistribution of power rises from the minute scale of events to those new entities that are able to monitor, manage and commercialize the flow of such minute power visible in the rise of small organizations that create new hybrid content that matches the desires of user-consumers whose power of choice is thus exercised. The illusion of individuality and free will is managed more subtly than before, as it was found that users exist in individual bubbles in which they move and that searches outside their own habitual virtual spaces are seldom. *The issue of space is also critical, as space in its literal meaning does not exist online*. Therefore, a more interesting phenomenon than virtual worlds is the one in which social media, use of content, news and communications, education and entertainment become part of an imaginary space of the user. Users articulate those experiences, and the distribution of ownership of user-generated *behaviour-content* is blurred. The commercial potential is therefore normally not harnessed by users as they form pseudo-anarchic entities, but such entities and their links and extensions can be accurately mapped out, analysed and used for commercialization of *behaviour-content* that 'floats' around the social web. The virtual nature of social media is not in some form of embodiment, unsuccessfully attempted through models such as 'second life'. The virtual nature of contemporary networked or distributed communications is that any direct expressions, communications or responses are frequently meshed with various types of content, links, other communities, networks and discourses. Therefore, the virtual nature of contemporary social media is the building of an online personality which is blended with the content (a respondent refers to the 'creative value of someone's lunch' on social media) and connected with the networks and discourses it adheres to. The content is the sign of a user's adherence, interest and identity within a framework of online media discourse.

The *improvisatory displacement of things* is therefore far from chaotic or liberating, as it evolves into a new structure of power that can be accurately represented by any number of models, depending on what relationships are examined.

Graphic models are particularly persuasive and structural models convey more meaning than geographical ones. There is indeed the opposing argument of 'activism', which has yet to be proven as an effective force in online media. However, this rarely affects any positive change in content management practices designed to benefit the creator. A number of established creative professionals, especially in music and the media, have spoken out against what they perceive as the disappearance of value from creative labour and consequent diminishing of the position of creative individuals who, they argue, are those who are the source of new value and the ultimate asset of all such industries. This is arguably structurally conditioned. The overall communications structure serves as a matrix, pattern, substructure that facilitates an ambivalence, a disengagement from content, where the content is perceived and used, communicated and exchanged albeit in a transitory manner, less committed to any particular discourse or *grand narrative*. The postmodernist displacement of content assets once postulated by Adorno, hailed at the very start of the twenty-first century as the opportunity to gain unmediated access of creators to audiences, audiences to events, owners to users and a multitude of voices in a neutral environment, is structurally impossible. Just as in the twentieth century linear creative industries formed their own structural landscape of patterns of ownership, control, communications and distribution, so does the more distributed but far more hierarchical structure of all the internet-based media and their formative creative industries. The Peer1 Hosting structural– not geographical – illustration of the internet shows the core competencies of a company that understands its role in presenting network complexity to potential clients and users, the latter for branding purposes. The interactive application 'Map of the Internet' shows accurately the highly hierarchical nature of the physical communications infrastructure behind the internet. Visually reminiscent of a jellyfish or –conceptually sounder – the ripples under water on impact, the diagram shows the interconnectedness of and penetration into local and operational nodes but also layers of influence depending on physical assets and global market positioning (Figure 3.1).

The 'map' structure may be read as a framework, a diagram showing how and why information ripples populate networks more successfully, deeply, thoroughly, effectively if they attain the support of infrastructure businesses, be it traditional (networked) or interactive (content-utilizing) media. More importantly, 'digital' in the case of, for example, the electromagnetic spectrum is a physical category, which is 'leased out' to media organizations. Digital costs are quantifiable. Therefore, even the innovative business models developed by new, enterprising creators frequently depend on a major infrastructure for bundling, payment and delivery – PayPal, eBay, Amazon, Google, TopSpin, The Orchard, etc. In conclusion, a new hierarchy has emerged, and with it a new set of challenges for future content innovation. The new ownership model concerns itself less with what is termed 'content' than with the means of using it. The shift of emphasis from content to communications meant the removal of control and a change of the fundamental interpretation of what is owned: not

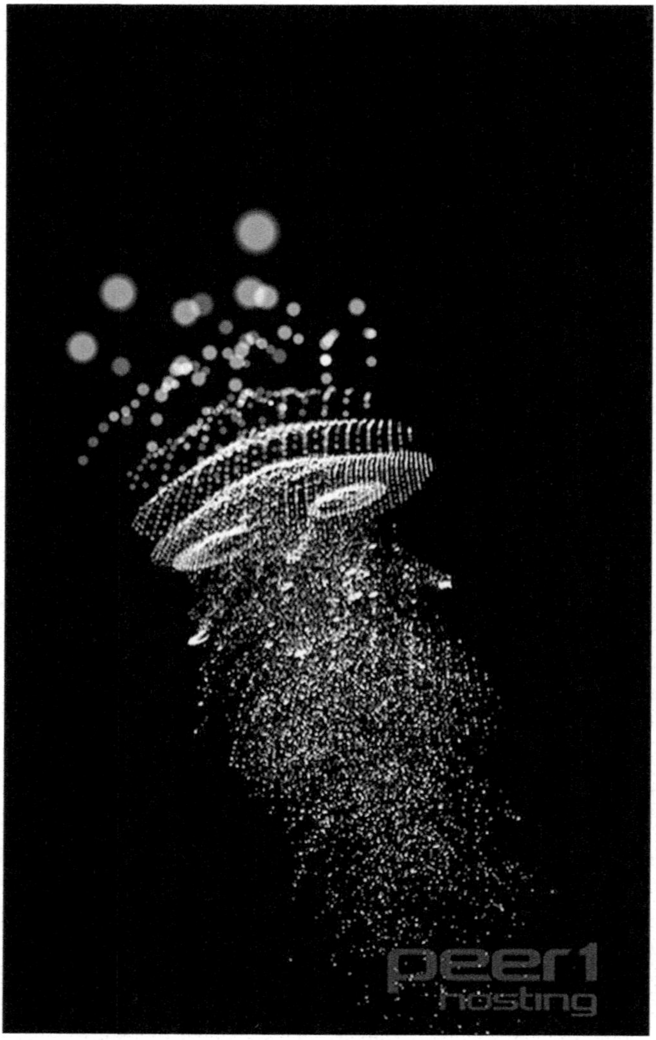

Figure 3.1 Map of the internet
Source: Cogeco Peer 1

only the inherent value but also the nature of the product or asset, from film and scripting to character branding, musical performance to artist brands, product placement across media narratives, in the bid to compete across the white noise of interactive communications. This signals the paradigm shift from 'pure' entertainment in art (artist interview) to applied, sanctioned use. The product of music, art or drama leads on to experiences such as dining, shopping for merchandise or destination marketing. In such cases, content owners may benefit from secondary use.

Share cultures facilitate such secondary value creation: if an online marketing campaign aims to attract attention to a creative phenomenon in music, video, art or film, it needs to define a value structure that does not end with the product. Rather, the product is used as a marketing asset to the experience sold. Limited access to content can no longer be controlled, so the ubiquity of a film brand (e.g. *Cars*) guarantees secondary income from merchandising (as stated in the interview with C. Schoenfeld) even if that means that some sharing of content would have undermined it somewhat. As a result of positioning within the market, its inherent value as a blend of technology and narrative and the hierarchical position of its owners, the brand benefits from marginal sharing of content. A number of cases affecting pirate services were set against a wide international policy change, with more effective content blocking and control of illegal or unsolicited use of content. With the case of a fantasy-drama soap-epic such as *Game of Thrones*, reported leakages of content resemble word-of-mouth marketing for secret events and raves. New content controls and restrictions of unauthorized use are substructural, attained by removing access to content links. This too is enabled through the physical infrastructure of ICT media sectors.

Control/ownership dichotomy

The control of content in linear strategies of the twentieth century (resembling a dam) were about the strict control of flow, where content was used in discrete numbers and aggressive promotion was frequently presented in tangible form, as retail and physical distribution were still the best way to get to use high-quality copies of material. Media were perceived as a promotional tool, and any number of recording technologies available to the public were perceived with suspicion and then co-opted by film and music giants. Similar patterns affected book publishing, print media, advertising, even networks themselves. Who could pirate a television station?

The redistribution did not come overnight, nor did it come stealthily. The new tool for communication was not at first understood as what it truly held concealed – that it was a production and distribution tool. By this virtue, the interactive media stemming from the web have challenged all business models based on scarcity to their very core. The mechanism of change resembles one of scientific revolution (Kuhn and Hacking 2012). The change of paradigm is not one of abandoning previous models: it subsumes them into its complexity, proving them to be specific cases of a more general rule. *Production can be done en masse. It does not have to be.* Dissemination can be done to all but it can also be finely targeted. The cost of those two improvements from which all other stem is that the control of content has to loosen. Physical – or more accurately stated, tangible – products of culture remain part of market offering. In some cases, they attain a new level of commodification and far higher negotiated exchange value, as scarcity is being replaced by veneration of the object or experience as a *singularity* (not to be mistaken for astronomical 'singularity' or the postulated 'Self' of artificial intelligence). Such singular items of creative value remain fixed in carefully crafted forms of books, events or designs. Just as with smaller media enterprises, the smallest remain in play and the new ones grow to significance while the middle, one-size-fits-all popular culture is fragmented beyond recognition.

This calls for the formation of new methodologies in practice and research. The ownership of intellectual works is the necessary but not sufficient cause in the new equivalence that creates the effect of market control. Irrespective of competition within it, an established sector would share such strategic aims at any given time. Such new methodologies are the result of the emergence of new dominant forces and the redefining of strata. These redefined participants and organizations use new models to create and commercialize value. User becomes participant, and participant observation becomes part of the narrative of interactive media, especially in the social media domain. Some of those narratives contain a substantial creative thread. Core narratives go further than those where innovation is captured and traded professionally, making the transition of amateur to professional apparently seamless; young game developers and software engineers attain the prestige once preserved for pop culture icons. This feeds into the emergent ideologies of new powerful sectors based on knowledge and IT engineering, replacing traditional creative pursuits. The arrival of new dominant sectors, the emergence of new types of enterprise, the increasing role of entrepreneurial creativity in public narrative, are the factors formulating new aspirational models. Their components are share cultures and innovation-based competencies, and their iconography is made up of new brands, practices and individual agents of change, the new leadership figures whose quasi-hagiographic public narratives help articulate the new culture. New ideologies and narratives permeate individualistic value systems of the industry. These include organ printers using stem cells, artificial intelligence, machine-moderated environments, etc.

Online cultures are deeply participatory. Immersion is revealed as a validated form of research. Therefore, it can be seen that a bridging of gaps between natural and social sciences is evidenced in a rather unlikely place: the 'Heisenbergian uncertainty' nature of immersive behaviours in social media, whereby the observer changes the observed by engaging in the very act of observation. The observer *is* the participant, and the notion of objectivity, epitomized by the quasi-scientific paradigms of business studies, becomes challenged by the evidence from contemporary practice. The impact of observation on the observed was proven in 1977 in a paper by Misra and Sudarshan. As advised by a respondent from the ICT sector, modelling of service software developed in his field is informed by a number of concepts from natural (and social) sciences, including mathematics, physics, mechanics and *thermodynamics*. Structures and behaviours of such logical or physical models are then applied to the purpose of the software. By design, therefore, some of these creative forms are thermodynamic structures that capture and analyse information.

Cultural identity discourse is no longer easily dismissed as fanciful at a time when new media giants define and capture value through minute observations of the longitudinal behaviour of their myriad users: the business models of Google, Facebook and other, newer online services are based on their ability to closely monitor and manage information pertaining to notions of cultural identity in the guise of 'psychographics' and other digital analytics. Examining the nuances of psychological, socio-economic, ideological and other identity markers can no longer be perceived as marginal, ephemeral pursuits without practical commercial end impact. *Knowing* the users, interacting with them, modifying that interaction and learning from it, then subtly manipulating the perception of empowerment by 'broadcasting oneself' (YouTube) or 'trending text' (Twitter) shows that discourse *is* power in a new, truly evidential and commercial sense. This opens many new subsets of business behaviour and delivery of finely customized services, from highly individualized ones to those that span global communities entirely based on discourse.

Here is a list of some notable new models of business behaviour, benefiting and learning from new paradigmatic postulates emerging from immersive user monitoring. All of these are evidenced in market reports and fieldwork data collected from some of the most important influencers consulted for this volume.

- Content as open utility and curation as flow management
- Service as product in design; the design–service–product continuum
- New, purposefully unstable art forms
- New types of games blending tangible and virtual reality
- New types of many-to-many interaction
- New forms (and formats) of media/events-driven entertainment, based on the notion of user empowerment, market impact, market research, value capture and value creation
- New modes of consumption, signifying value and user engagement, described as mass-customized, mobile, immersive, tangible/intangible, re-bundling of unbundled content, etc.

One main feature defines them all, and it is best represented through a mathematical metaphor (no room here for actual mathematical elaboration) as 'interaction to the power of n'.

The 'n' in this case represents any number of users within the limitless and potentially infinite set of natural numbers.

$$N = n$$

It is therefore not surprising to see new models of social-scientific thought based on such evident transformation of human-IT-mediated interaction, where statistical information becomes truly qualitative and interpretive in nature at the point of overall strategic analysis. One notable contemporary example of this is the emergent discipline of Cliodynamics (Turchin 2008, 2011, 2014; West 2011).

Returning to the distinct areas of merging practice in cultural and creative industries: all the new hybrid appearances and formats described above are based on the complexity of fundamental, traditional cultural forms and stimuli. Such forms and corresponding sectors, recognized as 'traditional', include for example literature, drama, art, music etc.; even film and broadcasting are now considered 'traditional', in the wake of the marked dominance of ICT-driven cultural/creative forms and corresponding industry sectors.

The core processes that define these 'traditional' forms are now intertwining and overlapping in new complex ways, which shape the new hybrid phenomena in the use and delivery of cultural and creative products and services. Such new hybrid phenomena include 'tweeting', streaming, blended events, product bundling and others. Their complexity grows with each innovation and creation of a new generation of cultural, creative and entertainment forms that are beyond books, print media, radio, television or games and yet are hybrids of those recognized formats. A definitive, fundamentally novel concept is the pervasive new approach dictated by technology, where the form (e.g. artistic) and format (e.g. an app) blend into one.

How far have new communication–production circuits affected deeply traditional forms of creativity, such as poetry, dance, pottery, sculpture, theatre – to name but a few? This question will be dealt with when the notions of 'artefact' and 'singular event' are examined later in this text. A different type of temporality affects such examples of creative/cultural value than the manifestly sweeping value renegotiation of multipliable products and services that belong to the legacy of twentieth-century media and entertainment industries.

Traditional participatory cultures such as drama and music were eroded by the rise of the culture industry, as originally termed to describe what are now the *established linear sectors*. The multiplicity of copies and high costs of production of a finite number of carefully selected originals – in the form of performances, plays etc. – have led to the establishment of high barriers between professional and amateur performance. This resulted in the creation of high barriers of entry for all but the well-established corporate bodies and the formation of powerful gatekeepers in cultural and creative industry production. This is not universally the case, as there are well-documented cases of disruptive innovation in business (independent business models) and to a lesser extent technology (highly cost-dependent) where business practice moved forward in few, albeit notable leaps, challenging the status quo and leading to strategic shifts and the adoption of ploys to incorporate those models while marginalizing such threats.

The participatory culture of the populace arguably waned in favour of highly advanced divisions of labour of a culture industry. Failure to participate in a shared popular tradition of socially-engaging performance (Sousa 1906, Lessig 2007), combined with industrial urban alienation, turned those potentially aspiring to express themselves through core cultural forms of performance and art into consumers and, at best, informed spectators of the fourth wall. Costs of technology and related distribution assets in cinema and music formed the added disincentive for wider reach of participatory cultures, which frequently bordered on professional engagement, such as in performing (ballroom) musicians and small-scale cinema theatres. This pattern led to further narrowing and higher specialization of exceptional performers or producers, highly managed by the linear culture industry, from dancers to directors, musicians to visual artists, forming a barrier of elitism and exclusivity between the industry and its consumers, not dissimilar from the widening gap between professional athletes and the spectator public. This sort of critique, presented in a number of notable works, shows the impact and mechanism of market concentration and professional commercialization of culture.

At its postmodern peak, the linear culture industry strategists identified the way to subsume the plurality of stakeholder voices relating to subcultures, movements, scenes and ethnic identities and co-opted those plural viewpoints through diversification. The market was only seemingly diversified, as the offering reflected the more vocal consumer segments and presented some products as independent, risky and unconventional, while strategic control of assets meant that profit would flow back to those who own them. Whether or not under their ownership or control, the linear culture industries presented a variety of products defined by genre, territory or cultural heritage.

The appearance of consumer empowerment enhanced the marketability of such diverse products owned or controlled by a small number of highly concentrated entities. It would be naive to suggest that the internet had changed some of the key mechanisms, but the types of players and their respective models do differ from the linear industry forms that defined the twentieth century. Independent films were no longer as independent due to the control of distribution and theatres; music, the press and others followed a similar pattern. The appearance of immediacy was well controlled from integrated centres of power.

The synergy of most centralized means of production, distribution and promotion is likely to remain as important as before, in principle, while its form may change. Servers are tangible assets, and their role in cloud computing combines the roles of storage facilities and stock management procedures with those of broadcasting technology and production studios of the past. However, participatory culture, amateur performance and production surpass blogs and online home videos; the membrane between the select group of professionals and a wider participatory public does become less prohibitive.

Such permissive attitudes to fan cultures and bricolage were developed over time after futile attempts to fight a groundswell of peer-to-peer phenomena. What may have been labelled parasitical, derogatory and illegal is tolerated for the purpose of promotion of many types of media content. Some of the user-generated bricolage created around major creative production is used to recruit artists, designers, directors, developers and other emergent professionals. This sort of flow and mobility is not surprising at a time of flux and broad-ranging change. Once definitive consolidation happens, if it does, it will be seen whether fundamental barriers will be erected again between the participating public and highly specialized industries. Final consolidation may not happen; most analysts agree that judging by the current state of things, change is the only constant factor in the interactive creative industries at the time of writing.

Freedom from format limitations came at a cost. No particular units are any longer the norm dictated by necessity. The question of packaging and marketing around distinct units had arisen in music and media. Television shows are available as virtual box sets, ready for immediate and full consumption normally spread over weeks, while the album format in music is under threat, as is the press-publicity circuit relating to new releases in music and other linear media. The film industry keeps its control of content due to cost and overall negotiating power of supply, and its investment methods become more conservative as competition from games rental and retail, added to peer-to-peer threats, become a drain on time and resources. The convergence of large synergistic corporate portfolios is possible and occurs. As in the well-documented cases of early commercial radio and consumer technology, one part should feed of the other in a convergent production–distribution–consumption circuit. This is not easily attainable in practice, as reported in studies on synergy and convergence in media corporations. Due to different supply mechanisms and lead times, different creative sectors have different operational schedules that cannot be easily harmonized with complex products such as the games that feed off film releases and market their secondary use (or vice versa). Add to this competing sectoral interests within corporations and it becomes evident that such synergic responses have a built-in causality problem (Jenkins 2006).

The 44-minute album and three-minute pop song were dictated by necessity but became recognizable units of marketing. Production cycles became harmonized in music, film and television so as to coincide with the annual and seasonal consumer leisure cycles. Even the duration of albums and pop songs, dictated by technology, stood in a close accidental correlation with human attention span.

The popular cultures facilitated by traditional entertainment sectors are often analysed from consumer subculture viewpoints. It is, however, worthy of note that such cultures permeate the production and business side. The articulation of similar stylistic interests between producers, business people and audiences had formed an alliance of trust which had in turn created the exchange value of cultural commodities of film, TV, theatre and music. Advertising is well analysed in a number of works as both the cause and the effect of change in popular culture formation. Assuming that aggressive campaigns and control of operations or market share are the sole contributors to the success of an entertainment product does not do justice to the consensus between creative/cultural businesses and their audiences. Practitioners (respondents) are often careful to use terminology that reflects their need to recognize consumer bargaining power. Such power resides within consumer culture, which may be manipulated or controlled by media within limits. Its newly rediscovered responsiveness is a factor that adds emphasis to that notion. The culture of linear media production created broad audience segments, fans and scenes. The cultures of non-linear media create their own definitions of audience, user and consumer relations fit for the ontological faculties of a different technology which brings qualitative change.

Technology influences creative businesses, which nurture a culture that defines new enterprises which in turn draw on technology. Forms of narrow subject specialization change, and switching to new areas of expertise becomes less infrequent than before due to job market necessity and improved usability/cost ratios of professional ICT tools. The new industry professional operates in an environment that is both convergent and fragmented. The fragmentation allows for convergence of different players and organizations. Such players and organizations must be prepared to adapt to rapid changes in the technology and methods used by emergent creative businesses that form the field that conditions them. The conditional nature of strategy requires agile responses. Those responses dictate a convergence of skills within organizations and between organizations. By implication, convergence of skills is required from labour and management alike. Focus on core competencies is the important precursor to the strengthening of the competitive position of emergent organizations that depend on such highly skilled labour. Management needs to understand technological and creative principles; sometimes those two are one behind the business goals of such organizations, and therefore managers frequently possess good production skills. This is akin to previous forms of cultural authenticity required of entrepreneurs in the early stages of previous paradigm shifts.

Focus on core competencies does not mean that these would not change over time. As the pace of innovation continues to rise, so does the number of parties involved, including very small independent production businesses, interns and start-ups with backing; the change of core competencies of such new virtual navigator suppliers may be both rapid and radical. The main principal component that is shared across such changes of focus is the digital methodology in communication, workflow management and supply.

Fragmentation of ownership and control

Fragmentation of ownership and control may not be self-evident. Rather, there is a well-documented process of fragmentation of demand. Fragmentation of channels, content, cultures, scenes, genres, styles, lifestyles, leisure preferences, degrees of activity or responsiveness, and consumer ideology discourses, whether conscious or not: many of these have been well documented in literature. The implication is that, if such fragmentation exists in largely uncontrolled online media where few enforced content restrictions apply, then it must correspond to an articulate action on the management side of content supply. Ownership, aggressive marketing and distribution aside, there are other forms of control that may subtly yet effectively manage fragmented cultural and creative markets.

Homogeneity constructs in mainstream products

Homogeneity of mainstream products seems unattainable on the scale on which it benefited concentrated market entities in the past. The *viewership* figures of individual television programmes are lower in significant relative terms as compared to traditional linear media. Predictions of the disappearance of broadcasting have failed to materialize. However, it is important to bear in mind that the expenditure per person in the developed world has reached a plateau and possibly decreased in relative terms; moneys collected for rights use across creative industries have been fragmented to a significant degree, and revenues have reduced due to user-endorsed unauthorized copying and distribution of intellectual property works. Those works represent the very essence of all commercial rights generating income for the industry. Therefore, the ontology of several industries has to change to accommodate the new environment. Any industry that depended on exclusive rights in content, manufacturing, marketing, distribution, processes and performances is now forced to change its own self-perspective.

A fundamental rethink is required. There are signs of evasion tactics, in addition to cross-industry ploys designed to buy some time while securing new and reusing old assets. Such signs of a changing set of priorities are visible through public endorsement of brand sponsorship deals, product placement in scripts and lyrics, and increased cooperation with the public sector. Art and other, more traditional cultural forms preceding modern music and media have long coexisted and collaborated with authority. Cross-sector cooperation or relations with the state were very limited in entertainment and luxury goods. A crisis of manufacturing and copycat models in design and luxury sectors coincide with the growth of new economic powers on the horizon. Those new economic powers may prove pivotal for the market for established creative and cultural sectors, being the places where intellectual property protection did not traditionally take root.

In such markets where retail of cultural commodities never took hold (Montgomery 2010), business models focus on the value around, not within, the product. The same can be said about recent business innovation in established creative and cultural sectors. Dominance and control in a market immersed in a changed environment depends on the ability to oversee the management of many flows of content and to benefit from user responsiveness.

Fragmentation across niches of culture

'Genre-rich marketing' can be a solution to the problem of the tagging of relevant products (A. Goodyer 2015 interview). This is the case irrespective of the fundamental nature of operations, whether the marketing narrative, integrated with genre network positioning, is designed by automation – i.e. software – or human design processes (e.g. brainstorming and bricolage based techniques and similar abstract tools, the latter described by Assa Ashuach in the field of design).

Empirical work in music marketing labs combined with industry partners' help in knowledge transfer shows that the best way to connect with fragmented audiences is to explore genre connections across verticals and horizontals with both likely (Rheinkultur and BMX or skaters, Deer Tracks** and snowboarding) and unlikely connections (David Lynch and cows on mobile or handheld gonzo camera). These unlikely links of concept and content drive online discussion and linkages, leading to the understanding of genre as a totality of integrated links, interests and associations a person could have across social and cultural groupings they adhere to as individual units of a complex demographic that changes per each unit-individual several times per day, week etc. – periodically, by different temporal patterns. Understanding what, how and when to post, connect and link, present and offer, has to be based (to a degree) on a bigger, holistic picture of different genres in different arts, lifestyles, product and industry sectors: travel and music, fashion and soaps, film, games and sports, cars, literature and cooking. Such imaginative links can enable marketers to package complex brand relationships that can be offered to multiple clients and stakeholders in a loosely connected 'coopetitive' (Graham *et al.* 2004) manner.

The non-necessary links of articulation (Hall 1980a, b) as culture form and reflect genre and business alliances which may or may not be temporary but are set to create value through artefacts, events, practice, discourses, stylistic forms and texts, all of which can be commodified and added to the revenue streams of creative economy (Hall 1980a, b; Hall *et al.* 1996; Todorovic 2004, 2008). In exploring such non-necessary alliances through genre connections, 'genre' may be understood on the highest level of abstraction. On that level an entire industry can be abstracted to the level of discursive genre: ICT as a science–design–innovation–use 'genre'; events as a transitory–periodical–experiential 'genre'; visual arts as an entertainment–introspection–experience–perception 'genre'; etc.

When we take a specific set of conditions and apply them to a given 'genre-rich concentrated-convergence niche' context, which is anchored in a brand or narrative, we have specific and rounded snippets of synergic content that attracts attention. 'That Dress', 'Flat Eric', etc. may not be engineered or controlled consciously but (1) their discursive power can be used to amplify a contextually and conceptually related signal ('see black and blue') and (2) the narrative and genre linkages defining them can be analysed *a posteriori* to inform the design of future public relations and marketing campaigns that do not have the ambitious goal to fire up the internet like the two phenomena mentioned above did – but may be quite helpful as was the case with now classic projects such as *Blair Witch* and its successful claim to authenticity, which amplified its signal to clients and audiences alike.

4 Strategy/creativity dialectics applied

One of the key tenets of this work is the equivalence of strategy and creativity. It is argued that creativity has to be strategic in order to bring sustainable results and that strategy is inherently creative. While in the area of cognition, components of decision-making can be seen – implicitly or explicitly – as 'strategic' (Harris and Sanborn 2013; Heilman 2006; Wilhelms and Reyna 2014), Bilton (2007, 2009) draws significant correlations between the processes of management and the notion of creativity, utilizing various cases in culture and creative management to embark on such explorations. Covered elsewhere in this book is the truly pioneering work of Bloch (2012), who dedicates an entire tome to the reconciling of artificially imposed disciplinary tensions between the respective paradigms of natural and social sciences. These are epitomized in deceptive dichotomies, defined as any of the following signifiers: positivistic vs. interpretive, hypothetico-deductive vs. inductive, measurable vs. descriptive, quantitative vs. qualitative, cognitive vs. cultural, etc. (*Anthropology and the Cognitive Challenge*). Implicit in this argument is a worthy debate on reconciling paradigmatic tensions, and possible contributory causes stemming from (post-) industrial divisions of labour, which not even intellectual work has evaded. For the purpose of this monograph, however, it is more than satisfactory to construe and benefit from overarching methodologies. As said in Chapter 2, these are postulated on the foundations of Kantian *transcendental illusion/synthetic a posteriori*, paradigmatic shifts noted by contemporary authors (following Kuhn 1962) – *evidenced in industry practice* – and Bloch's persuasive, powerfully thorough examination of multidisciplinary links between seemingly opposing paradigms of science, culture and, by extension, the arts.

There is adequate and growing evidence of the logical soundness of such approaches, found in the work of many contemporary analysts, and most importantly, field practitioners. Cognitive aspects of such strategic practice are explored elsewhere; it is now worth focusing on their organizational and interpretive counterparts, especially those focusing on the subject areas of culture and creativity. Notably, Bilton (2009: 30) cites the shift in the advertising industry from the aesthetics and individuality of creative concepts to the more integrated, strategic approach of the sector that defines creativity as business model innovation, thus elevating the notion of creativity from individual to institutional, and from campaign (tactic) to brand (strategic). Indeed, in this book it is argued that a systematic and encompassing approach that characterizes strategy is required for formulating and developing creativity in an artistic or scientific sense, and that the same is the case for being able to label a business decision or process 'strategic'. Namely, it is suggested that strategic processes are those which overcome, go beyond the generic and replicable character of project administration and day-to-day maintenance of business operations, whereby even incremental change requires the kind of reasoning that can be (conditionally) labelled 'creative' due to its cognitive characteristics.

Extensive fieldwork conducted for this book suggests that there are evident tensions between different ways of understanding creativity within the varied organizations that embark on strategies defining creative industries and sectors. In fieldwork, these notions of creativity have been seen to range broadly. The span covers respondent data/accounts, ranging from institutionalized models of organizational practice (including organizational learning), value structures and market operations (Bilton 2009: 31–35), to those of *inherently individualistic* decision-making processes. The latter sets of cases are especially notable in those areas where the value of the product, service or experience is a *direct function* of managing ideas and turning them into physical (whether material or digital) or cognitive (conceptual) form. The former, organizationally construed models of operational practice and value structures are more frequently, not surprisingly, a feature of corporate structures and approaches. The latter, inherently individualistic processes of creative strategy decision-making are more frequently adopted in small to medium-sized organizations frequently characterized by the focus on entrepreneurial leadership of managers, who tend to be creative specialists trained or educated within the actual core processes of value creation within the industry, sector or niche they occupy. However, drawing clear, binary contrasting delineations between 'institutional' and 'individualized' creative strategies would oversimplify the subject matter and not do justice to the complex nature of both strategy and creativity. Similar findings can be accounted for in other works (e.g. Bilton 2007, 2009; Pratt and Jeffcutt 2009; Christensen 2006: 39–41, 45–47, 54), leaving aside for the moment distinctions and nuances between the respective definitions of creativity and innovation. Moreover, this can be seen in other important treatises that define the links between business modelling, innovation and strategy and the adoption of novel operational models. This is especially the case in the broad, emerging pattern of sweeping transformation of entire sectors and industries where technology is the key driver of such change. Seeing change, strategy and innovation as a totality of all the fundamental transformations, encompassing all levels from the *minutiae of operations* to global paradigm shifts, makes it difficult to draw a clear distinction between the underlying technology strategy *substructure* and the business strategy *superstructure* (e.g. Casadesus-Masanell and Ricart 2010;

Garnham 2005; Markides 2006; Graham *et al.* 2004; Graham and Hardaker 2000). A relation of equivalence is drawn between (scientific) creativity and attainment of new forms of human capital (Garnham 2005: 21) while cautioning against the simplification of actual complex correlations between radical innovation in business modelling, technology and product design (Markides 2006) and understanding that this occurs on several planes and structural levels (Casadesus-Masanell and Ricart 2010; Graham *et al.* 2004).

In fact, some of the most noteworthy cases of strategic transformation that can be accounted for as 'creativity', 'innovation' and conceptual transformations of fundamental character can be seen as result of successfully managed sets of intersections, or *intentional convergences* of scientific, intuitive and pragmatic thinking. Some of those examples are so ubiquitous that they may not stand out: in digital media, search, communications and strategy tools as well as within the more traditional domains of product/service innovation. Global examples include Google, YouTube, Facebook, Twitter, Spotify, Netflix, *Angry Birds* (mechanics!), but also Lego, IKEA, the London tube map and even entire classes of culture-, experience- and service-oriented types of iconic product designs including skateboards and snowboards, the value of which is frequently more cultural, psychosocial and experiential than evidentially utilitarian. Many of the respondents in this study referred to the links between creativity and strategy, their responses ranging from pragmatically utilitarian (e.g. A. Bogucki, C. Price) to abstract and values-driven (e.g. M. Gallego, S. Funk). In some cases, components of the cognitive process were revealed – the strategy as a cognitive methodology in project planning, product/service development and matching of outcomes (e.g. A. Asshuach, D. Serrano). In other cases still, respondents referred to the inherent cognitive components of business model design, whereby business models are supported by an operational *substructure* that is entirely determined by ICT, and would not have existed without contemporary interactive technologies (e.g. A. Goodyer, T. Georgiev). Nonetheless, as argued in several places in this book, the *interactivity* of digital, ICT-driven models was created, designed and developed because of the inherently determined human need and ability for social *interaction*, which can be facilitated by ICT in such ways as to reinforce and create new forms of *intrinsic value* which can be consequently commercialized. Such need, desire and ability to interact is covered in numerous treatises; one case where its complexity is of particular relevance is the aforementioned work by Bloch (2012). Though not obviously related to business notions of strategy, tactics, modelling or commercialization, the fundamental philosophical, methodological and paradigmatic structures underlying this work reflect the need for business studies in general, and the notion of strategy in particular, to develop in tune with the times and realities of practice which is multidimensional, complex and therefore effective. The dialectic relationship between innovations in technology and creative business strategy can also be read in reverse, in order to identify governing principles and patterns of development. Why would this be of importance? One of the key tenets of well-construed strategy is its professed ability to anticipate and influence future moves and outcomes by understanding the role of abstract notions in concrete contexts. Strategic insight cited elsewhere in this book includes the understanding that led to the Apple vs. Apple case, brought about by the foresight[1] that music and computing would converge at a point at which there would be little distinction between the role of a record company and that of a computer-driven business.

This is not fundamentally dissimilar from the ability of advanced theorists to anticipate changes in technology that would make an impact on both creativity and business, or the artistic vision which may lack the appropriate vocabulary – as the technology has not been invented yet – but which can anticipate major innovations in form, format and corresponding market strategies. Notable examples of this include Andy Warhol's '15 minutes of fame' (the attribution of authorship and meaning of which are still contested), anticipating reality television, advanced celebrity culture and value capture thus attained. The leader of the Doors, Jim Morrison, reportedly anticipated the rise of sampling and musical forms such as rap and EDM (during a television interview); Adorno's prediction of internet/network-driven, content-focused and decentralized heterotopias has been mentioned elsewhere in this work. None of these people had access to information that would pertain to particular technologies, most of which were fully developed long after their deaths. Consequently, the vocabulary they used was conditioned by the technology of their own lived time era, yet this did nothing to undermine Walter Benjamin's understanding of possible consequences of format convergence coupled with potentially infinite copying of work, or Paul Valery's disconcertingly accurate predictions of what we now call 'streaming' media.

It matters little that most of these insightful individuals seldom focused on commercial implications, not having much interest in such outcomes or developments within the phenomena under their gaze. The ability to explore such complex phenomena through a seemingly paradoxical *combination of immersion and detachment* may be of great significance for future strategists. The strategic impact of technology on a market for creative products, services and experiences should not be overlooked in cases where key innovation occurred in the distant past, as it may lead to a heightened capacity for understanding fundamental forces driving the patterns of strategic change.

An obvious, relatively recent, and well-documented (even over-documented) example of multichannel recording technology is frequently discussed on all levels of understanding. Multichannel audio technology transformed entire product ranges, markets and underlying strategies in the 1960s and 1970s, giving rise to the power of global record labels (Frith 1990). Its increasing ubiquity and consequent reduction of cost, especially of digitized tools (and 'prosumer' product pricing), can be seen as one of the causes of the perceived loss of value in audio products. This was becoming evident even before the early Web, as compression formats and peer-to-peer networks beginning with Napster heralded 'the culture of free', as referred to by one media respondent (C. Price), and strategically foreseen by a charismatic industry leader (Maurice Oberstein).

However, the strategic impact of creativity, or the creative impact on strategy, can be traced into a far more distant past, centuries before Henry Ford's Model T and the twentieth-century assembly line. Arguably, the commercialization of art and culture is of a more recent date, just as stated by Tom Cardew, an artist respondent who operates in the loosely termed area of visual arts (though his media include non-visual means). A number of respondents, especially those who operate within the more 'traditionally' termed areas of art and culture, find the contemporary increased transition towards commercialization, institutional target-driven regulation and industrial professionalization of arts as disconcerting as Adorno, Benjamin and Horkheimer did in relation to the then emerging industrialization of culture and its consequent standardization (form, format, medium etc). Nonetheless, not only can the links between institutions, power and commerce be traced back into the distant past but the technologies now taken for granted played a defining role in this.

For example, looking at distant innovations in art technology, now perceived as 'traditional', provides examples of format characteristics so deeply ingrained in culture and Western civilization that global markets, cultural practices and audience identities become inherently connected to what was once 'novelty'. Oil painting was developed during the transition from high Renaissance to early Baroque, and its impact was not confined to style, form and representational aesthetics, all of which were results of improved technology. Qualitative transformation of technique led to the attainment of the illusion of depth, perspective and what was later to become known as 'suspension of disbelief' (Harris and Sanborn 2013: 58), especially important in the age of linear media such as film. Although art theorists or historians seldom if ever speak of any notion of 'marketing' in the distant past (e.g. the Baroque and Watteau in McClellan 1996), the 'trickery' of oil paint techniques first noted in the work of Van Eyck[2] would have subverted the older mastery of technologies preceding it and created a new sense of *intrinsic value* (e.g. Hewison 2006; Hewison and Holden 2004; Holden 2006; Gibson 2008 etc.), an experiential value previously unknown to audiences, patrons and buyers alike. Such innovation would have had a market effect, though 'markets' and especially matters resembling standardization or 'industrialization' of art and culture were not part of a common, public discourse of the time, neither quantitatively nor qualitatively close to what featured from late modernity onwards. Technological innovations in art technique or instrument design had a market impact, which needs to be noted irrespective of the necessary caution that one must take when construing a 'market' context in relation to a set of historically distant events and processes. The significance of culture and cultural goods during the transition from the late mediaeval age to early modernity and the artisan manufacturing preceding any notion of industrial production would not have been characterized by commercial signifiers akin to those of late modernity or this current epoch (Epstein 1998; Kieser 1989; Epstein 1991; Richardson 2001; Gustafsson 1987; Farr 2000; Epstein 2002; Pounds 2014). Nevertheless, the technology – including musical instrument design and craftsmanship – facilitated a set of developments that redefined creativity and its impact on the intrinsic value of creative work (extensive debates can be drawn on the basis of the approach for which Marshall McLuhan is famed). A strategy, loosely defined as a means-to-ends control relationship, would have existed, though not in the contemporary sense where all effects are quantifiable and many are means-tested commercially. A pre-modern notion of 'strategy', as a different notion of power, skill, control, plan, implementation, impact (etc.) and attaining a desired effect, would have been utilized for different purposes, as pre-modern discourses of strategy would have concerned themselves with religious, political and military power, where art and culture would have been tightly controlled to serve clearly identifiable goals. Such events, processes and discourses are very well documented in history literature (a plethora of texts can be found that reflect this, e.g. Holmes 1995; Stinger 1998; Masters 1996; Shneiderman 2003; Gilbert *et al.* 1957; Norris 1989; Anderson 1996; Wegman 1995; Leppert and McClary 1989; Dillon and Kallberg 2002; Holsinger 2001; Scanlon 2007).

Works on critical approaches to strategy, and to some degree those that deal with more established strategy discourses, examine the term's military origins. A particularly interesting notion is the analogy that Von Clausewitz, an eminent nineteenth-century military strategist, drew between war and business competition (Levy *et al.* 2001). Mintzberg's 'strategy as ploy' is an example of one that draws close to battle tactics and ruse. This comparison of business behaviour to military campaigns not only suggests a kinship of purpose between the two but also that *they are both arts rather than sciences* (Levy *et al.* 2001). In the ancient Chinese text *The Art of War*, instructions of a leading traditional school of military strategy are drawn in the style of philosophical allegory and poetic symbolism, with the apparent aim of abstracting the concrete experience and learnedness of the (legendary) author (Tzu 2002). This way of reading strategy as a set of logical riddles applied to different configurations, events and environments seems to have been purposefully designed to survive any particular context the authors may have referred to in their reflection on any actual or current events. Conclusions drawn by the reader may only become concrete through abstraction and understanding of the logical challenge presented in each section, and only then through specific application to the problem at hand. Situations are thus presented through the abstract representation of principles and key forces in a number of hypothetical scenarios derived through reflection. Any concrete situation would differ from the idealized setting of these strategic puzzles, where the moral of the story, the cautionary tale relating to the problem, is the key tool for instruction as it gives the reader insight into what components of the problem are variable and which ones are independent, offering a reflexive tool for understanding context based on supposedly archetypal principles. Frequently, the lesson to be learnt is that the opponents' strengths may be used against them.

In the Western tradition, one of the most notable examples of ancient military strategy is that of the battle of Cannae (Daly 2002; Goldsworthy 2007). The complex ploy behind the tactical manoeuvre on display there was long held *an innovative, if not a creative one* (it is more than a slight contradiction in terms to call a battle 'creative'). It should not be lost on the reader that Hannibal Barca explored configuration of the terrain and its east–west orientation in the context of choosing when and where to make decisive moves, analogously to the detailed market and environment research required for any major strategic innovation (Markides 1997) accompanying disruptive innovation in business (Christensen and Overdorf 2000; Christensen *et al.* 2006; Johnson *et al.* 2008).

It may be ironic to speak of creativity in such destructive contexts, yet this brings up the question of how creativity is defined in such terms. Schools of thought in modern cognition root creativity in regularity of practice and performance, while the term is also allied to the notions of sentient intelligence and talent, which is both elusive and problematic (Subotnik *et al.* 2005; Sternberg 1985, 1997, 2003). However, one of the ways of defining creative intelligence is that which learns to act in novel situations with very limited aid of prior experience (Heilman 2005: 70, 175, 177; Sternberg 1981: 149–155).

The links between such flights of imagination and understanding of the environment would have unsurprisingly appeared inspired to the contemporaries of these early innovators in the field of competition, since there is very little competitive activity as fierce and hotly contested as warfare. The quasi-hagiographic accounts of modern entrepreneurs of celebrity standing are shrouded in a similar kind of contrived mystery to that surrounding the lives of demigods such as Alexander of Macedon. Relatively recent works on social engineering in public relations are scarce and largely forgotten, and it is important to note that publicity takes a strategic ideological form in business and society alike. An author frequently cited in twentieth-century cultural studies and critical sociology draws inferences from the Renaissance principles of political strategy identified by a much vilified author, whose name became a synonym for duplicity and slyness. The utilitarian principles of discipline and control are explained as a rational exploitation of deviancy, and deviancy depends on context. Such covert organizational solutions as those defined in the panopticon are particularly effective in permeating the observed because they are built in to the minute aspects of a social or material architecture of the controlled environment.

This utilitarian leap too represents an innovation corresponding with the increasing role of empirical and rational thought over the punitive ideology of the middle ages which was seen as wasteful in post-Enlightenment Europe. Similarly, the modern panopticon was theoretically postulated in relation to the internet in early treatises focusing on the web. Having overcome the knee-jerk reaction to peer-to-peer networks of the early share culture, the linear media sectors are assimilating the panopticon model while being assimilated themselves by an innovation pattern that has changed their social, economic, technological, legal and policy environment. In this narrative, the creative – innovative – agents, frequently small groups of individuals to begin with, are credited with the ability to affect major field configurations by changing their viewpoint, reflecting and resolving riddles similar to those found in traditional texts on the philosophy of conflict. Examples are the improbable solution of using printers for the production of physical goods or medical treatment; the idea of systematizing and classifying online data links; or the idea of creating self-regulating peer-review systems of referencing informal user knowledge bases. All of these well-known examples have generated significant economic results, commercial or societal, and are triggering new creative experimentation that has strategic impact. The solutions offered in each of those cases were out of the mundane, repetitive nature of administering and sustaining dominant industry structures. Solutions to logical problems that few thought existed have imposed a disruptive shift of focus, turning the strength of the previous dominant industry paradigm into a threat against it.

Whether these metaphorical parallels and links are justified, and if so, what can be learnt from such discursive links to draw conclusions – these questions have methodological implications. The chief methodological consideration is, however, in a set of new equivalences, or dialectic relationships, between strategy and creativity that have been imposed on all actors in creative fields as a result of radical change of environments.

Ontology–epistemology–teleology of creative strategy

One of the key tenets of this work is the equivalence of strategy and creativity. It is argued that creativity has to be strategic in order to bring sustainable results and that strategy is inherently creative.

The second equivalence standing at ontological levels of each of the explored contexts is the equivalence between qualitative and quantitative information.

Below is a list of some core relationships between ontological components of value that lie behind the need to strategize in creative contexts.

- Relationships between tangible artefacts and free-floating content
- Relations of ownership and control
- Relations of control and use
- Relations of use and supply
- Relations of supply and value formation
- Relations of intrinsic value, use value and exchange value
- Relations of exchange and control

Every industry operates in its own context. That context is determined by *what it actually does*. This may be a blurred area; wherever such lack of clarity exists, definitions matter as they influence the outcome of development. The clarity of definition has been found to depend on complex and detailed understanding of content, context and form – examples corroborating the key postulates of creative industry ontology are found in interviews with experienced professionals and/or managers across creative fields (music, film, TV, design, etc.)

How a practice sees itself influences future practice. However, is there anything that is, as such, beyond the perception of those involved, the nature of the product or outcome of creative business work? Is it possible to understand the nature of what an industry creates outside of the perception of those involved? Is a musical work a value in itself? What is the value in itself of music outside perception? What is the value of a garment outside of its public perception? What is the value of a service in entertainment outside of the perception of those who supply or use the service? Does the work exist outside presentation, exhibition, performance, function, reproduction and consumption?

What is the function of music, text, film, industrial design, games? It is the ego–id function in metaphors of consciousness and pleasure. The gratification of conditioned and inherent drives for beauty, experience or engagement with the environmen: the id side. The rationalization of such consumption is in part defined by status and social identity: tribal position. It is the alienation of one's own labour by engagement with someone else's professionalized labour in art, much berated by the first cultural industry critic. This alienation is part of a conscious process, an ego-process of asserting status and identity through the garment, music, entertainment service or art. The link connecting the two is conditioning. How conscious the processes of selection are is less important than understanding that those who know how to influence consumption of pleasure in socially determined contexts understand the industry in which they operate. This does not mean that managers must be creative practitioners in the field, but the understanding of the creative essence of what the industry is determines the impact such decisions will make.

Also, similar notions may apply to change. Industry change happens both incrementally and in leaps. Incremental change is, as such, not abolished by disruptive technologies; incremental change continues as a feature of replication and the mundane running of business. It is the area of the blurring of boundaries where ever greater numbers of sibling assets are acquired by businesses that converge their forces in diagonally connected areas of activity. 'What *is* the product?' is a blurred question in portfolios combining games and film, for instance: the change needed to bring them together in supply chains may have been radical and disruptive at first, but the fine-tuning shows that the adoption of successfully convergent outputs requires incremental fine-tuning of supply mechanisms and operations, including communicating concepts and plans to different departments with varied methods and agendas. Where definitions of what an industry *i*, change from time to time, this serves as evidence of the sort of disruptive change that may come from fact – innovation, technology, radical environmental shift – or discourse: style, movement, social and political conditions that transform the pleasure principle behind what is deemed the right way to consume the creative output. This again is the matter of perception and the question of transcendental illusion – what is the value of creative output outside the shared perception of users, traders and creators.

The earlier stated notion of articulation is the one whereby an agreement is reached between strata and players: a consensus on what a product is and how it is to be used. If a digital form of storage and communication supersedes an analogue one, such as is the case with most entertainment media in highly saturated markets, then a consensus is reached between all (i) parties and (ii) strata: (1) users, consumes, middle men, producers, artists, engineers, and (2) levels of influence, from bloggers to news corporations and from local consumer networks to major policy bodies.

That agreement is renegotiated at every point of major change in the configurations on the metaphorical chess board: mass manufacturing of arts and crafts leading to modern industrial design goods; radio, personal stereo, personal stereo with infinite playlist; printing and customizing ones own clothing from templates; radical time-shifting in digital TV; using social media to attend live events; etc. The blurring occurs at points of such change. The blurring is now also a point of change that appears to be constant.

Constancy of change: the paradigm of infinite innovation?

To answer that, returning to the Self of what an industry does can inform policy and strategy for those able to plan or implement it, or those learning from analysis and aiming to apply it. What is the Self of music? What is the Self of communications? The Self of design? The Self of film: is it a hybrid art or a reflection of inner desire, the id of the user corresponding with the id of the author and of the marketing? Is it both? What the future holds for film can be understood if its Self is dissected in reflective analysis. It can be speculated that film is the hybrid of drama, inner-eye/dreamlike visualizations (perhaps a more constant human cognitive feature), and performance (with its unique protagonists marketed to the id of major media publics), confined to a particular duration and set of narrative tools. If what can change – or must be changed – changes without affecting the essence, there is film as a format and form remaining what it *is*. Product placement does not alter what films *are*; the Self of film continues to exist. Digital tools do not remove the essence of this hybrid form, but they do renegotiate the perception of believability between the creators, the marketers/traders and the user audience.

What crafts are has not changed due to technology, but it has confined them to the niche of highly dedicated connoisseur clients, thus narrowing down and opening the field to design and mass manufacturing before this started to give way to mass customization. The Self of an aesthetically designed utilitarian product has not changed radically enough to make such non-utilitarian focus obsolete – leaving room for choice based entirely on the id–ego plays of users. Still, the transformation of the value-adding processes, the reduction of cost per item privileging high economies of scale, and increased specialization and professionalization of craft-purpose products have led to radical concentration of power in elite markets at one extreme and highly commercialized integrated processes of mass manufacture at the other extreme case of utilitarian aesthetic for everyday use. This is not fundamentally dissimilar from what has happened in music or art.

What may be said of *all creative industry products* is therefore that they serve a purpose that can be postulated as an id–ego conditioned aim to satisfy a need that goes beyond biological survival. This makes it no less fundamental. What is the fundamental connection between all the so-called creative industries?

It important to look at their core products and services: art, theatre, dance, music, pottery, games, interiors, film, reality TV, apps, social networks, texts, garments, events, hospitality, poetry: they invariably satisfy an identifiable set of abstract needs. These needs are social, psychological and cultural in nature. They are both cognitively and socially conditioned needs. These products, services, outputs and artefacts carry an abstract value, a value not in itself but negotiated and perceived through the reflection of the user.

Their value is temporal. It is content-defined and context-conditioned. The Self of the output defines the ontology of an industry. Where a practice is surplus to the needs of a product-user articulated Self of an industry, that practice disappears: side-shows are confined to history, just as gladiator games were. Now reality television replaces the spectator sport of public humiliation. Records are no longer the preferred product, so they become marketing assets for campaigns that utilize the brand value of a music performer sold as unique, a public Self consumed by the public. This public is no longer merely viewing and purchasing content, and its varied levels of engagement with the public Self of a performer can be managed online. That becomes the new commodity value, where the commodity value of a record is renegotiated to be infinitesimally approaching zero in a majority of contexts. The Self of journalism is changing along similar principles.

In a similar way, the transformative nature of *interactive content media* changes the perceived Self of many traditional areas. Where there is demand for literature, it is partly satisfied by online creators, and some bloggers were recruited into script writing. While dance is an inherently essentialist activity that cannot be performed on high levels without necessary specialism and training, the fragmentation of *content-interaction media* allows for dance to fragment into as many forms as there are niche users willing to become viewers or audiences. Technology, on the other hand, improves the prospects for stage innovation on high levels of output and transform the format and the form of what performance itself is, through both media of stage delivery and media of dissemination.

Therefore even if the Self of a particular form remains unaffected, the transformation of its aesthetics into a genre-rich field area does affect the way in which the form of output can be stylistically and socially defined and commercialized. This occurs in style diversification and narrow niche definition and in the social context of consumption – viewing a stream of a live show, ordering tickets online.

Interactive media can transform the narrative of existing forms through the manipulation of perceived reality. Similarly, apps and services behind them redefine the nature of consumption of entertainment content. These hybrids perform one or, frequently, more than one creative *Self-function*, which existing analogue forms did in the past, normally in an automated manner. This is similar to the distinctions between film and theatre; or the ones between music video, televised live appearances and diegetic or non-diegetic music in film. The combination of dimensions of expression and experience does in some instances create a new quality. How sustainable such a new quality is cannot be foretold with the immense variety of models and media concepts competing for audience attention. Streaming or cloud computing in entertainment; printing clothes or design goods; customizing a hotel environment through digital media; mashups and user-edited footage in fan networks; all of these phenomena have components that are destined to reappear in many forms and media technologies. However, the sustainability of those models individually can only be asserted through ever-closer matching with the current interpretation of what the user currently perceives as the Self of a product or service. Negotiating that Self requires rapid responses.

One of the matters that transpire from recent work (e.g. Yin *et al.* 2012) on long-tail concepts is as follows. The problem with long-tail recommendation, search and other mechanisms, systems and models is that the blurring of metaphorical 'particle motion'[3] at the tail's end is too unpredictable to be managed with certainty. Therefore, the only ones who truly benefit from it are varied virtual navigators who have enough scope and scale to manage flows of information – and information is at least equivalent to content, mirroring the message/medium metaphor in new ways – so as to control matters of flow and benefit from the aggregate activity in the areas of unpredictability and uncertainty at the blurred ends of the asymptotic tail. The bottleneck managers of flow benefit from it most.

Convergence/synergy dialectics

The dialectic relationship between synergy and convergence is an important one. *With the two key respective terms defined*, it becomes evident that some connections arise between the two, in particular with respect to the nature of emergent ICT-driven communications that define the shift of power – a near seismic one – to those businesses that control the content flow, from those that traditionally created and managed content itself. The very phrase 'content' implies that there seems to be a diminishing perceived value of the works of creative artists, directors, producers and media organizations they work for, or with, depending on the particulars of business relationships set through contractual and intellectual property (IP) standards. While convergence can be seen as a set of technological conditions that enable the highly lucrative use of varied content across fixed and mobile platforms, media and devices, business synergy is understood to act as that type of organizational structuring that enables organizations irrespective of size (albeit predominantly large ones) to attain greater efficiencies in management terms, and in the sense of bringing different and varied departments and/or partners together for the attainment of market dominance. Though synergy may not be confined to the media or creative organizations, it is very well documented in the critical studies of corporate strategy whereby the nature of creative business practice attains synergic impact greater than that of most other traditional sectors.

Synergy is seldom mentioned in such treatises in the early twenty-first century. Without exploring whether this is due to its actual loss of significance, or causes relating to discursive trends in academia and commerce alike, it is worth examining what the term would have meant to the need for integration of allied creative sectors in the decades preceding the emergent 'digital revolution'. Diagonal integration, as defined by Doyle (2013), can be interpreted as that specific case of vertical integration that characterizes media, entertainment and other content-driven organizations. Moreover, corporate giants such as Apple clearly benefit from synergy: the attainment and close control of a closed system of operations, software and hardware, content management and applications in such a way that the ownership of IP in the form of patents, copyrights and licences acts as a necessary prerequisite for the continued control of large segments of the user/consumer market in advanced electronics and the content-driven services they deliver. This arguably goes beyond internal organizational efficiency and suggests that capturing large swathes of the market depends on synergic practice around any of the devices, products and services they support, especially but not exclusively in tightly controlled product–service continuums epitomized in the Apple brand. Indeed, the example given by one respondent (Assa Ashuach) who is a leading innovator in product/service design (such as 3D printing, networked production solutions etc.) suggests that in contemporary design, one should not make a distinction between product and service as one feeds off the other, attaining greater value and market efficiency. According to the expert thus consulted, this is namely for the purpose of integration that a discerning consumer/user requires in the current age of mass-customization and user empowerment. Those (creative, digital) organizations that do not understand the importance of creating and supporting a product–service continuum for any of their product or service lines are set to lose, according to this respondent, whose business thrives on the product and service modelling capacity enabled by ICT and mass-customization.

Once synergy is observed in this context, the equivalence with a definition of convergence offered by Jenkins (2002, 2006a, b) becomes evident. Whereas convergence does stem from technological advances (first used in enabling laser technology decades ago), making it work in efficient ways requires the kinds of organizational structuring and/or networking that encompass the notion of synergy. Being greater than the sum of its parts, a system of any kind, in this set of cases a system of product–service development, control and delivery, is historically connected to the technological solutions that were behind the original purpose of creating the internet (e.g. ARPANET). A computer network can sustain the sum of information greater than that of its constituent nodes. Preserving important information and communications data was essential for the defence purposes that lay behind the creation of the internet. Thus the convergence now manifest in the multiplicity of forms and formats across media, devices and types of data can be seen as a direct consequence of synergy that lay at the heart of the internet as it is known today. As previously argued in this book, the internet is *not* a democratic, levelling structure: it is highly hierarchical. The ownership and control of physical assets, both tangible and intangible, is essential for dominance and control in this communication, distribution and data/research system and its corresponding market. Widely reported controversies relating to privacy and control stem from that fact, as well as the understanding, that not all power is market power, as some utopian ideas about the internet as a democratic, levelling medium would lead one to believe. Large-scale, market-powered Foucauldian and other more traditional types of surveillance would not be attainable without such characteristics of that 'network of networks'.

The internet is highly hierarchical, though in some instances the Web and its constituent/adjacent digital media may not be so, at least not in their entirety. The hierarchy of the internet is significantly the result of its synergic nature: an efficient blending of hardware and software, communication networks, data storage and processing facilities, while the level playing field does emerge at points of significant disruptive innovation. Those successful disruptive innovations witnessed over the past 20 years frequently came from very small organizations and businesses whose key, if not only asset, was knowledge. This is the knowledge of key principles that govern the internet, its tools and media, as well as the understanding of research skills, software development and ultimately what it is that constitutes value that users and/or consumers may be willing or able to recognize, reward and/or engage with. This is the realm of convergence, where ownership is less important than control, and control less significant for business strategy than research and data. The vast majority if not all of the influential business models of these emerging and fragmented markets are based on research, which is the true asset behind the seemingly flat surface of an ostensibly level playing field of digital interaction. In their extremes, synergy and convergence are distinctly separate phenomena. However, synergy acts as a social, economic and organizational cause of effective convergence of skills, labour and knowledge that results in an organization's ability to create and capture value in digital markets. Respondents from the realm of digital media speak of curator services they offer, managing the flow of information in subtle ways that may be compatible with aggressive marketing but do not and cannot replace it. The users, audiences and consumers 'talk back', and they may at any point turn their gaze elsewhere. Understanding how and why this occurs may be aided by some key abstract strategic notions developed by Mintzberg. Key to this is a notion blending matters of *perspective and position*. The Plan is subject to any required Ploy, whereby those who can automate the Ploys, adapting their planning to the recognized and shared Perspectives between them and their publics, are able to adapt quickly enough so as to create and *modify* the means for a Pattern that is not merely emergent but also intended. The notion of 'intention', however, can be queried on a deeper level, and the loss of a single purpose that used to characterize the self-perception of role of the media, art and cultural endeavour is rather evident. This is a novel notion that has been much lamented by many a critic of the digital media, noting its impact on creative industry practice. However, to paraphrase the words of another respondent, with clear reference to disruptive innovation, 'we may not get what we wish for, but we will get it nonetheless, and it may well be something *greater than what we were able to expect*'. A highly influential respondent (Scott Cohen of The Orchard) stated in an early interview (2008) that the entire way we use, network around and consume culture would become transitory yet integrated. None of the respondents in this research overtly stated objections to the state of affairs that privileges knowledge over ownership, though many corporate reports do suggest that adapting to new practices may not work as seamlessly as is being professed in publicity materials.

The transformative nature of emergent knowledge-led alliances and the redefining of power relations in content distribution and communications is unsurprisingly unsettling for those large organizations that spent decades building portfolios now threatened by the insurrective power of networked nodes of content delivery, both legal and illegal. It is also becoming evident that policy has been developed to pre-empt illicit access to content as information, and a trajectory of policy development can be mapped out against the statements made by participants of the Oxford Media Convention 2009, when protecting IP in music was labelled 'choking innovation'. Compliance with new policies and actual active engagement in them shows that the balance is somewhat tipped back in favour of traditional content creators, yet it is hard to see how this is sustainable in the long term. The creators of *code as content* such as Facebook or Google jealously guard their own IP, as many a hacker, amateur or not, has been able to see. What is worthy of note, however, is that the size of an organization may not be the sole defining component of an effectively controllable strategy in digital media networks.

Also worthy of note is the fact that strategy and synergy may not be the sole and exclusive preserve of large organizations at a time when the convergence of significant skills, knowledge and comparatively small tangible assets creates (at first) minute market niches and hybrid, *fragmentary sub-sectors* that cannot and should not be dismissed *a priori* without great cost to those already established. Learning from new emergent strategies and business models has occured in the past. That process of learning appears to grow ever more important irrespective of the size of an organization or its assets. (To paraphrase the frequent finding of many a student of the humble SWOT analysis, strengths can easily turn into weaknesses, given the tendency to ignore the 'right' set of threats.) Such threats, in the case of digital communications and all the creative sectors they impact – and very few can evade them – are those brought about by disruptive innovation emerging from new forms and methodologies of knowledge creation. It does need to be said, however, that some of the deeply traditional forms of creativity and the corresponding practices, industries and sectors pertaining to such creativity and its outputs may not have been affected by the 'digital revolution'. Whether, or to what degree, they may be affected by it may not be a question of time or of degree but a far more fundamental matter of ontology. Nonetheless, the question of knowledge and power distribution is a matter that pervades all creative sectors, irrespective of the deep impact, or lack thereof, of interactive communications, content paradigms or digital networking.

Networks of knowledge power distribution

The work of the first progenitors of culture industry critique has been much criticized over the years (e.g. Adorno and Horkheimer in Negus 1999; Allen-Robertson 2013; Bennett 2001, etc.) for their inability or lack of interest in examining the fine nuances of relationships between corporate behaviour in culture production, creative individuals who generate works thus exploited and audiences who relate to such results of mass-culture (i.e. conduct fieldwork). Indeed, their somewhat sweeping generalizations on the motives and drives behind mass-culture formation in an industrial context did not do justice to the full complexity of the matter; the *a priori* negative overtones concerning corporate approaches to culture production did not resolve the issue of its apparent success. Treating the phenomenon as one of binary tensions between opposite poles of the exploited and their exploiters did little to strengthen the otherwise insightful understanding of the impact of power on mass culture and popular expressions of creativity. In short, a set of ideological prejudices undermines the core arguments pertaining to power relations that stem from political or economic factors at play. These shortcomings are also seen to stem from a lack of fieldwork or practical experience of the sectors and practices thus strongly criticized, and an idealization of past cultural formations can be seen to dominate the works of Adorno and Horkheimer. Nevertheless, what they did identify is what influencers and industry respondents as well as the majority of contemporary analysts have coined a 'paradigm shift'. The reference to a term originating from the philosophy of science (Kuhn and Hacking 2012) is not accidental. The invention of the internet, the development of the Web and all the innovations fracturing those two key events into manifold digital media and consequent business models have been hailed as disruptive innovations that stands to have an impact on civilization more significant than that of the printing press. Though it is impossible to judge the value of contemporary events by those who witness them or live in close temporal proximity to them, a fundamental change is evident in human communications, and even in some aspects of our core behaviours seem affected on many levels. Moreover, while the significance of the use of electricity and electromagnetism have undoubtedly led to the creation of entire new sectors, art forms and formats (film, art photography, recorded music, radio and TV), the intricate nature of distribution of power and its methodological nature (the 'How') is manifestly changing and its transformation is speeding and fragmenting in metaphorically exponential terms. (Whether that relationship is truly exponential or a different set of mathematical models applies is not the core subject of this treatise.) Some futurist writers and practitioners do seem to suggest, with varying degrees of confidence and with positive or negative prefixes attached, that the current 'paradigm shift' would lead to the development of a Singularity of artificial intelligence and the consequent transformation of human condition beyond recognition (e.g. Kurzweil).

Setting aside such grand discourses, it is worthy of note that ideological polarization has occured yet again, less than a century after the notion of culture industry was first postulated, originally in critically negative terms. Indeed, the discourse on industrialization of culture, and consequently creativity, has been so deeply ingrained into the meaning of what culture *is* that the terms of 'media', 'communications', 'music', 'design', etc are invariably followed by the suffix of 'industry'. This has occurred irrespective of the fact that the very notion of industrialization of culture and creativity has long been contested and debated as to its nature and benevolence. However, the 'industry' as originally portrayed in critical, analytical and pragmatic discourses alike is changing beyond recognition. The notion of mass production, the assembly line model, and centralized one-to-many communication, production, dissemination and distribution are no longer linear. Contemporary treatises on the transformation of supply chains into value and supply networks are contrasted with notions on management as creativity (e.g. the work of Bilton). Setting aside for the moment the fact that this is not necessarily an irreconcilable dichotomy, it is evident that linear production, distribution and consumption patterns of culture are on the wane across the world and that the very nature of human creativity is being contested in practice, *more so than in theory*.

Such contestations of human creativity come in two guises. One of them is the increased mediation between human and computer/device in many aspects of communication, most aspects of culture consumption, and the vast majority of creative production practices, all of which permeate cultures, states and communities well beyond the 'developed world'. (Moreover, the penetration of digital media modes and devices occurs at a rate and speed far greater than seen in previous transformations of communications and industrial development.) The second set of contestations of human creativity are those of originality/authenticity, and such contestations can be seen in two sub-categories. One of those is the very individuality of the author in collaborative (e.g. Creative Commons) and/or illicit modes of use of creativity (i.e. plagiarism, piracy). The second is the increased inability to capture value through traditional processes of retail, and/or remuneration for creative labour stemming from the devaluation of creative artefacts, the types of which can be copied, encoded and disseminated in digital networks. This crisis of retail and remuneration of creative labour for the units of artefacts perceived as 'culture' appears to affect the established, traditional creative industries and their individual workforces alike, irrespective of any twentieth-century tensions over ownership or control of the means of production, communication or distribution. Making matters more complicated, outmoded business power relations, epitomized by – and fixed in – ritualistic form through 'standard' contractual agreements between the dominant (major industry) parties and the weaker (artist/creator as labour) parties, appear to remain replicated in stubbornly immutable industrial relations. Automation and networking replace both labour and capital fixed in linear modes of authorship, ownership, production and sales. A respondent who operates his small yet influential design business reflects on this, stating that he often stands accused of reducing the demand for labour and individual skilled output by the very virtue of creating, developing new, cost-effective design, service and production solutions.

Such design/product/service solutions rest on automation, supply and value network creation, and mass-customization which do meet the growing demand of an increasingly discerning consumer base, fascinated by novel technologies. The Luddite approach adopted by both the 'traditional', linear creative industries, based on the assembly-line model, and the creative individuals involved on the labour side of these tensions clearly cannot 'choke innovation' and 'turn back the clock', as stated in debates over intellectual property preceding a broad scope transformation of IP policies (e.g. at the Oxford Media Convention 2009).

The degree to which networked technologies surpassed the expectations of even the bold artistic vision of a not-so-distant past is neatly illustrated in an example of a cult film produced at the end of the twentieth century. Wim Wenders's existentialist drama 'Until the End of the World' (1991) is set against the backdrop, seemingly, of a science fiction narrative and it features among its gadgets a payphone with videoconferencing. The payphone of such characteristics does not exist, and the need for it is already surpassed, therefore already limiting the demand to zero. The use of videoconferencing tools is so widespread that, at the time of writing, Facebook is set to develop a leaner data service for mobile devices set for use in developing countries, having decided to penetrate these tertiary markets, and having developed its own audiovisual interactive model for user communication. This example can serve as evidence of the increased speed of innovation permeating the world, and the fact that tertiary markets are not left as far behind as before.

It is therefore difficult to question Adorno's and Horkheimer's assumptions at their core. The evidence of tense labour and contractual/client relations in contemporary creative industries exists in well-publicized disputes over remuneration and contractual positions – especially those still replicating the linear, assembly line model which they wrote about. Similarly, it is difficult to question the wisdom, at least in its entirety, of assuming that a sort of 'old culture industry' alienation affects the public consisting of audiences, consumers and nowadays users, when it is increasingly transparent that Facebook and other social media *monetize/commercialize* the use of their networks by harnessing (or harvesting) the minutia user pattern data. The true commodity of the media is not its content nor its advertising but its audience, as suggested in an analysis of linear, 'traditional' media conducted in the latter part of the twentieth century at a time when interactive digital media were in their infancy. Nor is it fundamentally incorrect to note that media, devices, content and promotion feed off each other, as stated in Adorno's frequently cited text on the 'cynical' integration of production–promotion–distribution–consumption circuits. It is easy to observe not only the established nature of vertical and diagonal integration of 'traditional' creative industry corporations but also the new practices of networked supply/value structures, the acquisition of potentially threatening new business models and the disparity between the idealized 'long-tail' and the growing concentration of assets and data (as assets). This, however, happens under the corporate ownership of novel organizations that manage the flow and the research rather than multipliable creative artefacts of 'old' media. This confines the 'art' of yore (drama, film, music, etc.) within the category of 'content', the semantics of which are burdened with meaning. Such meaning will be analysed below, within the context of semiotics of creativity, and its capacity to map out the actual impact of novel structures of ownership, operations and distribution. Those novel structures supersede the 'traditional' creative industries where the originality, individuality and creativity of the authors and those who managed them were among the most important aspects of value creation and value capture.

This book, in spite of its abstract nature dictated by the elusive subject matter of strategy, does aim at the ambitious goal of suggesting pragmatic approaches and applicable modes of reasoning that should overcome the evident loss of value and suggesting practices that may 'turn the tide' and redefine creative industry practice through strategy. The most problematic aspect of strategy as a subject matter is its dialectic nature: if the analysis of strategy remains within the concrete and is solely driven by case study approach, it will remain limited in scope and impact. As such, it quickly becomes dated and hardly serves as a 'manual' for best practice; such texts resemble diagrams of antiquated devices or storytelling of events past. If, on the other hand, the analysis in this text remains entirely abstract, the ability to use it for application in practice remains limited. Such an abstract text becomes an entity which is too reflexive (Booth 2002) and it fails to inform planning.

Ultimately, the most simplistic and therefore most fundamental meaning of strategy is one of a highly complex plan, a plan of plans. It is therefore important to assert the reading that can have an implementation. Similarly, and nearly concluding on the value of critical theory of mass-culture, it is worthy of note that the works of Adorno, Foucault and others can have a very pragmatic aspect. Just as Adorno understood branding surprisingly well for a philosopher of Marxist inclinations, so did he anticipate, albeit idealistically, the emergence of decentralized media and communications that would subvert the status quo. On the other hand, Foucault's interest in the minute and incremental aspects of history, discourse and structure had some pragmatic aspects with far more immediate application. In order to understand the novel distribution of power within the emergent creative sectors, one needs to look at the connection between fragmentation, knowledge and compound effects of the two. The Foucauldian concept of heterotopia (loosely meaning difference of spaces) also plays an important part in this. The *non-space* of internet platforms, their ability to emulate a sense of belonging through means of orientation together with a designed perception of familiar 'environments', encourages communication.

Long-tail fallacy and commercial transformation of identity: a LASER model

The more revealing such communication may be, the more accurate the understanding of commercial engagement opportunities relating to the more passive audience segments, whose behaviour may yield results which may be used to influence large-scale chains of engagement and adoption. Among the metaphors of science actually adopted for the design and architecture of functional components of user applications (reported by respondents across the board), a proposition of an *inverse population model* may be of interest (see Figure 4.1).

This concept is borrowed from laser physics (e.g. Kononov and Koshelev 1975). The *light amplification by stimulated emission of radiation* is both the operational description of how a laser functions and the source of the acronym (LASER) that was later turned into a new word, now broadly adopted as a signifier of a technology and of many derivative metaphors ('laser sharp' among others). The use of metaphor in cybernetics and software design is well documented in theory and practice (Iivari 2007; Imaz and Benyon 2007; Wang 2007); an ICT industry respondent refers to the use of the laws of physics for the design of optimization software. Elsewhere

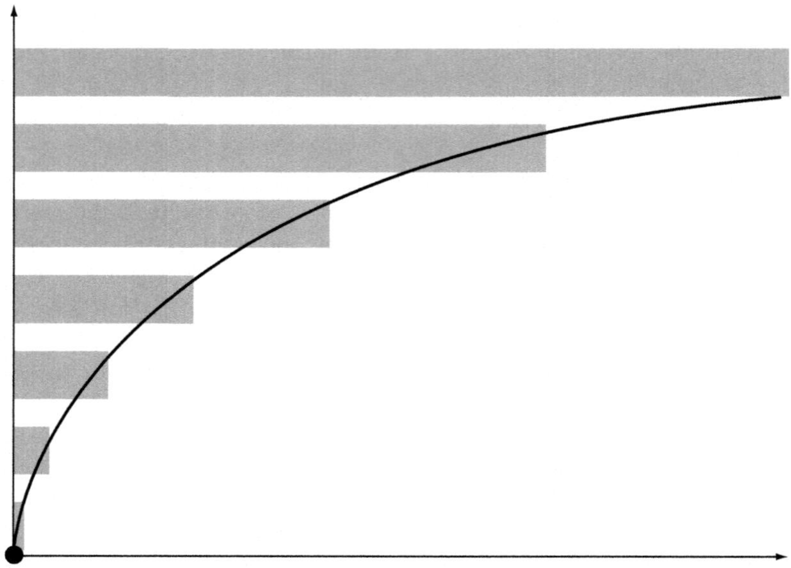

Figure 4.1 Inverse population model

in this book references have been made to the chaotic movement of particles and thermodynamic patterns and their applied use in some aspects of strategic management theory.

Put simply, the functioning of lasers depends on the phenomenon of inverting the natural position (distribution) of electrons, 'populating' (atomic) energy levels, which are inversely proportional to the distance from the atomic core. When a medium prone to emitting laser light gets 'excited' by energy input, electrons migrate to higher orbits en masse, thus attaining higher energy levels. In this position, not natural to the configuration of an atom, they remain unstable as it is their natural tendency to be closer to the positively charged core that attracts their negative electrical charge. Once excited, electrons migrate en masse, simultaneously, back to their natural position, again populating the levels closer to the core. The emission of energy during such migration, from the *inverse to the normal 'population'* closer to the core, is 'discrete' – all 'excited' electrons do it at once, all from the same (set of) higher orbits. Thus, the light energy emitted is 'discrete', or defined in terms of frequency/wavelength, of an identical colour. The identical colour/frequency of light means the amplification of energy, which is convergent (only one narrow band of spectrum) and, as such, highly focused in a way that results in narrowly targeted and high impact.

The metaphorical concept developed from the functioning of lasers is based on the idea that one can manipulate and control the engagement processes of internet media audiences. Since internet media resemble physical systems – hence the treatises and practice treating internet use as a physical environment – the same principle may well apply to the design of ICT tools that would facilitate the mode of communication resembling the *amplified* and *stimulated emission* of energy – as data. Reportedly, as in the texts that scientifically examine the actual effectiveness of a long-tail concept of use, and myriad other analyses treating the chaotic nature of user/data behaviour online, we are to find that *it is difficult to amplify a media signal* (as text or other data) and cut through the metaphorical 'white noise' of content. In short, without the support of mass media and major curatorial services (gatekeepers, as described in the Aaron Bogucki interview) it is very difficult or near-impossible to actually utilize the potential conferred by broad distribution of niche content (discourse, text or other data) – or put more simply still, to be known, heard or identified in the chaotic movement of content in online media and its potentially infinite amounts of content.

If a marketer using a convergent engagement tool based on such design principle facilitates an increased distribution of use that affects those users farthest from the core (ontology of a product/experience), any given online narrative may be amplified and focused in such a way as to 'cut through' the chaotic environment of online chatter, much in the same way as laser beams cut through gas.

This would be done by exciting those farthest from the core (of message or content being promoted), not only the closest of audiences or users, who are normally the champions of a discourse used in engagement, marketing, publicity signal amplification and commercialization. For this, audiences that follow such content most closely would be engaged in spreading the content to the farthest reaches of audience structures and doing so would generate far greater impact than normally, provided that an actual design solution can be implemented in such engagement tools, *and then managed (teleology) by those who understand (epistemology) the finest nuances of what the subject matter IS (ontology).*

In online distribution of information and related publicity strategies, those least engaged with a particular narrative are normally the majority of users, as even broadcast media channels consider 7 per cent audience share a mainstream product (36 per cent market share of the *X Factor* among talent shows is seen as worth sponsoring in a report relating to TalkTalk publicity strategies). Engaging such audiences, reading their behaviours accurately and being able to anticipate a pattern fitting an adaptive model to suit them would lead to the emergence of the kind of market control that characterized the mass media paradigm. As they operate in loosely connected virtual social spaces, these users are normally beyond the reach of even the more convergent of campaigns, their response being difficult to read or influence, as was reflected in relation to the nature of distributed/federation communications platforms which form decentralized meshes – Whatsapp, Blackberry messaging etc. The conceptual displacement, the virtual space being defined by concepts and ideas is the reason why it may be difficult to apply and attain the desirably heightened involvement of late majority users before engaging early adopters in advance of any official campaign launches. The social space is fragmented along a variety of themes, concepts, tastes and identity structures, so only a message that resonates across all these fragmentary social environments would be able to engage such more private, more passive, late majority audiences. Can 'That Dress'[4] be engineered along the principles defined by Bernays? To paraphrase a respondent discussing in 2005 a possible product placement case in a revered independent art film, if it does happen, the details will not be known to the public. This level of engagement across all media user segments and fragments would need to be supported by large, quality human assets such as social media managers and marketers who engage with audiences creating and connecting conceptually rounded and coordinated content. Just as thermodynamics, referred to in Foucault's treatise on space, were yet proven an important discourse for ICT innovation, so is Stacey's use of chaos theory to strategic management, finding its application in the emergence of unprecedented growth in the amounts of data. Perhaps a view attributable to chaotic movement of enormous numbers of 'particles' of information and discourse may imply that some user-generated phenomena emerge chaotically, as a result of the intensity of flow of content. Such content consists partly of creative works meshed with user discourses, and partly of user-generated text or linkages connected to user discourses. It is possible that chaotic patterns may produce temporary user-generated phenomena which may *later* be harnessed.

This adds further relevance to Adorno's visionary statement on the *clever fellows* and their ability to facilitate an 'improvisatory displacement of things' of a distributed and decentralized medium not known during his lifetime.

On the other hand, while chaotically produced user-meshed content can (interviews with A. Bogucki, T. Georgiev, S. O'Reilly) be useful for authentication of targeted messages, forming building blocks of discourse around a creative work, the creative work remains the focal point of all such distributed communications. The aim therefore is to identify how to derive the abstract concepts from these creative works and implement them in methodological terms. Moreover, it will be seen how these notions and abstract tools can be modified to complement the very pragmatic, deeply context-bound approaches to value capture prevalent today. As the creative work becomes commoditized (drawing on Pine and Gilmore), the dissemination of experience through fragmented user discourses requires assets to support it and, contrary to the Long Tail hypothetical model, privileges those products and experiences closer to the main streams of production and investment. The work to capture value through distributed, secondary use of creative works occurs in relation to the departure from *linear modes of mass production* and the overwhelming force of intricate communication, distribution and use governed by information technology and its influence on culture, creativity and consumption. A set of concepts covered in this book explores creative business innovation using technology to drive consumption. In terms of bargaining power and forces of paradigm change, the case study from the early days of a Concert Live shows how the buyer becomes supplier at a time of industry transformation.

Cultural coding of authenticity

How is authenticity construed and coded; where does it create greatest impact? What is an authentic experience, and is their inherent authenticity in the design of such an experience? Concept hotels provide an unlikely contribution to the subject: Citizen M Amsterdam, Michel Berger and Propeller Island in Berlin, Pantone Hotel and Be Manos in Brussels, Manhattan in Rotterdam, spa hotels in Belgium, Germany and Greece – all defined through special and regular events, designs and environments, blended experiences and methods of monitoring and control. Their brands are supported by content management and experiential strategies, sometimes long-term, as is the case with cooperation between Citizen M and Philips or led by networks of business innovation such as Serrano Brothers and boutique hotels in Colombia. These organizations utilize content, context, creativity, performance and art as part of their differentiation strategies. In each case, a digital media presence enhances the brand, however subtly or mundanely. The answers on return on investment can be sought by exploring the impact of such cultural and creative means on hotel differentiation and regularity of demand from targeted visitors/guests.

Sounds, audio strategies matching the environment, visual, functional and AV design, interaction and interactivity, spatial organization and stylistic references, concept and content, context and event environment are the means discovered and analysed covering this section of fieldwork (2010–2014). While Pantone Hotel in Brussels pays intellectual property dues to owners of all IP, it is differentiated by its conceptual roundedness and in its case the use of what is effectively library music does not constitute an experiential 'Muzak' effect of bland consumption of leisure. On the other hand, both Manhattan (Rotterdam) and Be Manos (Brussels), in very different respective market segments and levels of stratification, share the utilitarian feel of open access to piped content, likely due to their role as hospitality establishments servicing transport hubs. In such cases, Muzak is conceptually justified alongside stepped offers of audiovisual content and arms-length approach to any use of networked facilities such as wireless internet. These are high-flow, standardized environments that require clear and limited, cost- and time-effective customization of the minimalist travel experience influenced by the regional aesthetics of Zen functionality.

On the other hand, participant observation and reflective participation data from Michel Berger and Propeller Island in Berlin (2012) create a more definitive image of the use of specific audiovisual and spatial iconographies, references and integrated content tactics. For instance, the Big Lebowski theme at the former stands in coherence with its discreet patchwork design, squat-styled look (standardized) and a fluid approach to music policy outside DJ hours. The internal coherence of the experience across all its components constitutes value; such a coherent experience was designed to allow variations, and its standardized emulation of an art commune cohered with the city, while allowing the guests to use the near barren space as a stage with their own props. This, as with the immersive research in digital networks publicity, requires participation methods nearing Gonzo (Tamoni 1983; 2005) immersion combined with reflexive evaluations of involvement, bias and experience. In all cases, the research role of the guest was declared at the outset. This did not undermine the researchers' user experience, as it was novel in each case. Hotels were selected using purposive sampling, along a set of classes and types, with the aim of understanding sensory content and extension of culture strategies employed by these concept hotels. Traditions of technological innovation, standardization and design functionality directed early research to Netherlands, Germany and Belgium. The participant observation component of later fieldwork in Greece and Germany integrated alternative travel contingencies, location experience management, contingency planning in festivals, conference events and disruptive natural events (found in reflective fieldwork). In one such case, weather determined the course of the research journey, while the same storm affected the festival, proving that it had in place detailed contingency plans for the eventualities of disruption. Its identity, moreover, is coherent with the experience of focused craftsmanship involved in the planning and delivery of the festival; its free-of-charge character sets it within a separate niche from any of the large commercial festivals and it does not compete with them, its managing director stated during an interview held the day after the event. Its responsibility to the municipal authorities is institutional. It is therefore set to exist within the limits of the park, with strict noise pollution regulation in place. It remains autonomous in form, identity and image. This representation (more on image in Chapter 2 above) of the festival contains a number of ideas, concepts, memories, sounds, images and items and as such forms the value derived from the psychological-social *purpose* of an annual, one-day free festival. The description evokes images that constitute the experiential value of a brand described as: once a year, one day, free, festival. This is why Sabine Funk claimed that selling tickets to the event, however inexpensive, would fundamentally alter its nature, identity and appeal. It would also impose different operational structures of a closed event, different audience expectations and different governance implications. Such a seemingly minor change as an entry fee transforms the event and places it in a different competitive environment, altering its goals and therefore its strategy. The loss of relative autonomy, which for some organizations (as the case may be) is one of the ends, dictates an approach that brings lower profits but secures continued autonomy and relative independence. A 'squat' arts-venue model is covered in this research as a case of organizational culture centred on discourses of authenticity and innovation. Some of those discourses are ontologically founded, others are reflections of hybrid forms of 'hipster leisure' packaged in causes as means of value creation through promotion of values.

The full spectrum of venues includes independent art galleries. Such galleries and cultural spaces base their value proposition on authenticity, creativity and innovation. This is particularly important in their search of continued independence or autonomy, as increased competition means they have to seek funding and develop social media communications to maintain and attract visitors. A different approach to authenticity and IP as the normative source of revenue applies in fashion (Blakley 2001, 2010; Nixon and Blakley 2012). This is due to its distinct utilitarian character, combined with unique patterns of innovation and formations of brand and publicity. The industry structure, its economic imperatives and power relations differs from those in more abstract fields.

Political economy of creativity

> When we see policy change, there was this policy change where the government prefers everybody to do.... To have bigger companies 'we should not have these cottage providers with a fax machine under the bed, it is not very serious, *no*, we want big companies that are being bought by hedge funds and integrated with the multinationals' and so on.... Where that sort of balance between competition and collaboration does not happen. There will be some exceptional.... Discovery will cook to do something with the BBC though I don't believe they do that any more, that was only for a while. So you see this; you can look at all the history of Discovery working with the BBC so you see all the ills of – I think it was down to a political decision and say – 'we don't want any more cottage industry, *that's* not really good, we want big multinational broadcasting companies'.
>
> (C. Schoenfeld 2015)

In relation to policy framework pertaining to the allocation of funding for design projects and the impact of terminology on how partners and stakeholders connect, Assa Ashuach expresses dissatisfaction with the term 'creative', as it can be misread in such ways as to question the rationality of its purpose. On the other hand, and in a very different context, it is possible to see the emphasis on the impact of terminology, definition and professed policy goals on the ability of creatives and their management support structures to innovate and survive in the increasingly complex competitive environment. This is broadly reported by respondents from the areas of visual art, events and performances, especially in the more traditional arts and culture sectors. Respondents were particularly critical of the way in which funding is allocated and tested against targets, together with the measuring of impact and the imposition of control mechanisms through funding. The owner of the East End of London's iconic venue, Foundry, referred in 2008 to the problematic issue of funding structures and their closed circuitry, which privileges curatorial organizations and undermines the independence or autonomy of venues such as his. Laconically stating 'we supply space', Jonathan Moberly elaborated the reasons why Foundry never accepted payment from publically funded artists – as this was the roundabout way to establish a degree of control over an alternative arts venue. This in turn had the undesired consequence of the venue not being treated as a gallery and cultural space, and it was consequently closed down in 2010 as a result of policy interpretation by the local authorities and in spite of well-publicized campaigns to save the venue which drew attention across the mainstream media (including BBC's *Newsnight*). Not dissimilar to this is a complex narrative of two very different publically co-funded festivals in Europe, the respective fates of which were presented in Chapter 2 (Rheinkultur, Exit). There appears to be a trend transgressing national and regional boundaries and indicating that politicization and institutionalization (normalization in Foucauldian terms) of arts continues. In the words of artist Peter Jones:

> Most radical American art has been funded by the Reagan administration. Minimalist American art, conceptual, performance art controlled mandarin style ... Carl Andre sculpture for instance, you take it out of museum context it becomes completely invisible ... Warhol got lots of money from Reagan administration ... Leonardo worked for Cesare Borgia [*sic!*] The most radical forms of art only make sense in institutions.... The work of art is something cultural. Joseph Beuys's art fits perfectly within an institution whereas when it first appeared it was hard to even look at it.
>
> (P. Jones 2013)

The impact of policy is seen in deregulation and over-regulation: seemingly-free-market means of deregulation meet quantified societal goals of funding agendas. Creativity as a policy term was questioned as a derogatory phrase by a respondent, especially in policy contexts: the 'othering' of the 'creatives'. Admittedly an abstract process at heart, design planning is strategic. It has to stop its abstract aspects before the process gets out of hand and affects project targets and budgets. The tension between abstract planning and concrete evidence of value further problematizes the matter of goals and performance indicators.

Unique features of physical artefacts of creativity

At a time when the existence of a work is ultimately challenged through conceptual (art) and digital (media) re-representations of value, the material physicality, corpuscular tangibility and temporal, perishable character of relics and artefacts tend to aid the claims to value which are authenticated through the historicity of such works and their documentary nature. Abstract notions of 'aura', 'authenticity', 'intrinsic' or inherent value, etc. need not be consulted. The infinite limitation of supply, conditioned on the finite nature of events and processes leading to the creation of such products, artefacts and relics, is rooted in the object's continued existence. For hand-crafted objects information is coded in material, corpuscular, spatial form, and it is the analogue information of the movement of the arms and hands, eyes and synaptic processes of memory retrieval from training and practice, and the visceral information of the body and its mental processes that are encoded in the work itself. Aesthetic and interpretive transformations of the artefact commence at the point of creation and any subsequent representation of the work is negotiated through its indirect perception, as the sole direct perception of the work lay with its creator. These re-representations of the work are conditioned by a hybrid of cognitive and cultural factors and the scale and intensity, complexity of communications and representations of a work would be directly proportionate to its perceived value, provided that such constructs are a direct function of information. However, only full access constitutes complete delivery of information, and while in the case of encoded files reproducible as music, text, video or a design, such complete delivery of information equates to maximum access to the artefact of work, the spatial, corpuscular, temporally-conditioned works as artefacts can only be fully communicated through temporal and spatial presence: in short, being there and experiencing it then. Therefore, so long as information of an event continues to hold, any artefact or experience related to the event can be negotiated as part of commodification that leads to proving that it possesses market value. Similarly, the existence of the artefact and its inimitable nature is likely to promote its increasing experiential value. The resulting insight suggests that events and works of art created by the author do not diminish in value in the same way as those works, which are inherently susceptible to copying and dissemination.

The more abstract the core of an art, the more difficult it is to protect and use.

Space, performance and individuality as market value

The autograph is not identical to a retweet, but the two are used for similar purposes in celebrity PR. The former has the advantage of representing that visceral, biological information coded in a hand-written note. The latter has the advantage of mass-customized response to *the selected one*, and by extension, any given member or a loyal audience ('every soldier carries a marshal's baton in his pack') so such sharing of personalized information is modelled on the blend of opportunity, competition and random selection awarded by scope of such media. Individuality and uniqueness are parts of contemporary discourse, and self-representations fuel social media and celebrity branding strategies. The culture of self-representation, rather than a centralized model of the past (global role models presented across a few channels), includes the self-representations of fans, audiences, bloggers and trolls alike, to form a mesh of narratives referred to in both conscious and impulsive manners. This is seen elsewhere in the book as part of discussions with media leaders and in dialogue with advanced theory.

As also stated, early social research on internet phenomena included a well-coined query on virtual space: 'is there a There there?' (Jones 1999). The material space of the internet is greatly mismatched from its representational, virtual space. The first logical query that follows is, 'where is the There?' The presence of that 'there' is determined in cognitive terms. The user imagines a space, a context slot, connected to other context slots, that connect to a conceptual map in the user's understanding of place. Therefore, these spatial concepts and constructs depend on the value of significance allocated to a concept being searched, consumed or communicated. Frequently such nodes of interest, as was seen throughout fieldwork, are individuals and discrete discourses. The notions of space are determined by individuality and discourse, and users navigate those both consciously and impulsively, the job of the marketer being to facilitate, record and read both, with special focus on less conscious user decisions.

Actual material space is less complex and more effective as asset. Virtual space is modelled on it; the context in which it works effectively, drawing user attention from actual material spaces, constitutes part of the value proposition of all social media, many online services and a growing number of devices (some of them hybrid interior/household goods, as indicated by several respondents). In performing arts, the rise of the internet and its constituent media has not (yet?) devalued performances and events, leading to actual increase of interest and economic growth in events areas. Yet this frequently happens at the cost of growth by acquisition and as result of local-authority and national-policy-driven gentrification which leads to closure of alternative venues and festivals, as was also seen through several cases documented through fieldwork. Arguably, and as supported by a 2015 CIF report (CIF 2015a), the value of public arts increases the value of commercial creative sectors, as it feeds innovation into them. The marketization of culture appears, however, to be held as a more significant feature of policy makers across the areas covered both geographically and operationally. A number of respondents representing the thin end of the 'long tail', the concept of which was hailed as the model that would promote cultural niches and compensate for the loss of audience engagement, complain of the impact of combined forces of funding regulation, aggressive corporate competition and local policy. On the other hand, the increasingly stratified and hierarchical nature of internet media, combined with changes to search ranking involving mobile optimization, all contribute to the challenges facing smaller cultural enterprises such as galleries and their visibility through various online media.

Space is therefore a more fragile asset for those who aim to retain independence or conceptual autonomy. The paradoxical aspect of this is that some such spaces and venues, enterprises and projects in arts and culture were the ones generating substantive intrinsic value which attracted service businesses and investors and defined the space, local or regional area as a hotbe of culture. The value-capture is therefore becoming restricted to those who created the core value in its original setting – art and performances contributing to regeneration. The combined impact of strategic shifts across the creative sectors appears to be the result of two distinct structural forces at play. One is the seemingly 'levelling' commoditization effect of the internet and its constituent media. The other is the set of policy shifts affecting a vast majority of developed economies and leading to a change in regulatory discourse that supports marketization. The result of both is a thinning of the middle, with start-ups and corporations appearing better placed.

Live performances of major musicians, actors or other artists continue to attract audiences and this, combined with the value attributed to local knowledge, is at the centre of 'value-ontology' of bigger merchandisers, promoters and agents.

Performance/experience dichotomies

Before 'mechanical reproduction' of sound (with all its connotations relating to the Frankfurt School) the experience/performance connection was closer to select, individual events combined with the acquisition and maintenance of skill. This is what Sousa (1906; Lessig 2007) identified as a threat to the communal culture of amateur musical performance. The *talking machines* embodied the skills no longer needed to reproduce music through performance. The performance was thus delegated to a professionalized sector of production of 'expert' musical performance. (The term 'expert' in inverted commas to signify a negotiable notion of intrinsic value in industry environments, e.g. 'creative control'). The sunk costs of training, creative management and technological innovation were fixed in material form from the outset of sound recording and the copying of an image, still or in motion. Whereas no reproduction of visual art can equate to the intrinsic experience of standing before a singular artistic artefact, the experiential value of production and dissemination technologies continues to mediate the experience of a performance across different forms. The resulting stratification has been identified as an 'elitist' trend in arts and culture, while the ubiquity of recording and production experience continues to pose the problem for sustainable value capture especially with those creative works that lack major curatorial investment – this was evidenced across the fieldwork, from visual art to music and film.

The connection between performance and experience is among the dichotomies that can be found on the level of being, of ontology. What *is* experience and what *is* performance are questions connected on principal levels. A performance embodies an experience – at least that of the performer, and an experience can be connected to a performance both lived and perceived, though the notion of experience is more fundamental and it relates to constructs of 'Self'. Widening the communication channel between 'performance' and 'experience' generates value that can be captured through various means: from purchase of tickets to advertising integration in streaming or branded events. This has significant impact on business models and the design of core products, services and campaigns – from user experiences, 'lived' in leisure environments (boutique hotels), to redefining of merchandise (perishable relics; live CDs as evidence of participation) and of marketing analytics integrating the use of platforms in space and time commercializing the discursive elements of performance/experience.

Tangible and intangible products

This work aims to remove misleading inaccuracies which can have an impact on the understanding of core components of value. The significant impact of definition was explored throughout this book. Just as with distinguishing strategy from its constituent steps, or from underestimating the operational impact on business models of minor changes in governance processes – redefining creative products and processes means treating them differently, conceiving and developing them differently, or indeed acknowledging a change, a difference on the level of definition that results in an inherent impact on practice and policy.

The significance of such distinctions can be seen in documentary cases and original fieldwork accounts across the areas of research. This applies to the full range of data: from advanced blended architecture concepts ('you are the room') to links between catering preferences and merchandise (West-End or Broadway theatre-tailored wireless marketing), to bundling vinyl records as singular artefacts alongside concert tickets through advanced digital marketing and sales. Understanding is required across the full spectrum of experience: on the most fundamental level of *what the key products, services and experiences are* – to the most subject-specific (subject encompassing the user, the platform and the value model). This deep and broad oversight cannot be accomplished without automation – as reflected by all the respondents utilizing ICT, and the quality of such automation and the data thus used for improving user/visitor/consumer experiences depends directly on the design of the tools used. One respondent refers to 'design as strategy and strategy as design', while others speak of 'fluidity of user identity in socio-cultural contexts', 'emotive product tagging' or 'herding' the flow of content that emerges in curatorial media operations.

The distinctions of the physical nature of digital/material dichotomies are well understood by practitioners, even where the terminology remains convoluted. The physicality of human and hardware assets is understood by those who operate in digital environments. The abstract nature of the product of art is well understood by those who deal in its material artefacts. Removing erroneous distinctions would result in a more transparent training in transferable skills relevant to the emerging creative workforce strongly equipped to explore the varying effectiveness of combined tangible and intangible creative products. In conclusion, such varied forms of product promotion and delivery will depend on the informed evaluation of their position within the experience continuum.

Share cultures and their market impact

Before Napster sharing was chaotic. The threatening nature of Napster was embodied in its ability to connect people with desired content through other people who had access to it. Therefore, both the contribution and the threat coming from Napster and any other similar services that followed across media formats was their ability to identify content and its meaning, and to do so in a decentralized way – therefore both more effective and less subject to control.

Revenue stream analysis for cases in creative industries

As was analysed in a number of papers on the move from physical linear production and value chains to complex constellations and mass-customization of supply networks, the transformation of a number of industries well beyond media, arts and communications has led to a prevalence of a networked, values-based structure. This applies across the economy, to the smallest business models, such as *networked grocers* (boutique food services).

Two characteristics define such change from linear to networked models:

1 The meaning of assets has changed: for those in control of creative content it is the experience based on, but beyond that content that is commercialized, while for those in control of material, tangible assets it is the communication and culture that distinguish them from competition. The discourse and practice of media and communications has permeated markets and forms of value production from groceries to automotive industries.
2 Business alliances and operational structures are sometimes (intentionally) unstable (agile?) so as to allow for fluid forms of cooperative competition. This intentional modelling may occur a result of necessity, or partly by design, depending on the structural position of the practitioner in question (e.g. YouTube Partner collaboration practices or cross-media brand partnerships, contrasted with production requirements in independent film and TV).

Control of value chains does not guarantee dominance due to new networked hierarchies of power, and as a result business models are unstable and require continual, if merely incremental, innovation (Markides 2006). The equivalence between the strategy and a business model no longer applies at a time when interaction and communication technologies transform the key processes of value creation and value capture far beyond media, arts and communications where the whole issue of IP protection and cultural devaluation of product had commenced. Multiple business models need to be constantly planned and employed, competing for funding and development within an organization, as evidenced in the examples supplied by respondents in advanced ICT-aided design and interactive architecture. Fluid, unstable and highly competitive niche-driven business models embody the combinations of strategy-practice tools, from abstract thought and reflexive analysis to highly developed planning tools combining models of brainstorming and analytics.

The key conclusion that can be immediately derived from the above is that assets are used to create new value in a way that is fluid, as it depends on the dynamic relationship between different players, sectors and types of business dealing with creative work and associated products and services. These business models are fluid and multiple, accurately reflecting the fluidity and fragmentation of cultural and creative discourses. The same finite amounts of time and money are competed for by a variety of organizations, stakeholders and individuals so the fragmentation of offering which remains responsive to changes in user trends is the way to capture value across the spectrum of revenue streams. The core asset such as film, song, book, site or a work of art becomes the focal point of value creation and value capture for a number of revenue streams ranging from subscription to events ticketing, merchandise or limited-edition PR material. These revenue streams and many others, as well as hybrids between them enabled by ICT tools, add to the notion of strategy as a convergent and synergic sum of intentionally realized business models. Indeed, though this may be correct in principle, conceptualizing such an approach and consequently controlling the imagined process to full utilization, is seldom if ever the case. Emergent revenue streams and business models frequently replace one another and transform regularly, therefore acting as a sum of complex procedural plans both conceived and realized. Strategy is therefore seen as a plane of planning and action, consisting of different complex plans and business structures, embodied in business models which were more frequently networked than linear (constellations vs. chains). Those business models are the new tools (means) that justify the ends (e.g. market share) in a more complex innovative market context. Rational planning methods involving those such as SWOT and business model design tools are used complementarily with brainstorming, abstracting and inverting, free association and similar methods. Often the focus is on immediate results and budget imperatives which leads to complex results developed in an incremental or chaotic manner. When used in retrospect, the classic tools of analysis such as five forces do contribute but are not credited for the planning itself in a fast-moving entrepreneurial contexts (especially in strategy as practice). The competence of an organization's strategy is reflected in its business models and its ability to adapt them to rapid and constant changes in its environment.

A seemingly marginal product such as a smartphone game – *Angry Birds* – becomes a cultural item beyond meme but of a similar nature. Doing so, it encompasses all the merchandising, vertical integration and promotional synergies across partnerships, control and support models (Hasbro, Inc. 2012; Robertson 2012; Staff 2012). Therefore, while generally unclear as to the actual growth of the market as a result of such innovation, the multiplying of business models in traditional entertainment sectors works to maintain the engagement of audiences with the aim of maintaining the commercial value of such entertainment content, now competing with values that form the ICT discourse and aid in the commercialization of creative services other than those connected to 'content'.

The importance of formulation goes into the pragmatic aspects of industry operations and beyond the matter of definition from a narrowly analytical perspective. With what is alarmingly termed 'art becoming content' and the transformative formulations of creative industries as those containing disparate and frequently conflicting areas of practice are matters that have a very tangible impact on the commercial value of different areas and types of work, varied policies and approaches adopted in relation to such formulations. Revenue streams on the other hand show that networked, complex relationships (Graham and Hardaker 2000; Graham *et al.* 2004) between stakeholders replace the traditional relationships of supply, downstream value adding and product–service divisions. Data is supplied by the user.

An enterprise that uses and therefore requires exclusively licensed content may develop a business model architecture that would generate new forms of value such as data capture, which can be commercialized through continued direct marketing, branding and push-supply promotions. In this way, such an enterprise becomes the supplier of its suppliers, as with the early operations of Concert Live, which improved (in 2007) its bargaining position regarding its much-needed access to exclusive content by generating added commercial opportunities for all involved. Similarly, software developers behind a heuristic tool (e.g. some fieldwork respondents) used for mass-customization and product–service bundling create more than a tool for user-experience management or sales. They create methods for the capture of user data that can be then sold or licensed to third parties, as such finely targeted user information is likely to generate more sales in relating and overlapping areas. Therefore, new revenue streams added to sets of creative industry models are made possible through the conceptual and contextual alliances involving data and rights uses – sometimes labelled 'cooperative competition', and sometimes through confrontational or subversive methods of innovative disruption. References to Lego bricks in opinion-leader treatises (Osterwalder and Pigneur 2013) indicate that the complexity of business model innovation may in many cases be reduced to individually mundane components of a commercial value-structure, the combination of which is what adds specific value (e.g. brand, sales, data). This configuration is key to effective strategic formulation of business models, rather than the number and individual value of each 'piece on the chessboard' (Levy *et al.* 2001).

The process of articulating what a business model is about therefore involves the ability to plan and manage unique combinations of value creation and value capture that formulate and sustain revenue streams. The uniqueness of such combinations, rather than their individual constituent components, is what sustains value processes. It has been seen that ontologically any product or service, work or labour in the creative industries is about experience. The value of such experiences is discursively formulated, both intrinsic and utilitarian. The formulation of value and its effective commercialization resembles broad, deep-rooted negotiations close to the concept and impact of the *social contract* between stakeholders: the value of values comes to the fore in a utilitarian manner formulating probable, legally and mutually agreed revenue stream models. These include methods of licensing and subscription such as streaming services Spotify and Netflix, bundling such as Mobile Roadie and Topspin, crowdfunding such as Indiegogo and Kickstarter, and others. Such negotiated values are arbitrary by definition and are entirely context-dependent, as the functionality of a creative product is directly linked to the subjective character of experience and its potential to generate extension through new experience and user engagement. Such user engagement may trigger further value creation and value capture across 'verticals' (that is, integrated and/or connected markets for conceptually related products and services), thereby increasing the potential for the involvement of other sectors, sub-sectors and niches in commercial use of experience-driven creative work.

Negotiations between different parties across the types and classes of stakeholders determine the market exchange rules stemming from creative work, and it is therefore not surprising that some respondents question the very definition of 'creative' or 'industry'. Where concerned with the policy impact of terminology, the notion of 'creative' is rejected as divisive and pejorative in a case of someone whose innovative approach to design function has evident and necessary components of strategic product–service design and scientifically-informed experimentation (Assa Aschuach). For this respondent, the importance of investors, clients and public regulatory bodies is matched by the need to prove evidential value of design innovation, and fuzzy terms such as 'creative', significantly because of their 'soft' connotations (see Chapter 2), are not seen by this respondent as favourable to agreeing the definitive, evidence-based commercial value of his work.

Similarly, a respondent whose entertainment media career spans years in radio, television and online streaming prefers the term 'cultural' to that of 'creative'. He does so not only to delineate between the editorial and production nature of the two respective formulations, but also to assert the type of value that forms the core of a market proposition of such a medium, whether private or public. A similar terminological tension arises concerning the term 'consumer', again not only on aesthetic or ethical grounds. The ethical, *values-based* notion of 'audience' carries with it some significant utilitarian connotations: the 'audience' is seen as a subject and therefore a stakeholder in media strategy. Neglecting that fact is strategically unwise, especially in the context of increased interaction in media communications. Also, this more culturally empowering view of the role of 'users'[5] of entertainment media indicates the concern of a media producer/editor/manager with the audience as the core 'product' (Smythe 1981; Negus 1993) of media. An audience's experience can increasingly be evaluated beyond statistics and case study research, with detailed and refined analytics that can point to potential income generation showcased to clients, whether commercial (advertising, sponsorship, product placement) or public (licence fee, investment in programme or technology). These revenue streams sustain a media business model, the meta-tool justified by measurable and researchable resources such as audience data, which are the essential means for attaining the ends in need of justification. Such ends are market share for commercial media and public service support for public media organizations. Therefore, the content and programme, structuring and editorial features, supply chains and networks – all tools of a media organization – may be the core components of what a medium 'is', but the key 'variable' that justifies the existence and market position of a medium is its audience. Therefore, the semantics of 'consumer' vs. 'audience' are not mere reflections of jargon; they represent the distinction between different revenue models.

Value capture is most difficult to attain in the leap from the utilitarian value of user experiences (teleology) to their actual commercialization (quantification). The existence of intrinsic, ontological value ('music', 'art', 'game', 'event') is the necessary but not sufficient cause for the successful formulation and agreement on commercial value. In the cases of architecture and design, functionality is intrinsically connected to experience as an aesthetic, subjective categorization. The value of more abstract forms such as text, entertainment format or music is more obscure, connected to psychological, social, cultural – i.e. 'soft' – categorization of creative work. Therefore, the sufficient cause for the effective commercial capture of value is a consensus across different stakeholders who agree (formally or informally) how to recognize, regulate and implement engagement and commercial exchange pertaining to creative work. The need for policy, regulatory frameworks and rules of exchange is counter-balanced by the dynamic nature of creative markets, where change is the main constant and any framework may be perceived as a limiting factor that slows down, chokes and threatens to reverse the pace of innovation.

There is an internal contradiction, a dialectic tension between the protective nature of regulation lobbied for, across the creative industries, and the needs of enterprises that drive such markets (Garnham 2005) to remain as unrestrained as possible and engage in continued innovation.

Notes

1 Attributed to the late George Harrison in a *Los Angeles Times* article of 1991.
2 Oil painting is considered to have developed centuries earlier.
3 A metaphor used in relation to chaotic movement of users, data and content patterns is fit for purpose, and it relates to strategic management theory (e.g. Stacey) and software design practice, especially concerning networks, cloud services, search and engagement practice etc.
4 A well-documented internet/Twitter meme from 2015.
5 The term 'user' is cited on purpose due to its neutral character devoid of description.

5 Business modelling and interactive contexts

Commercialization of share cultures: promotional role of consumer/user/bricoleur

Music forms a prime case study for the analysis of the impact of online media. Music and text-centred forms of creative products, and to a lesser extent OLD multimedia content-driven forms (film is convergent, as is TV) such as broadcasting and film, set the scene for analysis of alternative and somewhat *'oblique' strategies discussed earlier in the text, were most affected by the transformation of supply processes* (Graham *et al.* 2004). A delay caused by the fundamental structural issues of bandwidth and software development had given film and broadcast media additional time to adapt to the near identical threat from free sharing of creative produce and the challenges of participatory culture (Jenkins 2006a/b) to the centralized linear models of broadcasting or film distribution. Indeed, in this case the richness of multi-sensory content such as film or television, further enriched by experience of theatrical events and social media interaction, seems to have balanced out the threat from unsolicited content reach. Online narratives on media narratives such as the reportedly leaked episodes of a given trending television series create added interest in the licensed product obtainable through various media platforms and 'verticals' which are both user friendly and cost-effective. User-friendly nature of such services can be read in an inverse manner to define its position in value generation and supply: user-friendly content services are those which need to be highly integrated and supported by assets, both physical (digital and tangible alike) and knowledge-driven (content, skill).

The multifaceted nature of an audiovisual media product involves several levels of narrative, each of which can be commercialized, especially if it is linked to related content genres and formats. Narratives include the impact of David Lynch and his experimental project Twin Peaks on recurrent and multilayered media narratives embodied in The Sopranos, as one respondent stated (interview with Carl Schoenfeld). In adapting to the new media environments and the fundamental changes to media and communications operations brought about by the internet, content-driven media organizations have somewhat reduced the risk to their core business propositions. They did so by engaging the audience in different types of content and platforms (*at least in the case of commercial broadcasters*), anticipating the impact of digitization of all broadcast content delivery, diversifying and engaging in policy development during time lag in disruptive innovation of the kind that impacted on music and text media. The impact on text and music was felt and those two concepts of content delivery (Kindle, Google Books) remain challenged by the need to constantly adapt and develop new forms of value-generating mechanisms, including audience engagement and utilizing user-driven narratives in which process concessions had to be made regarding strict interpretation of IP principles.

'Engage the fans', says one highly influential artist manager, 'and pay them for their work', the work of promotion and user generated design, 'but make sure you pay once'. Fan payment and fan thanking appears in different forms: music, rare recordings in box sets, tickets, names printed on sleeves, merchandising, public thanks, meeting their favourite artists etc. In most cases these are objects of symbolic value: reward the asset (active, connected, agile fan) with asset (content, event, product). Thus *closing the value circuit* also amplifies the publicity signal through media, both interactive and non-interactive, digital (any format) and human (word of mouth). Every user capable of influencing the marketing and publicity outcome of a product, brand or service campaign in entertainment, has the opportunity to earn Warhol's 15 minutes of fame, which seldom captures any sustainable value or is *monetized/commercialized* to benefit the user who produces such value for the marketers, brands and content owners. 'Star Wars' fan content discussion groups and 'Blair Witch' clips for 'documentary' authenticity were the two key events in the relatively distant past that helped kick-start and define user-generated and user-supported campaigns. Harnessing not fighting the chaotic mass of audience/user voices was a decision made multiple times *'for the first time'* in different industries, sectors and segments. These important events in decision-making and policy reassessment were those moments where a producer, content owner or creator, marketer or media organization would decide to follow the chaotic flow of user information and communications, choosing to use its power rather than try to stem it, which proved costly, counterproductive and ineffective.

Influence the influencers – a phrase coined by Edward Bernays, the founder of modern Public Relations contributes to promotion with added weight. Therefore, a highly positioned respondent refers to the ability to read and understand the behaviour of innovators and early adopters who move swiftly across the changes in digital platforms, and using such ability to communicate with them directly and entice them to endorse a campaign and therefore amplify it. The engagement of such key nodes in the online network of opinion formation requests immersion of the kind where the distinction between observer and participant becomes blurred. As stated elsewhere in this book, interactive media have that additional feature that is yet to be fully understood and effectively managed: the quantum-like blurring of boundaries between observers, influencers and participants as previously postulated in Heisenberg-style notions in physics (Misra and Sudarshan 1977). Refined, light-touch involvement with deeper 'expert' layers of communication online seem to breed more reliable, 'authentic' results based on decisions to interact with influencers such as bloggers. (Other reasons why online communications resemble a chaotic system of particle movement are explored elsewhere in the text, with special reference to Stacey's work and the emerging disciplines within Big Data concepts such as Cliodynamics (Turchin 2008; Gaddis 2011; West 2011)).

Such decisions were not as widely publicized as their counterparts in the form of perceived threats of piracy, IP violations, and new business entrants epitomized in early peer to peer networks, whose actual contribution was overlooked by many. At a time when Lycos was one of the key search engines and mp3.com the big source of online music, the problem of searching for music and identifying similar tastes and audience patterns was near impossible. Napster and other peer to peer models changed that, by establishing a fan community that formed the conceptual precursor of contemporary social media, cloud services and streaming models. Before advanced search engines were developed, identifying subjects of interest and their connections with content were operations that most users could not perform. By bringing the threat of exponential growth of the use of piracy, Napster and others in its wake provided the future tools to marketers by revealing the structural nature and media amplification potential of culture- and concept-defined user networking. Contemporary curator services online are, in the words of a media respondent (C Price), not editorial, top-down or linear in nature. Curators of online media content take good care to manage the flow gently. The management of such curators' online media workloads involves understanding, overseeing/monitoring and supervising chaotic cloudlike behaviour of large numbers of users across a large number of platforms discussing and exchanging information/content across a large number of topics. This is the precursor for the next, necessary step of guiding such flows through a combination of software and conceptual/content expertise. This is where Stacey's work attains a new application (Stacey 1992a-d; Parker and Stacey 1995; Stacey 1996a/b; Stacey 2013). Managing the flow of chaotic particles of human-digital communication resembles identifying chaotic weather patterns and organizational patterns described by Stacey in his work. It is in this case true that less is more: management of flows of online information has to be subtle, therefore suggesting an equivalence in Stacey's suggestion that systems are self-managed.

Strategic means used by curators and virtual navigators do not, in such cases remain confined to strategy tools presented in business school literature (which may be used in any case to inform the discussion). Contemporary online curator-type services are conceptually close to social networks, search services, cloud content services and streamers. In each of those cases, a strategy is defined with the aid of analytics tools, whether own, proprietary, outsourced or free. The novelty and fundamental added value in such services and tools they adopt or develop is that these are not speculative tools but evidence based, mixed methodology tools that overcome the crude divisions between quantitative and qualitative, positivistic and interpretive, scientifically-modelled and social-science-driven tools for data collection, analysis and interpretation. Emotive, cultural and cognitive aspects of user behaviour and content use are as important for the strategic management of such services, as are statistics on the frequency, place, time and volume of use, payment and impact. Overcoming the academic limitations, the models used for data analytics by any organization capable of harnessing such data, treat online information about human market behaviour in digitally-mediated communications, as a continuum of natural science and social science paradigms tested in practice. A truly multidisciplinary, cross-paradigm planning methodology exists beyond the scholastic arguments of academic schools of thought and its name varies from brand to brand: Google, Apple, Spotify, Netflix, Facebook, Twitter, etc.

The changing nature of engagement with online media is one of the important factors influencing the market and management practices the same user can interchangeably be a fan, audience member, consumer, pirate, tourist, reporter, essayist, citizen, client, voter, learner or hedonist. Social media features are likely to spread to all online media. A balanced policing of IP rights means that many uses of content are tolerated and some encouraged. An intelligent (in an IT sense) licensing framework model such as Creative Commons enables mutually agreeable arrangements between multiple interests and parties without any, or with minimal mediation. Users create a patchwork of information, interpretations and conceptual content links between trends, discourses, forms and formats. Such a patchwork may be difficult to predict or keep under control but it can be influenced. The semiotics of '*That Dress*' meme is an interesting example. The use of celebrities to amplify the signal and the creation of online celebrities of transitory but lucrative 15 minutes of fame are cases worth investigating as examples of a definitively postmodernist patchwork culture of user commercialization.

Promotion–distribution equivalence

There are evident paradigmatic transformations of marketing practice and strategic marketing, influenced by the relative interactivity and consequent impact of users and their treatment of content. The very use of the term 'content' was discussed in the section on semiotics, Chapter 2. The shift from 'art', 'music', 'performance', 'photography', 'text' etc to all-encompassing IT term 'content' reveals some important and novel dialectic relationships. Anything that can be encoded as data, is. This goes beyond traditional perceptions of media, shifting the notion of content, information and material existence on levels of ontology: what is the work, is there a work, what is its value? This bearing in mind that the existence of the work is the evidence of value which may or may not be commercialized at later stages of promotion and distribution.

'Not being able to download an ironing board' was a metaphor used in an early study of internet music (Todorovic 1999) to examine the immediate impact of the internet of the time on music and other, less complex or bandwidth-intensive data. With 3D printing and its constituent design solutions, the data of this kind can be encoded, transferred and reproduced in tangible, corpuscular physical form. One form of data encoded by the producer may in this case become tangible content produced at the users' end. This example serves as an illustration of the considerable transformative impact of ICT on the very notion of physicality, creating a visible equivalence between abstract forms of data and concrete distribution of products through an ICT-driven service. The semantic shift therefore shows the shift in the balance of power from varied forms of art, design, text and performance – results of creative work – to 'content', a term defined by a new force in creative industries, because in ICT terms all of such creative produce is placed under the general umbrella of data. Therefore, ICT and the internet now fundamentally underlie all aspects of any art form which can be encoded and transferred as information.

The equivalence between promotion and distribution existed in historic media, both analogue and digital. Such an equivalence led to the well documented Sony Betamax and Amstrad cases, just as when in the more distant past, live music on radio was perceived as a threat at first. The value is being reproduced and delivered to the user directly in all such cases, and it is delivered free of charge. The only notable exception is the historic class of models where non-interactive digital television services were covered by monthly flat fees. This relates to the stages before the internet and online media became truly influential in creative asset content management. An infinitesimal charge for each type of media content can be calculated on the basis of licensing costs and subscription fees, therefore serving the evidence that content capture through a form of video or audio recording was paid for by subscribers, however little for each potentially recorded viewing. The capture of content amounts to distribution and the Betamax and Amstrad cases were brought about because such content was captured free of charge, without payment to content owners or performers. The same principle would apply to any method of content capture through media delivery – audio, audiovisual or other.

How can performance of a work be defined if it is presented through the media? Its role is not limited to performance as a right or singular event. Events, however special, do not generate utilitarian value unless recorded in some form, even participant accounts. Moreover, there is the underlying work that facilitates, gives shape to and defines the very existence of a performance. The next layer of analysis is performance beyond event or work: performance as communication. Performance itself is a form of communication, ontologically; not communicated, a performance may not be proven to exist.

Promotion can be perceived as applied communication; promotion relates to an event and a work. That event is recalled, remembered, recorded or fixed in the form of a copy. The full experience of the event cannot be recorded as it is multi-sensory, multi-subjective and socially interactive by definition. Any recording of an event and therefore any performance embodied in such an event constitutes information, which, however rich is limited as events and performances are unique and singular by definition.

Promotion is an applied form of communication, and in the arts, it is frequently an event and associated performance that is communicated in recorded media. It is therefore not surprising that dramatic performances promote the texts on which they are based; also, copies and adaptations of such performances and texts in different media *('verticals')* while the performance of musical works, recordings and films also communicates the underlying work. By virtue of licensing agreements between broadcasters and content owners, some aspects of such agreements show that a work is being promoted through such performance. Strategy of a sector or firm, as well as industry policies can be read into when examining any standard industry-wide agreements in fine detail. The balance of power can be checked through changes in industry-wide policy, government or trade area initiatives; modification and interpretation of the law; at present, as in the recent past, a shift to new market leaders and emerging sectors and industries is evident. Some examples in this particular context come from tensions over licensing fees and usage charges in BPI and PRS/MCPS Alliance, Netflix's tensions with ISPs, or the strangulation policies over internet broadcasting licences (Adhikari *et al.* 2012; Cook 2014; Leonard 2014; Wallets 2015).

Content is secondary to digital media and their licensing reflects this. Irrespective of the type of content, when it is reproduced with minimal mediation, it resembles the original so closely that it may replace it, thus removing the need for retail. The distribution is done *through* the media so the product that satisfies reasonable requirements of the public is copied on to a memory drive at the point of performance. Performance, previously a form of promotion, becomes fixed and copied and therefore constitutes distribution. This applies across a number of media and creative digital forms. This leads to a definitive collapsing of boundaries between performance and consumption.

The greater the flow of content, the more significant the earnings of the current generation of ICT-driven media/communications corporations. The embodiment of the threatening loss of control over proprietary content use which more traditional creative sectors share, is the potentially infinite number of copies of works being transferred across the online media, with its innumerable variations among the connected public. Such potentially infinite number of content transfers accompanied by data such as comments, re-tweets, tags etc is what generates value, both commercial and non-commercial, for online media corporations. Therefore, an artificial and temporary alliance is being formed between policy makers, who need to respond to influential linear media established in the twentieth century, those media, and suppliers of content through advanced digital means. As a result of policy influence of guild-style bodies across the creative sectors, some IP protection has been enforced by means which are non-coercive to users. How sustainable such alliances are depends on the targeted development of technology that further removes direct links between mediator and content. It also depends on the adaptability of any creative organizations which are originally based on linear, mass-modes of production, copying, and controlled dissemination of information (promotion) and content (distribution). Originally driven by entrepreneurial practices of the analogue mass-production, mass-communication era of linear value structures, *these organizations are in the process of learning the new, and unlearning the old modes of control.* Control exists in digital environments but it is not restrictive. Therefore, a number of respondents question the wisdom of tight IP protection, suggesting that it is the management of the flow of content related communications that matters. This also applies to those models that still utilize sales of discrete units.

The promotion-distribution equivalence is brought about by the very nature of digital communications whereby a copy remains on the receivers' end and can be captured depending solely on the ICT tools and skills available to the user. Content, therefore can be captured and even reproduced in material, corpuscular form; it is not difficult to imagine 3D printer piracy and its consequences across creative sectors and beyond. Information is encoded in the form that can be reproduced irrespective of form, format or medium.

Therefore, knowing about something in online environments frequently means possessing a copy of it. This devalues the copy unless it is connected to some other context based on experience, which is rooted in the psychological, social and cultural aspects of how cultural or creative value is being constructed by users. A highly positioned digital distributor refers to the need of being heard above the 'white noise' of contemporary digital media where much of the flood of content remains commercially untapped and does not break even. Some of the leaders of new generation artist management suggest that music business may never generate large revenues on the scale it did in the latter part of the twentieth century, due to the game-changing nature of the internet. (The 'fallacy of the long tail' was discussed elsewhere in this piece. Similar cases can be found in the media, news, print, publishing and advertising.)

The result of this is that strategic planning has to move to more abstract planes, and that competitive advantage once attained is lost easily without continual reassessment, reflection, testing, development and innovation. The linear creative professions and associated sectors are identifying their new role, the new means which they can use to create and commercialize new value. The old models persist but they are becoming segments or niches of broader markets. Manifold new forms of entertainment exist, from interactive content in social media to multi-player games and collaborative online production. The result of this is a fragmentation and reassembling of different established creative forms, formats and media and a growing user-audience interest in such fragmented and hybrid entertainment phenomena. The same happens to discourses in the fluid environment of online communications, where, however grand, narratives just form part of the flow.

When speaking to an executive of a major music and media corporation, whose focus was on digital marketing, there was little interest in the notion of cooperative competition, postulated by Graham *et al.* Creative industries are represented by stratified fields of practice, where imperatives can vary significantly: from small artistic venues that strive for independence at the cost of loss of revenue, to highly integrated corporate bodies where project management and return on investment preclude many decisions on the long term value of artistic merit. A simplified and idealized view of the internet and its online digital media subsets is one of equality, neutrality and liberty is contrasted by highly hierarchical ownership structures, media regulation and asset control matters, market capture and model acquisition. Contemporary user empowerment and interactivity are set to remain low on individual levels, because users do not control media assets; this applies to content media as well as to software or hardware.

Promotion-distribution-data-consumption

This is a subset of the concept explored above. It is part of the product–service continuum referred to in interviews, especially those connected with design, virtual/physical architecture, leisure and music and media.

It relates to activities, which may not have to be sequentially ordered but are connected in a parallel manner. The production-distribution equivalence opens new opportunities in responding to audiences: narrative and online chatter, expressed interests, connections with other leisure habits, potential for strategic cooperation with brands – Burberry, Bacardi, etc. The ploys of adaptation to new market conditions and changing audience trends include tactical alliances with the other media, brands, products and services, consumer technology goods innovators or software developers. Data informs the consumption-distribution relationships in a number of industries and sectors susceptible to the 'multiple originals', which remains an important discourse succeeding the era of linear mass-media production and which can be copied without conceptual limitation at negligible cost enshrined in pop art, *a conceptual root* of reality media and mass-customization alike). A combination of *'push' and 'pull'* marketing approaches, the ability to monitor and respond to changes in use patterns is cost-effective, but also beneficial to user experience. Examples of methods combining *parallel, sequential and mutually responsive* structures can be found across the creative industries, as can be seen from the following list, which is non-exhaustive and likely to grow with the proliferation of hybrid media platforms and creative forms and formats. Licensing income for example, in the use of any content on digital media through any legal format; echoed on a farther end of the spectrum by product design strategies and production workflows in design also evidenced in field research interviews. Examples from streaming media include the impact of audience analysis on script-writing and production (Netflix) with its less interactive precursor in the form of BBS on Star Wars and Blair Witch Project. Streaming media examples do need to involve music services epitomized in Spotify and its predecessors, competitors and *future 'mutations'*, the key to its effectiveness being the ability to analyse, monitor and respond to user data in ways that combine applications of set theory, genre-related data, structural content analysis and cognitive patterns of music listening. Therefore, the analysis of patterns involves all types of data sets in quantitative to qualitative user information; the logical structures behind the core *product*, forming the software and its functionality, are the actual strategic formulation behind the value created by such a service. Data that informs consumption in this case combines many varied principal components. These form the strategy behind the aims of developing the software as a means of identifying and capturing value by effectively feeding fresh user research data into the content stream. To create effective software tools such as those behind Spotify, it can be seen that combining conceptual elements of seemingly irreconcilable paradigms is what creates significant improvements in using data to manage distribution and influence consumption across channels related to the medium and its content. These improvements involve content management planning, responsive implementation of data-content tactics (Ploy), accurate positioning, identification of use patterns and adapting to user preference, conceptually nearing the point of anticipating user/audience choices and accurately targeted content recommendations.

The principles and phenomena behind the thinking required to create an effective streaming service involve different paradigms and discourses embodied in the disciplines required for the attempt to understand, and interact with audience choices and tastes. These disciplines would involve among others, the understanding and implementation of logic, *advanced set theory*, probability, cultural contexts of content aesthetics, and cognitive responses to content structures (streaming services and predictive playlists are a prime example).

Use of such tools in marketing and Public Relations online is implemented in a manner similar to the one described above. Within the context of data use in influencing consumption, the ability to benefit from immediate links of promotion and distribution means that audiences can be engaged, or believe to be engaged in designing the product, service or the media concept itself. The former relates to advanced marketing campaigns that benefit from online curator services, social media, streaming and other content platforms. The latter relates to those models in entertainment where the media-integrated event and its underlying discourse and narratives serve as a focal point for a multifaceted exploitation of various rights, licenses and uses – such as televised or streamed talent shows or awards ceremonies with notable audience engagement through digital communications.

In the case of contemporary online marketing campaigns, the equivalence of promotion and distribution and the accurate reading of user engagement data, aims at modifying the campaigns and driving consumption through engagement. According to several respondents, the product, service, promotion and communications form discrete parts of the same continuum, reported in literature and notable cases studies (e.g. NESTA). Consequently, this serves as conceptual evidence that research capability helps inform product, service and project strategies in media production, and increasingly across related creative and cultural sectors, as varied as design, merchandising, events, leisure, interactive/blended architecture and more emerging ICT hybrids between them and established cultural/creative forms. (NB: this was accounted for in detail by respondents in 2012, including Angelica Vleeming, C Legrande, the Propeller Island Hotel manager and others).

Product as service: assets and PR ploys

A need to redefine the role, use and purpose of 'creative industry products' (Adorno 1991; Bilton 2007; Garnham 2005; Graham *et al.* 2004) became apparent with the asymptotic reduction of value in many creative products which 'cannot be seen' or 'known of' against the backdrop of white noise in continually fragmenting niches of culture and content. Product units, such as copies of content or performances of recorded content are losing out on *exchange value* and strategies needed to compensate for this have to consider links across allied industries and markets where the product can generate value through thus linked products, services, events, brands and projects. Moreover, products become integrated with services (Time Out music, Burberry etc) so as to create synergies across sectors and partnerships. (With Concert Live as a prime case.)

Irrespective of the artistic value of self-referential audience discourses, the societal positioning and subcultural (Thornton 1995; Geldder and Thornton 1997) capital of fan communities can lead to the commercialization (frequently referred to as monetization) of fan discourses and narratives as means of amplifying the signal of publicity campaigns. If strategy were to be defined under the general heading of formulating and implementing certain means, tools in a utilitarian instrumental fashion, the means and tools adopted here would be defined as social-networking, sub/culturally embedded communications and would as such resemble the models recognized in the work of Weick (Krackhardt and Hanson 1993; Krackhardt and Stern 1988; Kreiner and Schultz 1993; Torenvlied and Velner 1998; Weick 1976; Weick and Quinn 1999) or the muddling through model of strategy implementation analysis.

Marginalized to the point of niche narrative, the unlikely contribution from the work of Hunter S Thompson may inform the understanding of such audience discourses, harnessed for the purpose of metaphorical or actual *publicity signal amplification*. Beyond that, such seemingly self-referential work also assists in the understanding of the need for full immersive *method acting* in forming and nurturing communities of online followers through subtle PR campaigns. Paradoxically, the self-referential nature of gonzo writing and narrative methods adds to the deeper understanding of fundamentally subjective processes of online communication and immersive word of mouth. The user numbers engaged with content and communications on multiple levels, genres and platforms also allow for a proposition that observing the system is equivalent to influencing the system. This is a concept from quantum physics, the metaphorical connection to which was postulated earlier in social sciences (e.g. Booth 2002) and may be proven in the case of digital interactions, as the impact of any narrative thread can be evidenced and assessed through digital analytics. Bloggers, content addicts and internet trolls represent some of the manifest forms of such deeply immersive participatory cultures.

At a time when the arts and humanities are subject to funding cuts, the creative industries lobby for their position before governments and policy bodies, aiming to preserve the protection of IP rights for their content and operations by reconciling their varied, sector-driven interests. It appears that the methods of 'pure' social sciences such as reflexive analysis, thick description and deep knowledge through ethnographic immersion into the community or culture create considerable value through 'sub'-cultural capital, which can be commercialized through the internal use or sales of detailed audience data, especially its participatory aspects. This may appear surprising only on the surface: scores of analytical texts were written about the societal (Mafessolli 1996) and economic (Negus 1993, 1999) impact of sub/cultures and lifestyle-driven pseudo-tribal behaviours, considered marginal, ornamental and self-referential and thus not normally used in an applied business context in mainstream business literature.

Not normally driven by commercial imperatives, discourses of modernist, post/structuralist and postmodernist analysis fit into the models of planning the influence over the flows and utilization of content and audience narratives. The neo-tribes postulated by Mafessolli (1996) are embodied in the analysis of best means to meet user expectations and reach users with the means of presenting content in order to amplify demand for commercial transactions with media. Tactical ploys such as 'E4M', email for media are the subset of 'D2F', direct-to-fan relations that were developed as a medium-term strategic ploy to keep engaging fans and audiences as an active response to the crisis of content. The crisis of content was dubbed 'the culture of FREE' by a respondent whose expertise covers entertainment media both public and private, linear/broadcast and non-linear/streaming. The semantic difference between the researcher and respondents are indicators of deeper contextual and conceptual differences rooted in the varied respective positions of respondents and the researcher whose stance contains inherent disciplinary bias, just as the case is with respective purposively sampled respondents. Therefore, a highly advanced designer and product designer dismisses the term 'creative' outside of its cultural context, explaining it in its policy context as limiting, *othering* and somewhat derogatory to rational design strategists and innovators.

Though not mentioned, the subject of innovation remains present throughout the interview: the respondent refers to two equally important cognitive and organizational processes. Those involve two methodological aspects. One of them are design strategies for the development of product and service design solutions without 'closing' the project solution even though the concept planning stages reveal the most likely outcome, and before selecting the optimal design under the utilitarian imperatives of budgeting, time constraints and delivery of functional results. The second is a reference to an entirely different cognitive approach, which appears to be less organizational and more entrepreneurial in form and method. This is the approach to the concrete design subject as an abstract problem, to paraphrase the respondent, 'inverting it' and resisting the limitations that may have been imposed by education, training or experience. This respondent (*Synthetic a priori, Kantian*) considers such abstract, cognitive processes as essential for design strategy development and implementation as those that relate to optimal planning of design functionality outcomes under the constraints of budget and time. In a statement that echoes some of the critics of other large creative sector organizations and industry policies, this respondent states that 'he is not interested in something that works in San Francisco', and replicating a working solution is not his area of interest. He pointed out that funding policies and acquisition strategies continue to resist a necessary fundamental rethink of IP and of the practice of opting to assimilate successful business models based on functional design solutions through corporate acquisitions rather than investing in innovation.

Business modelling and branding processes

The role of the designer is similar to that of a dancer, in that neither dance performance skills, nor design solutions can be 'faked'. Therefore, the approach of this respondent to design is 'as strategy', and this is reflected in his drawing of equivalence between inherent value and use value, by suggesting that aesthetics of a design solution are similar to those of a business solution, labelling the case of Spotify as design strategy, 'beautiful'. He contrasts it with a case of a green, recyclable airline bag as ineffective merchandise as it was created for the sole purpose of publicity exercise due to excessive costs of design, which was outsourced to a costly service of a highly established design brand. The beauty of that product diminished in his point of view upon realizing that this particular design idea was not intended for user application, nor made cost-effective or sustainable. The conceptual framework of green, recyclable branded merchandise is closely aligned to the concepts of sustainability both economic and ecological. Thus, the mismatch between the professed, intended and actual purpose of this design item was rendered aesthetically flawed by this respondent due to its unsustainable nature and tactical purpose. Business models relate to such coherence between the overall strategy, tactics (or a policy framework), and the specific use of value-driven solutions. The branding experience forms part of the business models developed by Serrano Brothers in cooperation with clients reflecting the considerable impact of Hartley (2004).

User involvement and identity marketing

Concert live is not just a live music business; it is not just an events business either, nor is it just a merchandising company. It operates in all of these areas and it covers, cooperates with and develops business models and strategic relationships with many events, arts and music businesses but at its heart, this company creates value thorough data management and mass customization. Its approach is empirical and it creates experiential hybrids to draw audience attention in physical environments. Part of its labour on the ground, public facing PR and sales staff are provided by university students across the areas of operation whose volunteering serves as a gateway to further placements and employment across related sectors and industries. The audience facing engagement is the first step in a refined data-for-service process using a number of tools to capture data and turn it into specific sales propositions to (1) users/visitors/audiences, (2) partnered businesses up or down the stream of value depending on particular aspect of the model arrangement and (3) third parties/future clients to whom services are be marketed on evidential basis.

The latter include new partners from other sectors and industries in leisure, hospitality and sales. Partnerships with West End theatres serve as evidence of this emerging model connecting experiences in material space. The plans to expand to Wimbledon connect cultural aspects of sports with leisure experience and design through means of creative industries of data collection, push value supply and agile marketing.

The essence has not changed, the strategy as a core concept in every business model remains based on the same value creation and capture principle. Concert Live use services and products to capture data, in the most nuanced and detailed way awarded by the context of value offerings. At different times and stages of their evolution, these would include live CDs, downloads, customized discs with various data/'mixtape' designed by user though the cloud, wifi experiences, offers and conceptually tagged personalized marketing, or any other emerging variations and integrations of technological means, experiential assets and services. In every case, the company generates value by carefully collecting and responding to user data, targeting audiences and users in their multiple roles and identities through refined psychographics, geodemographics and analysis of visitor response patterns. In past instances, such as CD sales or early mass customization of – a probable project in – festival mixtapes, scope for user data collection and analysis was relatively limited compared to later technological development. Still, the use value data would generate was attractive to partners, both upstream and downstream in potentially connected sectors, and therefore sufficient to award Concert Live the opportunity to act as both supplier and buyer across multiple licensing/revenue streams. (This was explored in Chapter 2 in relation to the methodological empirical learning connected to Five Forces.)

This company nurtures a direct relationship with audiences, visitors and users (the same people in multiple roles), supplies them goods, services and experiential substructures and by doing so collects rich, detailed and systematic data which is used for further refinement of marketing and sales which generate value for clients, partners and complementary models across various industries connected to events. Users supply demand (patterns) enabling Concert Live to commercialize such demand through multiple and growing numbers of global and localized partnerships. Means – the ICT prowess combined with human interaction and (still) 'emotive' Most Relevant Product tagging justify the ends: market share and market/sector penetration/integration. Their founder, Adam Goodyer reflects:

> we still have to tag the products ourselves; user data patterns are not a problem, it is the understanding why and how a product is best tagged and offered that is not yet scientific, it is still based on emotive decisions.

Perhaps the key question here is whether 'still', a quantitative term (read as 'a matter of time') apples or is the process of offering the most relevant product (service, experience etc) a qualitative problem that can only be solved by human intervention, on a case to case basis (emotive, read as 'interpretive'), representing a theoretical dilemma between Stacey's chaos theory approach to large numbers of data and Georgiev's (respondent) heuristic evaluation on the one hand, and an interpretive role of the manager/marketer who needs to brainstorm 'manually' as the aid of automation is limited *in principle*, by definition. This being qualitative matter would mean that a machine cannot sell as well as a human, however well programmed to do so. If, however, matters such as tagging can be automated and made 'scientific' in only a matter of time – a matter of degree – then the answer is that this is a quantitative problem which can be by definition resolved by tools that do not require human intervention past the point of design and initial engagement. This has considerable implications for cognitive, management and labour related matters.

Discursive power of business models: marketing and fragmented identity in application

The following relationships will be examined in relation to discourse (ontology) and its impact on modelling (teleology applied in concrete processes). To understand the workings of discourse/model dialectics, it is worth postulating the following relations:

> Discourse as meaning, utility as meaning. Meaning as utility. Utility as discourse.

An example of *crowdfunding* is a contemporary snapshot of current flux (no guarantee that it would persist as a model in the future). The model and its sustainability are of lesser relevance than the case study explaining its discursive impact and its position within economic structures that facilitate dissemination of such discourse through commercial application online.

Every online identity is fragmented and this fragmentation can be readable given appropriate tools. A number of interviewees work in the ICT and digital areas of creative industries and use software to respond to, identify, categorize, analyse and target user requirements. While some design interfaces, services and environments with preset customization (as is the case with Serrano Brothers' blended architecture designed for leisure), focusing on material space and tangible environment, others focus entirely on intangible digital assets. External interactivity has not yet populated such spatial material environments and is so far being used as an add-on through content or social media – Serrano Bros integrated social media into their room interface which may be of use in hospitality environments with which they cooperate, reinforcing the marketing of ongoing leisure experience through self-narrative and networking. This may be in some ways similar to the refined reading of user data in wireless networks for venues and promoters Concert Live work with. However, no media, social or content-driven are a central feature of architecture or hospitality models analysed in this research. Varied uses of media and blended experiential environments can be accounted for, but they play a secondary and intensionally passive role. Intrusive media and data collection are not part of the core value proposition in such models and may stand at odds with them on ontological grounds.

It is therefore logical to suggest that user fragmentation may not be directly measured through such blended leisure material spaces. Indirect measurement though travel, design and leisure portals, forums and apps. User fragmentation is therefore measured indirectly in case of leisure architecture and hospitality; directly, only in cases of direct engagement. Elsewhere in this book it was stated that such engagement may appear to be passive – mundane examples such as search for content, may reveal a pattern of interest, reflected by any search entry (Firefox Collusion) that can be commercialized. Respondents also described users occupying different social and psychological profiles, depending on the purpose and time of use. This sort of information is fragmented across genres and channels. It is not unsystematic and understanding how it is structured enhances user experience and with it the opportunities of effective targeting.

Marketing and the online ID: the panopticism

The wordplay of id and ID is presented on purpose. 'You know what they say about slugs. They always leave slime in their tracks' (Angel Heart 1987). This quote describes the ultimate panoptical paranoia felt by the main protagonist of the film, Harry Angel aka Johnny Favorite aka Johnny Liebling. The possessed main character creates a trail of destruction by which both law and his conscience, epitomized in his nemesis 'the client' trace and convict him.

Firefox Collusion, a browser add-on is an effective tool for representing the use of data tracking tools in simple graphic semi-animated form showing geometrical progression of tracking links at any point of the searching and browsing process. This tool was referred to in other sections of this book, in order to illustrate the other side of user experience most users do not consider or evaluate in relation to gains from use, networking and browsing. Another conceptual illustration relates to two very different purposive networks; this stands alongside search bubbles inherent in personalized and customized search technology/design. *LinkedIn* utilizes a functional feature 'who looked at your profile' as a push tactic for premium services. Facebook lacks such an open function for a reason: possible interactions leading to various forms of social tension and discord may have arisen soon upon enabling and opening such user features. This is due to the very different purposive function of the latter. Personal, focused on reflection and self-representation (Bloch 2012: 118–138) through personal 'I' narratives, Facebook would facilitate very personal and contentious communications if every user were able to observe any search through their profiles. The design features of both networks vary significantly in meaning and purpose, and the impact of seemingly minor changes to the structure of activities and the communication model would radically alter the business model, its functioning, commercial value to advertisers, legal aspects and overall effect (Casadesus-Mansanell and Ricart 2010: 198).

Evidently, panopticism is part of the paradigm shift: the more accurate the user data, the more valuable deemed the model in the bidding for investment – as media-respondent Chris Price stated scepticism over value capture through many social media and streaming models. The value of regional, national or supra-national interactive media audiences to advertisers and by extension, content owners and businesses controlling network substructures is a function of evaluating an economic area or national market for consumer goods and services, which would explain content barring in areas of lower GDP or the unavailability of email/subscription-free components of some streaming models. One contrasting example which shows the importance of global network coverage and user data collection relates to (FB) offering less processing-intensive social media interfaces in tertiary market penetration of broadband services mainly supplied to mobile users. The statement – and finding – referred to elsewhere in this book that '*Users are Who They Are*' on Facebook, can be seen as the resultant sum of a user's longitudinal behaviours, both conscious and less so (emotive). Data is longitudinally collected; not only relating to interaction with other users, their use of content, own postings and discursive linkages. What would be of value as user data is the interaction with the interface which contributes to data, including user responses, e.g. a degree of passivity in making choices regarding options which are continually modified and pushed through different levels/forms of user targeting.

The user becomes equivalent to an ID, which is an emerging pattern of purposeful, utilitarian and experiential, emotive and substantive actions and links characterized by place, time, periodic nature of use, search and content/link selection criteria. Such data can allow suppliers or services to anticipate user's actions save for the critique that such data also shapes user actions by narrowing the options for users and *creating search bubbles*. ICT managers who work on optimization generate and utilize such information interview with T Georgiev.

Metaphorical and evidential connections between complex user ID functions of data collection used for analytics, benevolent service delivery and user targeting is further explored within the observation, that internet and its constituent media, applications, niches and channels may be seen to represent an ego-structure with a model resembling the repository of unconscious content links. Such observations are not mere guesswork, but based on recent breakthroughs on connecting cognitive and anthropological paradigms in Bloch's work (2012: 128). Moreover, in informal talk, a respondent/ICT expert corroborated the allusions to likely design features allowing social media to facilitate emotive responses, which are valuable as they supply user data on impulsive and irrational interactions. On the other hand, many business models across media and entertainment sectors online benefit from user data trade-offs such as '*contact for content*' barter.

Finally, increased immersion in blended environments is a feature of media events, from blended music videos and blended streaming events (Foals 2015; YouTube 2013) to events media environments such as immersive use of wireless fidelity networks used for leisure marketing customizations in West End theatre. This type of modelling goes significantly beyond ticketing or merchandise, as a functional feature of 'white label' services (Adam Goodyer interview July 2015). Gadget-software partnered[1] interactive music video by Foals uses Google Earth Street View as both aesthetic and metaphor, and the creative innovation of such promotional videos is conceptually rounded and synchronous with interactive media discourses. In the YouTube music video awards a blend of interactive reality, live event, stage play acting and music video is achieved through the use of editing and streaming tools to the effect of creating a virtual reality stage more sophisticated than any avatar-based experiment of the past. The emerging information technology presents its innovation as a functional feature of interaction and content-driven entertainment as a conceptual prerequisite of a new design aesthetic. In either case, evaluations of creative experiences, products and services are based on the understanding of user identity and how it is construed through interaction with the medium. Where a functional aesthetic is built into a design based on interactivity, the perceived value of shared user experiences can lead to capture through content-related commercialization (ticketing, merchandise, subscription). It remains to be seen to what extent interactive music videos will generate value beyond publicity and whether such format innovation tactics adopted by some artists and producers would generate lasting stylistic, aesthetic transformation and thus generate new value creation beyond synergic publicity branding effects already attained through cooperation and experimental format redesign showcasing such cooperation across verticals.

Information as innovation and value

The context in which information became the core, ontological component of Concert Live and their business models was explained in other sections. Models such as Netflix, iTunes/iPod/Apple Music are explored in the context of ruse, manoeuvre, envelopment and disruption on the level of substructure elsewhere in this book. Similar attention was paid to software design strategies in Big Data and the opinions of seasoned professionals in ICT and digital media regarding the transformative character of analytics, curatorial services and infrastructure. With all of these cases and classes of cases, the use value of digital physicality (spectrum, networks, hardware, operations, content) is evident on the level of ontology. Therefore, it was not a challenge proving that information as tool (epistemology) and as substructure (control of information reproduction, teleology) directly relates to the meaning, i.e. intrinsic value in such cases. However, it should be observed that information/innovation evaluations apply to those works, concepts, models and *commodification* processes beyond ICT, media and abstract, coded forms such as music or data. Having been forced to innovate due to being first affected by the improved richness and reach of internet-based media, the music industry has come up with some noteworthy user tracking and loyalty models derived from audience and genre structures. However, while this was characterized by elegant conceptual initiatives such as 'In Rainbows' which represents an un-credited precursor to 'freemium' models, a campaign driven by artists, the transformative nature of ICT created a tidal wave the effect of which have not been absorbed by a novel and overarching business model. Such a business model should resolve the – now material, not abstract – loss of the work's 'aura' through reproduction (perceived value), supersede controlled scarcity of content and information, and underlie a transformed conceptual approach to overcome *commoditization of content* (Benjamin 2008; Eco 1995). Benjamin and Eco dealt with mechanical and magnetic copying respectively; due to their analogue and unconnected environments, such storage, copy and dissemination media did not have the commoditization capacity subverting content exchange value to approaching zero in an *asymptotic long tail* of infinite *copying* (Anderson 2009; Pine and Gilmore 1999). The content commoditized this way, forcing the managers to develop audience-driven adaptive models as an interim, incremental *Ploy*.

In an early text related to value of data and at the same time a text hailing the end of radio eras Negus (1993) referred to Smythe (1981) and commodification of audiences to utilize the value of audience data. Audiences as commodities in appeared as an important concept in the analysis of pre-online media. This happened in connection to 'narrowcasting' (Negus 1993; Thornton 1995) that predefined a thought process behind more focused media targeting enabled by narrowed channels of genre-communication (before ubiquity of the internet), as the increased profiling of media sub-genres created the data on audience character that would be presented as use value for advertising. Information has therefore been perceived, formulated and therefore used as exchange value – as *representation conditionally determines value* of abstract matters such as 'experiences'. Such information therefore traditionally serves to justify expenditure – this is the case with audience research in the 1970s as much as it is through the use of social media and streaming service analytics – the evidential component continuously involves a statistical appendix and a logical framework explaining impact and related sales potential. The slippery component of this is that such evaluations are based on products with no finite use value, therefore the negotiated value of creative triggering can range from infinity to zero. Returns on niche products at the end of the long tail – which has been proven a form of distribution, not a function over time – are low for those entrepreneurial formats that remain autonomous from virtual navigators and traditional linear industry structures.

Those that belong to the visual arts presented in space, belonging to the more discursive, socially-engaged and thus policy-driven areas of culture and the arts remain confined in a different model of fragmenting framework. The public funds bodies in the arts increasingly define their projects policies on the basis of utilitarian/institutional value aims, confining independent and autonomous enterprises into a more fractured and narrowed policy-driven space, defined by funding targets (and complementary restrictions). The double circuitry of independence and funding that forced venues such as Foundry into the area of relative autonomy carrying risk, is transforming into a regulatory framework that prescribes an increasingly specific descriptive nature fragmented discourses to be invested in, focused on and engaged with if the funding and other support were to be utilized, according to multiple respondents across visual arts. As an artist/respondent claimed Tom Cardew, 'the absence of sales or pricing (...) suggests that artist is a charlatan', while later referring to a creative practice structure that was not centred on commerce and economy (as contrasted with some observations on Vatteau's agent's marketing methods). Yet this stands in coherence with a very specifically and articulately intoned statement by another artist of very different sensibility and history, suggesting 'it is not surprising that neo-liberal Reagan administration spent major funds on conceptual art'. Both artists seem to present the same conflict from different viewpoints – the conflict between stated 'purpose' of art either from a 'market economy' viewpoint or the one on 'institutional value' that encompasses all and commits to none (as implied by artist-respondent Peter Jones). Therefore, information becomes value as visual arts beyond the mainstream or community/causes-funded projects remain starved of publicity.

Those interviewed at the innovation side of the upstream network of visual arts such as artists, gallery and venue owners and independent dealers presented their concerns over funding policy and dominant discourses which only seem paradoxical and contradictory. This is due to the paradoxes and contradictions in the art environments emerging from interviews and reflexive data. These seeming paradoxes combine *marketization* with the fragmentation socially engaged and ideologically charged niche discourses within the same narrowing band of the continuum of visual arts, labelled 'alternative', 'countercultural', 'outsider', fringe art etc. The prescriptive means-based management of 'institutional' and 'intrinsic' values of policy organizations that dictate public funding is contrasted with a narrowing field of commercialization of works that fall within what could be defined as the long tail of visual arts. The '*glocalization*' (Swyngedouw 1992; Mok *et al.* 2010) through internet does little more than to expose the small providers of new art content to the white noise of internet discourses and channels on art. A gallery becomes a venue and its signal as a node of substantive value creation is muffled by the white noise of clearly profiled commercial or PFI-modelled projects; art-venue fragmentation continues and smaller spaces compete to attract new audiences following gentrification. In the light of this, the key issue for such conceptually uncompromising and articulate autonomous spaces (and events[2]) is the one of '*does the work exist if I not know of it*' and '*what is the impact and purpose even if it does*'? This, as postulated by Montse Gallego, shows that those independent and autonomous enterprises and creators need a clear and open, multifaceted channel for conversing publics. Such audience reach of 'presence', whether digital or spatial/material (corpuscular) is costly and does not fit the means-tested approaches of the role of art or the market-ready-made models that involve profiled commercial genres defined by lead players. The matter of visibility of niche art/s, and therefore the problematic evidential basis of its value (in whichever public form) is directly related to the matter of investment and the very question on the nature, character and existence of a work. This clearly has direct funding and value implications.

Two notable examples questioning the existence of the work and its agreed value are indicative of the same problem of balance between public reception and exchange value. In 2001, Martin Creed's Turner Prize for 'Work No. 227' presented an entirely conceptual work where the evidence of a 'work' as 'labour' was entirely removed from value-formulation processes. A similar example relates to Carey Young's Beck's Futures 2003 entry competing for the prize of £20,000 where the work was 'invisible' and the artist refused to reveal whether the work exists at all, citing a non-disclosure agreement which details the fact of the work. Soon it was reported that another artist, Ms Anna Livia Lowendahl-Atomic, had complained this her work was plagiarized in relation to her own non-disclosure agreement relating to works consisting of 'secrets' for sale (Telegraph.co.uk 2003). This case represents an interesting intersection between on the one hand some highly conceptual notions of the *disappearance of* creative work, and legal implications of intellectual property and definitions of the existence of an original work. Invoking legal comment fixes in binding form interpretations of artistic ontology.

Related to such radical conceptual tensions, comes the court ruling in 2015, requesting of Dahn Vo to deliver Kreuk a work deemed 'Large and impressive' to the value of $350,000, by agreement with the commissioning collector, which is to be done by consultation regarding the design of the work (Maneker 2015). Therefore, the issue of tangibility and substantiality of a creative work – art[3] in this case – is not merely affecting media, music and film. To relate back to Cardew and his philosophical take on creative – artistic – strategy, 'a painting is not a sum of pieces of wood, canvas, nails and paint'. What connects them is *the work*, an underlying synergy attained by *virtue of 'a reality'* (what of the test of 'impressive/large', quantified in commercial terms, as defined above?)

Information (e.g. copy of a work, knowledge about a work) is in itself no longer treated as user value. Newly redefined, exchange value of works in creative sectors is postulated through other material and experiential links. Art is required to be of material, measurable substance (by legal precedent) especially in the context of commissioning, and media-related contents are required to create other experiential substance beyond the reproduction of recording in any format or mode of delivery (this being affected by deregulated market affected and by related free use of content). The similar double-edged approach applies to media: where regulation is looser, as in commercial contexts the standards are set for redefined push–pull entertainment models which in turn influence public broadcasters whose remit is re-examined and debated through the funding mechanisms ontologically close to those redefining the impact of art, research or education, and consequent policies, targets and evaluation models. The areas of innovation and impartiality, such as independent and autonomous creators and dealers, as well as of those whose unbiased public role in culture are both facing challenges from commerce and streamlining of innovation funds.

The visibility of non-mainstream art and the right of public media to experiment were identified by art-respondents as important aspects of the social contract, referred to in other parts of this book in connection to the redefining of many fundamental rights and social practices through the impact of the internet. As public funding bodies are required to follow broader policies professed by governments and trade areas (e.g. the EU/EEA), the approach to publicly funded art at a time of reduction of funding becomes restrictive and risk-averse. It is this risk-aversion that affects the creation of new value that would renew the process of feeding innovation into commercial creative industries (CIF 2015a/b).

Attempting to resolve this, organizations such as Creative Industries Federation (CIF) representing the top strata of creative industries formulate and implement campaigns to governments articulated through a causative economics-driven discourse focusing on *impact* – the term *impact* becoming a key word for elusive creative economies, including education and research (as will be elaborated in Chapter 6). By doing so they reinforce the notions developed at the top end of market with formulations suited to large-scale policy initiatives that treat internal contradictions as nuances of form under a broadly inclusive umbrella of creativity and production. This approach is dictated by the structuring of the market with hierarchies of ownership, control, processing and goodwill, and the necessity to address policy bodies, from regulators to governments and supra-governmental forums, with a coherent discourse on the creative economy. They do so by reconciling many internal idiosyncrasies and presenting the data in an evidence-based framework with the aim of providing the case for the direct or indirect actual economic impact of creative industry funding. The market-defined discourse of policy dictates the discourse of evidential and publicity materials.

Commodification of creative discourse formulated a policy response that works to prove a causal correlation of value creation and capture, means such as public art justifying the ends such as commercial impact of artistic innovation in other areas of creative industry practice. Such causalities are difficult to prove as discussed with an established cultural planner in 2011. Yet if proven, these causalities (ROI, etc.) would justify the utilitarian treatment of art and culture without necessarily creating concern over intrinsic or institutional value. Those two may become part of the utility and therefore concern over authenticity, rooted in experience and shared meaning would not be of primary importance so long as the market operates by recruiting innovation into the commerce through models of acquisition or replication. In this respect, Blakley's analogies with fashion (Blakley 2010; Nixon and Blakley 2012) are not entirely contextualized to fit the ontology of other, less utilitarian creative fields, while Ashuach's (interview) critique of replicating, adopting and acquiring innovation through purchase, licensing, reverse engineering or acquisition, innovation is redefined as singular and discrete, qualitative and noncompliant, free of the normative rein of funding, regulation and policy definition. This context also provides one possible reading of Assa Ashuach's rejection of the term 'creative' as a blanket phrase signifying his practice.

In his case, *information is innovation, on the ontological level.* The concepts in design strategy and experimental applied work are primarily functional, the function of them being defined at the core level of: *what software is, what networks are, what materials are*, etc. This is done by connecting the science and technology principles behind the design and service tools, design principles behind these tools – as designed at his studio, and the cost-effective, sustainable functionality of his projects, which he labels *aesthetically pleasing* due to their logical elegance and design solution elegance. Such innovative information takes up physical form – relating to both meanings of accurately defined connotations of 'physical' – as data/digital content, which may in many cases transform into corpuscular, material existence (a design object) or information-distribution services complementing the product or project delivered by such designers. Printable encoded information objects and operational solutions are among the many value creation forms integrating information, innovation and value, where utility is equivalent to intrinsic values defining the function and ICT substructure.

The examples presented above serve as evidence that information is not confined to media and abstract, copy- and meaning-driven creative forms and constituent value structures. Material products, functional services and events, artistic concepts and discursive values are susceptible to competition with the white noise as well as push-services in the arts and entertainment and the Kantian notion of existence as evidence of existence matters to them by means of richness and reach in ways equivalent if not at times near-identical to those of media content. As will be seen in Chapter 6, attempts are made to redress the balance through public funding of regional arts and culture portals (e.g. EU/EC projects). Those initiatives too are subject to limitations of project management discourse epitomized in logical frameworks that need to show compliance with policy targets, definitions and formulations of impact (TING Project, LMU/UTT 2010/11). These projects were subject to interactive value exchange models whereby initial start-up funding for the arts portal integrated with tourism and hospitality would come from public funds while the sustained operation of such a portal and value creation through related industries would depend on effective, transparent and well-documented communication and cooperation with other stakeholders. These would include hotels and travel in commerce, local government for policy, research units for incremental improvements, artists and media for content and PR, etc. – managing and sustaining such operations would depend on the model, the effectiveness of hierarchies of governance and transaction costs between different parts of a licensing and experience marketing model. Moreover, the marketization of such a culture-investment project would be reflected in the fact that the information portal would promote culture as a component of destination marketing. The most complex aspect of the actual implementation would be the cost-structures following launch: media, local businesses, operators and events organizations would need to pay for promotional value of the portal, which would therefore require regular innovation and upgrades, costly in cases where one or more of the stakeholders were to consider sunk costs sufficient investment. Quantifying the evidence would be challenging if the role of the portal consisted of redefining the visitor experience. Collecting such data would be best done through the design features of such a portal but to make the business model sustainable after launch, licensing, cost and evaluation procedures would need to be fully designed and fixed in contractual form to warrant sustainability.

Cost structures of interactive value exchange

Even the minute of changes in the policy formulation relating to the use of assets in business models affect economic their structures in ways that lead to substantive changes to value creation and capture (Casadesus-Mansanell and Ricart 2010: 198). The tactical effects of business models should therefore be examined through value exchange, in advance of development and design planning processes that run concurrently with business model implementation. The role of interaction here is twofold: as a value concept in itself (ontology) and the value-catalyst character of knowledge-(epistemology) and communications management (teleology). Such ability to catalyse other ontological, epistemological and teleological relationships within and between creative works and value structures in which they are set is a highly disruptive force that generates and subverts value. There is limited capacity to anticipate and plan for the specifics of value-subverting processes. Yet, examining the fundaments of what a creative work is within its value structure, how it stands in relation to other works and structures, and how it is known, understood or communicated can provide insight and foresight to the analyst as to the more global, conceptual moves within and between creative industries and sectors affected by interactive ICT. In addition to that, processual methods and cognitive models developed for such purposes can aid in anticipating the patterns of strategic environment development (Christensen 2006).

This stands in clear correlation with the means-based value of strategic application of business models developed by a number of contemporary creative industry organizations. They sell value to clients, users and public stakeholders by proving their proclaimed ability to anticipate, respond to and influence environments by creating, developing and refining the tools used to aid online business activity. The immersive, social and subjective nature of large-scale chaotic patterns of online interaction results in the fact that observing (knowing, researching) the system (online content and communications) is equivalent to changing it, influencing it – interacting with it. This is the result of the actual crossing of disciplinary boundaries in online models, eliciting a recognition of deep fundamental integration of subject different disciplines (Bloch 2012), between cognitive and other, scientifically-supported and subjective, immersive social components of new methods of analysis and action in online value structures. Moreover, the value of software structures used for interactive models is based on their ability to learn from, and adapt to mass-customized user behaviour, therefore designed to interact with the cloud of communications just as described by the analogy between quantum mechanics and radical ethnography including Gonzo (the latter of particular value for online PR strategies).

This conceptual feature of design in networking, analytics etc. discussed in Chapter 2 is understood to combine knowledge tools and value creation/capture models, thus calling for a reformulation of methodologies underpinning the academic disciplines in business studies. Such new methodologies should recognize the evidential value of 'soft' data such (e.g. culture) and the need to design analytical frameworks that overcome the artificial boundary between 'objective' and 'subjective', 'positivist' and 'interpretive', 'quantitative' and 'qualitative'. Since such disciplinary limitations were ignored by entrepreneurs and knowledge management professionals from ICT, design and creative backgrounds (as found in interviews), the disciplinary divisions never arose to limit the scope and direction of business model development. The evidence for the need to reassess the fundamental rift between 'natural' and 'social' science approaches (Bloch 2012) can be found in the success of such knowledge-based business models, esp. using science tools from ICT (Garnham 2005) to create analysis and response tools, complex hybrids of 'social' and 'scientific'.

Value creation and value capture in such complex business models is based on users' subjective, learned, unconscious responses, as well as on rational decisions. Structural, indirect analytical approaches are required in order to analyse the processes of creation of value and its exchange in contemporary business models. This is partly dictated by the non-disclosure nature of most business data, as well as the actual value creation processes embodied (intellectual property) in ICT-driven business models (Kagermann *et al.* 2010). Moreover, an analysis based entirely on the level of concrete information and business case narratives has considerable limitations if it remains on the level of description (Jarzabkowski and Fenton 2006; Jarzabkowski and Wilson 2006; Yin 1994; Gaudesi 2015). The lack of capacity for generalization is not the main issue with case study approaches; *any* successful and distinct business model owes part of its success to its *unique fit* within a particular context, so *creating one* should *not be about replicating another* (interview with Assa Ashuach). Learning about generating sustainable business models therefore combines of the concrete facts and the abstract methods of depth-analysis (*transcendental illusion, from ontology to method*).

Analogies with artistic *plastic anatomy* (Chapter 2) suggested an analytical approach that awards equal relevance to the general and the specific. Proposed is an X-Ray portrait of a business model by examining its visible features in the context of what is known about underlying structures. Such well-postulated underlying structures include economics of value capture and value exchange, any licensing and IP assets, market position, the structures of competition or cooperation with other businesses and their models, information flow reach and richness, etc. The *thick description* (Geertz 2000) of a business model is necessary: the appearance is important as it relates to user experience and investor perceptions, among other things and detailed sets of varied data need to be created from components available in the public domain. Those sources may fall within a number of disciplines, purposes and levels of competence from blog entries and social media posts to global market reports and operational analyses. Any fieldwork should include interviews with decision-makers able to comment on driving principles not concrete, justifiably protected value-adding operational procedures. In this approach, the representational nature of abstract thought is applied by contextual use of matching structural, process-based tools (e.g. business model canvas, Set Theory, feedback loops to explore the visible manifestations of a business model). Such visible manifestations include sales data, known partners and competitors, any licensing information available, descriptions of user interface design – if any, reviews, opinions, policy documents, PR presented as features, branding implications, etc.

The multi-level, multi-disciplinary 'X-Ray Modelling' approach has two evident implications. One, the comprehensive analysis of business models is, and should be done by teams of analysts, in ways that resemble industry teamwork. Two, in planning and developing educational strategies for the paradigm shift, policy makers, academics and educators need to place an emphasis on a convergence of skills in their students and trainees, combining multidisciplinary approaches with various levels of application from abstract/depth ontologies of business modelling to concrete, detailed description of plans and procedures in use.

Adaptive innovation: insurrective and top-down

Insurrection is a discursive category as well as a material act and process. In order to formulate any goals and means that may amount to an insurrective concept, participants and entrepreneurs involved need to arrive at a degree of consensus on the method and aim of such organizing. The disappearance of oppositional charge from many of civil society meta-narratives was originally registered in relation to post-industrial late twentieth-century diffusion of tensions across the threads of lifestyle identity discourses, a fragmentation through variety of popular forms and modes of consumption. Such conceptual fragmentation of genre into minute niches was further reinforced through the opportunity 'levelling' appearances of the early web and 'commoditizing' effects of actual internet media, tool and asset stratification and concentration. The devaluation of content occurs at the asymptotic ends of long tail/distribution of content across a niche or fragment continuum, as it does not attract sufficient attention to generate revenue through traditional or alternative means, and though it remains attractive to connoisseurs of creative niche content, the individual units of enterprise creating and disseminating such content are not self-sustainable in commercial terms. This applies to music as much as it does to film or visual arts. Adaptive innovation is thus frequently a result of long-term project investment and intentional push-supply of well-distributed tools, services or content: major media services or social network models, as well as experimental art projects part financed by public funds. An innovation of a capillary spread, through a metaphorical '*osmosis*' of discourse, content and skill, can be facilitated in education and some of the models that have transformed interactive media from the ground up include formats, services and tools developed by research teams. Indeed, some entrepreneurial businesses adopt such insurrective models of innovation. Those businesses operate in the experience, design, data, events and gadget-innovation sectors and sector niches. The deep level of design, level of concept is the level of disruption and adoption through pull-push tactics. Whether these adaptive add to the '*whole pie [chart*]' (Markides 2006) or create new Schumpeterian niches (Garnham 2005) depends on the relative position of the business, its output and emergent strategy, planned steps and overall market attractiveness. In many cases, in those industries, sectors and professions most directly affected by digitization this is a tactical *Ploy* to buy time and extend the period of speculative bargaining over new value transaction concepts until a new opportunity for sustained value capture is created or seized. The qualitative test, just as in the question of Most Relevant Product tagging is whether the ontology level of market substructure facilitates any new blanket method of value capture.

Top-down adaptation rests, however, on the economies of scale, scope and sunk costs of R&D, coupled with a curious inherent feature of internet based business models that '*there can be only one*' identical, singular, specific leading model which is more often than not linked to a single company or brand. Diversity may appear under brands and major online media organizations, but the model in which horizontal competitors do nearly identical things and operate in near-identical ways applies mainly to the most unstable of market segments and emergent sectors. The uncertain position along the long tail – contrasted with the clearly profiled core competencies of leading virtual navigators shows that top-down adaptive innovation, though distributed through fragmentary/capillary structures has a far greater expected impact than an emerging discourse which may aim to innovate and lead the way in redistributing power to creators.

Disruptive innovation and subversive technology

There is a growing body of literature on disruptive innovation (Christensen (2006), Christensen *et al.* (2006), Johnson *et al.* (2008), Markides (2006)) to correspond with a growing number of cases emerging from the shift from steadily paced patterns of change to a flow and flux of business models both dictated and facilitated by the impact of IT (Kagermann *et al.* 2010; Osterwalder 2013). Innovation is no longer seen in its Schumpeterian sense alone, and this is attributed to the transformative character of the combination of factors that define the dominance of ICT in innovation. The pace of change is such that the socially redefined cooperative business funding model transcends established markets and presents internet-discourse as a *modelling logic of crowdfunding*, which is set to transform beyond its current form and irrespective of its fortunes represents an effective manoeuvre away from the problematic mainstream discourse of financing innovation (Braet *et al.* 2013; Lawton and Marom 2012; Mollick 2014).

Technology in itself is not subversive; its purpose or application may be. The meaning and resultant impact of ontological shift in its purpose depends on context. An ICT specialist whose interest in optimization tools spreads across the reaches of online media and their impact on culture, states that a deep and fundamental innovative disruption will require unwitting compliance as it would wipe out all previous models of utility in its area of influence. This disruption being defined by networked computing technology will as a result leave few things unchanged. By 'things', it is worth imagining actual objects in material space, connected to some form of interactive media. Business models of Serrano Brothers, Concert Live, Citizen M Hotels, and others referred to or anticipated by respondents, benefit from the interaction of lived environments with various media feeds and integrated advertising revenue models. A leading designer, however notes that his disruptive innovation in production and delivery processes, characterized by intelligent design tools, the circumvention of traditional supply chains and the reduced cost of increasingly functional products – faces a somewhat Luddite response citing concerns over the impact on labour practices and demand patterns. In this respect, the current shift does resemble the industrial revolution as labour – both applied, material and abstract, analytical – is being streamlined, restructured through networks and somewhat automated.

Describing the kind of software developed by his company and how it improves effectiveness and efficiency through the example of sales decisions, the respondent claims the following:

> [The generic product brief requires] comfortable level of accuracy to make a decision. If it does not have enough data to make a decision, it passes it to humans. In theory there's no limit [to possible field of application of] ... what level of decision-making a client would like to give a machine ... [it deals with] Supply accounting and sales – optimise the decisions where from ... where to deliver, plus automate the delivery process. Based on [key questions] 'How long does the process to go through the system' and 'how much money this brings to the company and effectiveness delivery bonus'.... Actual processes of sourcing and additional deals that eat up the profit margin – actual, final delivery of the deal.
>
> (T Georgiev interview 2014: TG 2014 below)

The automation component redefines established work patterns and roles; moreover, the efficiency/effectiveness claim in the area in decision-making processes has an impact on human decision-makers and how their choices are perceived and evaluated across the firm. The former results in potential transformation of labour practices, bargaining and changes to skills requirements, while the latter affects the position and role of lower and middle levels of management. This reasonably mundane use of ICT innovation leaves a disruptive impact on the structuring and management of key sales operations of a client. In relation to the nature of disruption and contingent content management solutions brought about by major data management organizations, the respondent claims:

> Disruptive innovation – we won't know what technology they will have in 2020/30 ...[now it is] just a lack of understanding how to capture and promote that content because the content is there. [It is about finding the means of] ... how do you make them pay for it [the content]?
>
> (TG 2014)

Another respondent whose past covered entertainment media, including MTV, Radio 1 and last.fm is less optimistic. His insights come from the point of view of a music radio and television professional who focuses on media policy within the context of change and the ways to continue delivering the most competitive programming in the era of personalized media and music discovery models. The analysis he provides relates to the commercial viability and economic sustainability of specialist media in the non-linear context, and the viability of emerging models of content delivery and content discovery such as streaming.

> [upon acquiring last.fm] CBS have not made any money on last.fm ... [they are] scaling down ... that model has failed because value proposition of music discovery is quite a niche pastime. Music discovery being their USP.... Most people aren't that bothered about discovering new music. And yet their business model demands huge scale in order to be profitable ... And Spotify though it's much bugger and well known is not any better placed than last fm to say 'we're successful' ... they have 24 million subscribers, six of whom are paying [at the time of the interview, early 2014] ... 24 million people around the world is actually pretty small.... It needs to reach much bigger scale. At the moment it's going for scale over profitability ... though I am sure they could become profitable if they want to.
>
> (C Price interview 2014, CP 2014 below)

As seen in Chapter 2, the disruptive effects of the launch of the iPod/iTunes product/service continuum were deeper than initially accounted for. The fundamental disruption was not merely technological and a result of pure empiricism of R&D. The emergence of novel models that incorporate large-scale transformation of the ways of thinking about a product, service and experience are changes of conceptual nature and cannot be attained by chance or as a result of 'spontaneous' effects triggered by a product or service 'wild card'. It was shown that this process was designed and developed with the aim of transforming the substructure supporting the market for content, which covers any number of types of data, as laconically stated by a respondent when tracing the notion of deep disruption brought about by ICT and its treatment of all matter that can be encoded and transferred across digital networks as 'just data'. What transpires from any interview concerning any of the complementary matters of '*using data for content*' (traditional creative fields) or '*using content for data*' (ICT businesses utilizing traditional creative forms to underpin their trade), the in-depth understanding of *just how the technology transforms practice* is pivotal.

> If you go.... 'We've done this before, this is how this is what I think works' ... but until you start understanding how important certain parts of this chain are, [which] you're gonna start focusing on more, spending money on those areas, focus, resource or time and thought on those areas, and other ones would lose out.
>
> (A Bogucki interview 2013, AB 2013 below)

The insight of this respondent, highly positioned within a major music corporation shows that every technological tool that makes an impact needs to be understood both generically – what is it specific functional nature – and in fine detail. The latter is a direct reference to the necessary evaluation, which of an ICT tool's particular operations facilitate what sort of method for communication or delivery model that can be utilized for the integrated processes of marketing, promotion, engagement and sales relating to content, brand and artist. Specific features of the operation of a communications tool of a music discovery application, for instance, need to be seen as value-creating or capturing mechanisms that may contribute to user experiences, ending in sales. The dichotomy between technology and business concept is a false one, he claims; moreover, if a model emerges and appears superior, others will be evaluated within the part of a broader ecosystem or infrastructure and given precedence. That way, disruptive innovation occurs within a niche of operations and subverts the structure in such a way that it aids organizational learning feeding into practice. In relation to matching tools with goals, he uses an example of the now established marketing operations in music – exchanging user data for content (email for media or E4M, elsewhere in this book coined *contact for content*).

Regarding the techniques for key marketing operations such as collecting emails in exchange for music and other perks, requires seeing what specifically is used on social media (Facebook or Twitter), 'you need to *understand what to* do and then get the technology *the other end*'.... The management process of matching messages with methods (media/message equivalence) requires a high level of user proficiency or more, within the context of creative sector specialism. Not just data, but data in context. The decision-making processes therefore require the in-depth understanding of key principles and value structures. This is equally important for utilizing or modifying existing technological means, as it is for the ability to adapt to a wave of fundamental innovation that threatens to make a business area obsolete. Aaron Bogucki states:

> Formats live and die ...
>
> When you're gonna dispose of those things ... [models, catalogue etc] when they're:
>
> a redundant
> b the consumer does not connect with them any more, or the end user ... I keep saying *consumer* but we have *different kinds of terms* for creative industries ... a lot of it is consumer-driven.... Consumers want, we know, access to the cloud ... they're not going to go to the Blockbuster round the corner anymore ... dispose of the video store.... Models change. It gives us this little thing to play with ... improve things ... can we do this more efficiently, or cheaply?
>
> (AB 2013)

The decision to dispose of a format, model, campaign or product, especially in major media, music and entertainment corporations is a rational, utilitarian one. It concerns cost, revenue and returns on investment, subject lead times and reporting. However, the creative practice of digital marketing involves some other strategic decisions which are less clear-cut and therefore more interpretive. Aaron Bogucki speaks of consumer journeys and experience architecture in further detail, providing further evidence that internet-defined media and ICT in general have revealed the already existing socio-economic, cultural and psychological processes of consumer choice well beyond the crude statistical models of traditional marketing research, opening new areas of experimentation and innovation in marketing strategy. Those processes of identifying more refined and nuanced measurements and evaluations of user behaviour include processes of engagement and influence, so the data feeds into the system where it came from in order to capture value, while also generating new data on how efficiently this is done. Observation-interference dichotomies (Atkinson and Hammersley 1994; Jorgensen 1989; Misra and Sudarshan 1977) already explored will now be analysed within the context of business practice in ICT-driven environments.

Cognitive structures, innovation and organizations: Value and values: a dichotomy revisited

On the subject of consumer experience architectures, Aaron Bogucki states:

> We know that this consumer journey exists, we just haven't mapped it properly. We haven't thought about it properly.
>
> It's fluid, not every artist on every journey is like this. When a new system or product or experience comes to market then you plug in, and go how does that affect everything else? … will people stop doing this because they're doing this, or maybe … why don't we test that a few times?
>
> (AB 2013)

Values as means were discussed in Chapter 2. Festival concepts based on an endorsement of social, ethical, aesthetic and cultural values have been analysed in the context of utilitarian application of values-based discourses. The quasi-consequentialist proposition was there to indicate a relationship of equivalence drawn between consecutive the components of planning, implementation and realization of strategy. In Chapter 3, the inverse consequentialist proposition 'means justify ends' was revisited. This time when observing how structural change, a transformation of one hierarchical structure and part replacement with a new set of emerging hierarchies and the interim uncertainty, whereby established creative linear models and forms require methodological justification as sources of secondary value for related industries and sectors.

Manufacturing, service provision, geodemographic monitoring

Concert Live transformed its business model numerous times but the key links remain between live events, experiential marketing and operations, and data that facilitate this. The combination of these three factors has meant that

Adam Goodyer and his company were able to transform (disrupt) a niche of live events and merchandising, and move into more complex fields of technologically-driven experience management through various models mass customization that followed them from the outset and early break into the market, covered in Chapter 2. The focus on mobile networks as means of data collection, analysis and promotion/engagement platforms superseded live recordings and cloud-supported personalized mixtapes. The respondent agreed that data was always at the heart of their business model and especially the client value proposition. On the subject of changing degrees of automation, geo-demographics and planning involving more sophisticated methods emerging from such IT tools, Adam Goodyer, founder of Concert Live says:

> [in relation to the need for manual input of product descriptions and tagging] in spite of our ability to analyse user patterns ... with Most Relevant Product tagging ... we do have to put something in ... [in relation to traditional market research and inputs of large sets of statistical data] sometimes you get the data that looks surprising ... we're doing Broadway, New York, as well and working with a local data company there for our credit card purchasing analysis across all the major shops, these are millions of transactions, and they discovered a correlation ... you wouldn't normally think about it, but when you actually see, of course, that's how it works. When you see that in major grocery stores, there was a consistent pattern of increases in Friday purchases of nappies – and beer. And you think hey how is this correlated? And then you go back to the data and they found that they were by men, of certain age, who were on childcare duty so not necessarily going out to the pub on the weekends, so they go and get the nappies – and they go and get the beer!
>
> (A Goodyer 2015, AG 2015 below)

The example cited above is closer to traditional statistical analysis but the volume and accuracy of data is significantly improved – as is the analysis of external causes, the scope and catchment area being geographically defined and clearly identified through the tools integrated into the wireless service offered to event visitors. Triangulating the data with focus groups and commissioned market research analytics aids Adam and his team in deciding how to formulate the personalized targeting through '*emotive' categories* (as he labels them). As was shown across several areas and classes of cases, imagination and human decision-making are a necessary complement to even the most advanced technologies that enable mass-customization (covered for example by Moser *et al.* 2006; Obermaier and Hofmann 2012; Rayna *et al.* 2014). Similar reflections come from other advanced practitioners: Assa Ashuach emphasizes designers' strategic intervention when selecting between several projects aided by ICT and deciding which one will need to be fully developed at the expense of others. The same kinds of decisions reappear across media and digital music marketing.

Notes

1 A video editing virtual reality package and brand, aptly integrated with the music interactive, street-view-culture-inspired video: strategic genre-rich marketing, integrating deep-level concepts with luxury technology goods. Technological excellence is treated as aesthetic discourse and integrated with ICT experience genres using music as a point of convergence carrying the brand through music video as code.

2 As the case may have been with Exit and as it remained with Rheinkultur or Foundry until closure.

3 The artist's potential ability, as formulated by the Dadaists, to redefine the boundaries of a work's existence is thus being commoditized, as in Pine and Gilmore's observation of services (1999), and art is thus requested to have material form of negotiable value based on size and content.

6 Ethical and methodological implications for research and practice

Education and knowledge as power: educating creative professionals

Empowerment through knowledge, structure and understanding is presented in contexts that go beyond the Foucauldian knowledge-power equivalence, and include components of cognition, thematic structures, economic relations and data. Education is undergoing transformation and creative industry education is significantly affected by the ICT-driven paradigm change. One respondent discusses at length the educational importance of importing state of the art industry practice in film and media training. This respondent speaks of the practice in education and active plans to implement online media training in preparing the students for organizational work in production as well as production itself. He emphasizes the importance of real-time training of film and media practice students who may be physically remote distance learners by leading them to focus on the full contextual application of technical and organizational knowledge. They are encouraged to do so within their own environment and in real time through digital interaction tools used in training.

This way the trainees are made fully aware of the practical implications of key features of their concrete socioeconomic, cultural and localized environments where the specifics of practice or market characteristics may differ from those employed by other students/trainees but governed by the same principles taught to all of those involved in an emerging type of ICT-aided courses. In such a way, this respondent argues, a conceptual roundedness is achieved without undermining the contextual specificity of the circumstances in which a student engages in industry practice. In such hybrid educational models, the same tools and methods are in use in education as are in industry practice.

This includes but is not limited to instant messaging and AV conferencing, cloud services e.g. for content editing and product development, project management and mentor leadership. By agreeing a set of tasks, targets and skills with the student, the mentor/tutor agrees a learning contract which is tailored to the specific needs of the student in their concrete contextual setting, within the abstract framework that can be modified within the limits of generic practice and with clear to transferable skills. These skills involve practical, production-focused decision-making, i.e. production as management or design as strategy. The process of experiential learning thus attained involves working within a specific environment that is driven and managed by media tools used in industry practice in a given sector. Therefore, through an attainment of skill, skills are seen as cognitive precursor of creativity (Subotknik *et al.* 1995). Such effective vocational knowledge should be, ideally, assimilated through practice and abstracted on the cognitive level of decision-making in creative project management.

The social isolation of learners from each other and the trainer, accompanied by added emphasis on self-motivation are the inherent limitations of distance-learning methods including digital media-aided ones.

At present, there coexists a number of hybrid, pragmatic and empirical models of education in creative industries. Replicating the forms, formats and fortunes of the industry, the current flux and seeming levelling of playing fields is likely to be a precursor of a more hierarchical, established order of educational models. It is clear, however, that higher education in creative sectors continues to involve an increasing number of combinations and variations of practice, theory, tools and methods, within changing frameworks aiming to mimic, respond to or anticipate industry trends and frameworks. Such trends and frameworks, important for education involve employment markets matching the development of industry practices, structures and strategies. Contemporary creative industry education is therefore highly context-driven and dependent on research in its pragmatic application.

Experience is the key factor that defines creative industry work and constitutes core value in education as well as design, development and consumption. As stated by Pine and Gilmore, in consumer 'visitor' experiences, those range from 'emotional' to 'spiritual'. This has two consequences for education in the experience industries such as music, events, media or film.

One, the actual need for the transfer of experiential value through courses, training structures and knowledge partnerships, empirical models of teaching and learning industry practice and quality models that suit such experiential education models. These models resemble industry practice in two ways: not only in content, which is transferred to academia through industry relations and fieldwork. They resemble the experimental thinking required of contemporary industry professionals when designing their own business models. Therefore, modules and courses, along with industry partnerships and research input/output circuits, should themselves resemble business models structures that can be modified or 'mutated' to stay synchronized with the most advanced industry thinking. By thinking like the innovators of the industry, academic institutions may adopt a methodology of business model incubator thought and integrate it into the curriculum not only on the content level, but in conceptual, structural terms. This may be applied to any future structural projects through institutional funding, including Erasmus programmes.

Such structural change may be enacted in leaps such as revalidations and quality assurance processes. However, neglecting incremental development would make this process more complex due to a lack of institutional learning where small-scale module development is not constantly planned and mapped out.

Incremental educational strategy development, however, may involve structural change module by module, where a business modelling *logic* is built into modules one by one, which are so modified as to correspond with one another structurally, as to resemble the structural networks of value relations in the industry. Some examples include the following relationships – an events practice module is modified to correlate to the one in digital marketing, which draws content from the events module and uses it for student enterprise campaigns in the actual market; a business modelling module is modified to provide an entrepreneurial business development/incubator component to the digital marketing module. In this model, industry partners mentor, evaluate, partake in public events and student showcases, advise on, and analyse the curriculum or its components of particular interest (own sector, branded module, etc.). This way a new model is developed, based on experiential structures and methodologies adopted in the industry, while maintaining educational autonomy through the development of own models of innovation in training and education-based enterprise.

This leads to the second consequence of the impact of experience economies on emerging creative industry education. Branding is directly related to the transfer of experiential value within the educational institution and through industry partnerships. Educational brands as experiential models; industry branding evidenced through knowledge development (creation), transfer (engagement) and attainment (capture) experiences. The relationship branding with the industry may create further synergies, and requires careful strategic planning due to the need for sustainability, transparency and intellectual independence, one of the most important value components of educational structures and norms. Therefore, structural learning, and close, clearly delineated knowledge transfer alliances are preferred to models where education services the industry in exchange for work placement opportunities and content use privileges.

The autonomy of academia is one of its most significant strengths developed strategically over history. Therefore, its claim to value creation is not in copying the external environment, describing it, mimicking or servicing its protagonists, but by learning from it and engaging with it through its own models of thought applied in training, teaching, research and analysis. The ongoing transformation of knowledge structures, experiential economies and roles of those who work in them is an opportunity for creative industry education to overcome the fallacious boundaries between critical, technical, and business knowledge. In business reality of the creative industries, sustainable careers require integrated, adaptive and convergent knowledge structures: the expertise of a sector manager involves the understanding of the nature of the creative work they manage, just as the experience of a practitioner, developer or artist requires a structural understanding of the market (and preferably more). Education needs to reflect this through strategic industry relations, while maintaining its autonomy through own value creation.

Longitudinal practice in industry education shows this goal is attainable. When encouraged to act, given clear parameters, students have shown impressive reflective ability in practice-related work. Some of the case studies cited in this book come from the pool of student-developed reflective knowledge. Management participant observation from actual, current and cutting-edge cases created by advanced students contributes to the body of knowledge in specialist areas across the creative industries. One module alone led to the development of 45 case studies on student-managed industry practice. These were fed continually into the module curriculum as critical training exercises, pointing to a set of management tools and strategy layers in analysis and subsequent application. For example, students are asked to reflect on the long-term career positioning of industry clients, mainly creators or performers, in relation to the specific campaigns led by student teams. A set of key questions is examined through reflection on practice. These include: conceptual coherence between the campaign, brand and creative content; the nature of services supplied to the client; the importance of analytics combined with detailed description and conceptual analysis; the application of semiotics in branding and PR practice online. Of special importance is the combined use of data and brainstorming to increase the target market by crossing over different segments and sectors through tagging and links. This is done as a result of a combination of workshops focusing on past experience and current research, in open debates on best solutions and critical reflection. Fundamental analytical concepts are seamlessly integrated into practical examples discussed; such workshop experience is then applied to student enterprise, conducted in ICT labs. Formative feedback is thus reinforced until the final weeks of teaching, when an industry-led discussion of campaigns forms the final formative assessment event, followed by submission a week later. The module itself forms a spiral of development through reflective learning implementing Kolb's experiential principles.

Just as in industry strategy, contingency planning ('ploys', manoeuvres, adaptations) may be required: in relation to competitors, adapting to a changed environment, planning for an undesired eventuality of weakening of industry ties, adapting to new patterns in student demand – change of educational operations and paradigms, driven by increased commercialization of education, etc. It can be proposed that a clearly defined educational curriculum in creative industries involves a set of operations resembling the development of a creative industry product or service, the inimitability of which is based on experience, educational and practical, through events and processes of knowledge transfer and practical experimentation. The sustainability of such educational models depends on a number of factors.

These include: quality, conceived in such a way as to match – and safeguard – respective needs of all stakeholders (students, institution, industry, public); research and practice being fed into curricular structures, targets and aspects; industry relations policies; assets in software and hardware; operational practices; purposefully designed feedback loops, channels and communications. Many of the above characteristics define the creative sectors for which students are being primed in contemporary creative education.

Creative industry higher education: experience or application?

A highly experienced industry professional involved in industry education states that a successful manager should be 'a jack of all trades'. It is not surprising that this is the case as contemporary managers in CCI deal with convergent phenomena which they strive to commercialize. These practices are constantly changing and forcing industry professionals to adapt to an environment driven by ICT and changing governance mechanisms. Therefore, the knowledge of a fragmented creative industry needs to be fragmented to match it – this does not mean skimming the surface of various disciplines but identifying key links between them in given context, combined with the understanding of 'why' (epistemology) and 'how' (teleology) of such connections. Therefore, when a change occurs in the market, policy or technology, understanding the principle of what had happened leads to more effective adaptation to new market conditions. A new type of manager, as with the many interviewed for this book, adapts quickly to such technological changes by learning 'what it does' and demystifying the notion of a business model by examining the relations between its constituent parts. Very frequently, these parts consist of different disciplines, industries, sectors and markets spread across platforms, geographical regions and creative forms – a game that feeds of a film with added marketing through music, for instance (Adornian).

Which ever is being managed: the core, traditional, creative products, experiences or offshoots involved (e.g. merchandising, festivals, apps), the contemporary creative manager needs to be adaptive, aware of various conceptual connections across industries and able to learn new skills. The combination of incremental and deep reflective conceptual development is evidenced in contemporary managers interviewed in this research and worked with in education on all levels.

Therefore, an educational model fit for purpose consists of a strategic component, which is the broader, long term conceptualization of curricula, and the tactical component which is subject to change, employing a number of manoeuvres through various models, as postulated in business model research (Casadesus-Mansanell and Ricart 2010). As in the case of industry business models, minor changes to educational operations such as the use of ICT as module assets, lead-time-operational division between lectures and seminars, and practice policies may significantly impact on the quality of student experience and thereby, value capture – the intangible notions of 'enterprise' or 'employability'.

An established manager or practitioner in any of the contemporary, ever changing creative industries may influence the way in which new managers and creative practitioners are trained and educated. They would do so either by engaging in research or educational cooperation, where knowledge demands are fed back to students and institutions. This transformation of educational practice is negotiated through normative models and educational policies, academic legacy and value, quality procedures etc., frequently on a case by case basis, within the governance structure focusing on skills.

The educational brand in a changing environment greatly depends on the set of models supporting it. A notion of business model can be taken as an allegory or in literal terms; however, the latter requires thorough conceptual analysis, especially on legal and ethical grounds where students create profit. Knowledge units as products, training as service, practice as experience; the newly adopted market categories that define education especially in creative contexts reflect the paradigm shift in education. This leads to a seemingly unexpected, increased significance and impact of the learning contract as an ontological feature of quality.

Education is transforming into a market structure across many developed countries. The removal of state funding, a steady process that reached a qualitative turn in 2012, is morphing university students into clients and universities into suppliers of services. While this is not the case with all European education systems, it certainly is in the UK and some other developed countries.

This does indicate that new commodity models in education, especially in creative fields, may spread more widely in the future. The importance of creative education is enshrined in the UK's CIF policy, as is in the governmentally controlled CC Skills programme. Investment in creative education is seen as an investment in the future workforce of creative sectors, which amount to £76 billion per annum and a growing number of jobs in the post-industrial UK economy (NESTA, CIF, CCS,). Several respondents in arts and creative industries, some of whom interchangeably engage in education creative management and culture-production covered such client relations and ensuing pragmatism of education. The curriculum strategy of educational institutions is seen as a value-creating and value-capturing process connected to branding and publicity of courses and units aimed at the professed ends of enhancing employability, student enterprise and industry cooperation. Indeed, as observed from Chapter 2 onwards, these aims are the *meta-ends* used to achieve value capture through, in this case, client engagement, retention and processing. Students become the units of advertising and revenue generation and as clients, they request evidential return on investment measurable through industry opportunities, collaborative knowledge alliances, applications of theory, skills and knowledge, convergence of skills and disciplines and synergies between education and career aims. Transferable skills include organization, leadership, enterprise, business model development, communications, marketing and understanding evidence-driven analytics. The list is not exhaustive and though specific to creative industry education, many generic areas of practice in business utilize similar educational and training tools.

Creative industry curricula therefore aim to attain competitive advantage through professed, as well as actual blending of creative, practical, reflective and analytical skills on the one hand, and practice opportunities through industry approval, mentorship, cooperation and endorsement on the other. The arts and humanities roots of creative industry education no longer inform the key discourses which are now reflecting the paradigm shift towards value chains and networks of meaning in a pragmatic, evidence-based interactive environment inherently connected to the morphing of education into a commodity-driven model of client-driven practice. Where possible, clients and suppliers of funding include key stakeholders in pure and applied research, skills policy, knowledge transfer, aid/development and education networks. Such cooperative models may create mutually beneficial relationships between academic/educational institutions and the creative industries, generating value for both sides. Such value can be subjected to the same classification as other forms of cultural value, defined through the principles of intrinsic, utilitarian and institutional value. However, treating this as a binary dialectic would not do justice to the full complexity of the emerging cases of this class.

First, the removal of state support for the vast majority of higher education subjects has led to the further separation and divergence of interest between educational establishments and students. Public control and state support somewhat cushioned the traditionally complex relationships between students and institutions, which may arguably operate on the level of oppositional ideologies of the tensions between 'parent' and youth cultures, and charged discourses of mainstream society, subculture and counterculture. (The author is aware of the contentious nature of such propositions, and of the ideologically laden discursive foundations of many such terms and interpretations. Therefore, such discussions will be set aside and the text will resume a pragmatic tone.)

With the disappearance of state subsidies and commodification of education, new processes of *othering* actualize tensions between the clients, who, for reasons of quality still need to engage in learning contract with the institutions, which, as providers of services need to act as marketing- and operations-conscious business entities while continuing to enforce the learning contract with student-clients. An artist-respondent (T Cardew) who also works as an educator refers to the logical shift from abstract analytical skills to measurable outcomes at the point of commodification of higher education. In parallel, another respondent, a film-maker and creative educator (C Schoenfeld) pragmatically observes the best possible *means of cohering with industry practice* – for example, immersive and context-driven online distance learning techniques, emulating collaborative work in contemporary practice, while fully immersed in local production and business practice. Without need to travel, knowledge can be delivered through the transferable skill of advanced online communication, which is indeed used in creative sectors as a feature of collaborative organization. The educational context is thus conceptually rounded, enveloped within a new model that is pragmatic and user-value centred. The educational establishment navigates the process of knowledge transfer in ways which are evidence-based and subject to novel quality procedures fit for such value structures based on novel operations in a competitive knowledge market.

The emerging set of value exchange relationships do not naturally conform to traditional educational goals, and the pronounced commodity aspect requires the delivery of 'goods' and 'services' beyond knowledge, such as industry contacts and employment opportunities. The inherent inability to guarantee to every student/client the utilization of industry contacts through employment or other tangible benefits is contingent on the inherent interests of industry partners who help validate the vocational commodity of creative courses that operate in new, market conditions, as will be seen with the second part of this increasingly complex dialectic.

The inherent interests of industry partners define the second aspect to the changing, increasingly complex dialectic relationship of creative education institutions and contemporary learners. A sustainable and mutually beneficial relationship between industry and education needs to go beyond personal contacts forged by creative education professionals, which are frequently the result of educators' industry experience past or present. There are myriad reasons for this, including the fact that in an increasingly commodified education system, institutions providing knowledge need to remain as autonomous as possible from external influence, in order to continue to claim quality, impartiality, and operational control in teaching and learning, which forms part of the deepest fundaments of the value of education, as such (ontologically). Therefore, a reliance on a single provider of industry goodwill carries multiple risks. On the other hand, many aspects of industry culture embody the notion of exclusivity.

While this may not necessarily be the case in collaborative outcomes between industry and education, the risk of over-branding and over-dependence on industry relations should be countered by well-developed operational models based on skills, astute knowledge of industry structures and internal relations, and the ability to develop own empirical models for training and analysis. Such clearly formulated foundations, would clearly facilitate the development of various incubators, business modelling service labs, and own branded events. This strategic approach would make educational institutions increasingly attractive to industry partners, while safeguarding against over-dependence on a single, or discrete selection of suppliers of industry goodwill. There are varied degrees of effectiveness of forms and examples of institutional response to challenges of commodification and increased emphasis on industry relations. Industry partnerships initiatives should represent more than a mere response to an emerging challenge of commodification and the need to prove methodological relevance as an increasingly utilitarian supplier of institutionalized knowledge.

Third, the changing role of the state, policy and governance bodies, research councils and trade area policies for education. The reform of funding for higher education research, the dominant notion of impact, and the emphasis on skills and knowledge alliances with stakeholders, have resulted in an emphasis on market-driven approaches to education with an increasingly vocational approach directed towards such modification across a number of curricular structures. Creative industry related programmes are a significant test for this transition. The fourth component of a more complex dialectic between educational and student aims is the managerial discourse reflected through organizational practices in higher education within the context of fee liberalization. A *marketization* discourse permeates the sector, and a new professional workforce is being profiled from academics, administrators and academic executives (Hanlon 2004, Ouchi 1980). Its policies and strategies emerge within the continued state of flux, result of fee liberalization, and matching them is an internal imperative for those involved in negotiating industry-relations-driven programmes or programme components.

Mintzberg's metaphorical use of *perspective* can be suitable to describe the need to take steps to resonate with both internal and external environments. Several emerging, dominant stakeholder discourses take precedence on high-scale decision-making, and thus cannot be modified by practitioners alone. These emergent stakeholder discourses include: institutionalized learning contracts (in the context of emergent student-as-client '*paradigms*'); industry interest in education and recruitment filtering; policy-maker discourses of change, quality, control and targets; and an emergent marketization of institutional processes in higher education. The results, articulated in the form of curricular innovation and sustainable industry-education relations, rest on minute negotiations between these discursive drivers of the shift towards a market-driven experiential creative industry education.

Harmonizing the expectations and managing cooperation is complex between such multiple stakeholders whose respective positions of interest are as varied, fragmented and loosely aligned as those of educational administrations, students, industry partners and the funding, policy or sponsorship bodies. This results in fluctuating connections between key nodes in the networks formed by these respective parties. Alliances may be temporary or medium-term, and it is too soon to speak of strategic alliances that would prove sustainable over long periods. The main implication in this supply structure is the position of industry partners as key suppliers of labour and enterprise opportunities, source of knowledge and IP assets, and client of research and teaching institutions in more advanced models of cooperation. Creative sectors' quest for autonomy is counterbalanced with their labour interests, whereby their involvement in the filtering, refining and profiling skilled labour secures an attainment of human assets at the heart of a sector.

The *part-time*, transitory involvement of students can trigger some concerns on employee/trainee commitment within advanced placement, mentorship and practice modules. Equally, it is important that industry partners are not perceived or do not act as employers or clients – unless agreed specifically so. This has ethical, legal and experiential implications on the relationship of trust between the institution and students and has to be consequently reflected in the implementation of the learning contract.

Conclusions and implications

Notes on science, method and philosophy of creative industry strategy

The main postulate in this book was that strategy context should be understood at ontological level, what it 'is' the strategy in its particular creative form. The second postulate was that strategy is inherently creative and that creativity can only be strategic if it is to be enacted to full effect. The axiomatic foundation of these propositions is that interaction predates all media.

The methodological proposition is to explore business strategy as both art and science, situated in social contexts of control, market behaviour and key processes. Case studies and theoretical innovation support the concept of qualitative/quantitative equivalence in research and interactive business practice.

Purposive sampling of case studies and respondents reflects the permeating nature of creative industry innovation, especially in IT and media, which formulate the new ideology of business, its discourse and practice, direction of innovation, processes, research methods and the philosophy of business. The specific nature of general principles is reflected in all key cases, from quantitative and positivistic methods of production and value-adding processes to new intelligent quantitative methods in production, innovation, marketing and service networks of a *post-linear* creative industry strategy. The service-product-sales continuum is now required of creative industry organizations and thus substitutes the previous focus on product, manufacturing, marketing, and distribution of linear methods in mass-production – and mass-communication, as reflected.

The medium is now frequently part of the production circuit, and diffusion of content, ownership and control privileges leaner businesses, clusters of creative management and those large organizations capable of managing such flows of content, intersected with production and user feedback management.

It is therefore not surprising that in such emergent patterns those leading organizations invariably possess significant IT assets whether developed in house or acquired. Moreover, many businesses only marginally connected with culture and creativity now use interactive communications to add value, change image, process orders, cut cost and increase efficiency or survive in a changing market where processes and labour divisions are influenced by ICT, and new models – and associated corporate structures – compete with old ones of established markets subjected to disruptive innovation.

This shapes a different labour market and dictates policy frameworks, bur also places the vast majority of non-creative businesses under the philosophy/discourse of interactive communications and supply methods; it creates labour empowerment of IT trained staff and managers and thus infiltrates the business culture across non-creative sectors through management, marketing or supply power of ICT services from portals to telecoms.

- Mass market but also a fragmented one
- Every minute bit of user identity, consumer preferences or audience appreciation and experience can be analysed through both qualitative and quantitative means irrespective of the fact that such analytics use large numbers. The composite image is multidimensional as it reflects the emotive, multifaceted and transitory complexity of user individuality in social context of its tribes or social-cultural-links, psychological patterns and classification, as well as the *quasi-thermodynamic behaviour* of large numbers of interacting individuals.
- *Immersion* appears to relate to the physics-rooted *uncertainty principle* as the most minute types of media use amounts to observation that can impact on the system being observed (e.g. traceability of use). This is used in marketing, order processing, design, intelligence and analytics.
- Mass customization is affordable, stock control revolutionized through accurate flows, communication becomes a component of user/consumer generated design, visitor experience is improved through rating and online user commentary or in interactive media used in venues or leisure and hospitality premises.
- The product becomes the service and distribution of assets is frequently not the key to value capture. A product is treated like a marketing asset. Value is being captured through varied types of multi-custom-options blending tangible with intangible products and services and charging for experience as well as offering stepped models of loyalty based information or finance exchange. Virtual value is quantified through its qualitative contributions such as member recommendations that may trigger added free services.
- On the other hand, the principles that define a singular artefact and govern its value do apply, as is the case on the other end of the spectrum, that of the mass-customization and *infinitesimally fragmented* communication/data analysis. Returning to what the strategy context 'is', the ontology of the market, product, service, process, control etc is defined through the product/artefact itself, its perceived use value, uniqueness, perishable nature or socio-cultural, historical and intellectual significance. In such cases, interactive media and IT are most frequently a marketing or publicity enhancement of the artefact while its singular nature may not

in most cases be undermined by the multiplicity of custom, choice or product management of the new.

- A similar paradox can be found with performances which do not by definition exist otherwise than in their real specific time and place, as events, which are by definition experiential and unrepeatable, therefore allowing to render their value substantial. Having a look at music, drama, dance, or literature, none of these age old media exist in the present or material form. The text is a carrier of narrative but the narrative itself is temporal and therefore only in existence in the process of creation or therefore reproduction. Consumption, use, experience of those media is always temporal and recreated anew with each use which invariably requires decoding – reading of music from a sheet is therefore no different in principle than the laser disk reproduction of a performance by a singular artist. In this case, however, the multiplicity of copies is theoretically infinite in ICT context and both the value of such reproduced performance and the very singularity of the artist in question can be, and is undermined by the very mass-customization and infinitesimally fragmented interactive communications that greatly benefit networked businesses, market research analytics and emerging user-driven models at the fore of such innovation. It is evident that such innovation disrupts most of the established hierarchies in economic, cultural, and consumer strata, and undermines the established relationships of power, production, distribution and marketing processes, positions of stakeholders and policy makers, and the social contract in some ways.
- It would be naive to presume however, that the 'old' structures are inert or weak. The flow of new blood from companies, start-ups and ideas, innovative practices fixed in patents and other IP, goodwill, organizational know-how, and can be acquired through rapid organizational learning and adaptation on one hand, or assimilated through well managed acquisition of services, companies and human capital of skilled and entrepreneurial labour force. The negative outcome case studies are matched with cases where such acquisition of business culture, know-how, and practice did work.
- The infiltration of clan like professional structures into some of the mass-manufacture, one-to-all – push-media and creative industries led to a change of internal culture, further exacerbated by mergers and acquisitions that shed some of the key know-how assets has led to the weakening of goodwill, operations, capacity for innovation and risk-taking, leaving many such organizations oversized, inefficient, risk-averse and vulnerable. Risk aversion led to weakening of portfolios and ageing of product life-cycles, combined with a disposable short-term strategy of management pet projects. Embattled in the emergent culture of sharing and multiplicity of content links, those organizations were weakened by the previous stages of capital growth through acquisition, and actual reciprocal shrinking of assets and production-management innovation

processes. Thus a conservative approach focusing on only one key business model links its fortunes to the ageing business model, assuming seemingly that the linear growth of market share can be repeated with every incremental format innovation under the control of such a mature medium or cultural asset model. In short, those processes result in the corrosive organizational unlearning, the uncoupling of intellectual assets from their creators, weakening the internal market aspect of the organization and therefore removing it from its core context of innovative management of culture production.

- Once a multipliable product of the temporal culture media – drama, dance or music, any type of game or book, become treated as singular artefacts, the value proposition proves conclusive to the improved market potential of the product. For this, however, a long term approach works best, supported by innovation in production, with the necessary condition that the product itself is not solely treated as a commodity. This type of production is more costly, of higher risk in both market terms and socio-cultural terms and it is the principal opposite by assembly line model favoured by large, risk-averse organizations chiefly concerned with maintaining their mature competitive position.
- Some acquisitions resulted in quick organizational learning though. There are case studies where a complex structuring of mature market players and shared interest with other supply sectors leads to absorbing innovation through slowing down of disruptive change from new players. Such is the case with Netflix.[1]

Notes on politics, consequentialism and warlike manoeuvre in creative industries

Machiavelli is more relevant than in the past. Corporations resemble strict feudal pyramids of renaissance kingdoms and principalities and are as powerful on the global scale as those sociopolitical formations once were in his time in Italy. This has interesting implications on culture and creativity bearing in mind that the post-economic-bubble world, developed parts included, contains narrowing and deepening pockets of wealth where high-end innovation is captured and then disseminated in copies, hybrid firms and convergent formats through various levels and types of engagement to mass-customized audiences who believe to be partaking in interaction with one or more parts of the innovation process, in an experience that may involve perceptions of empowerment enacted through responses resembling both the democratic process and customer relations.

Concluding notes on the nature of creative industry innovation

Following the logic of Kantian conceptual modelling it can be concluded that '*Innovation is synthetic a priori*'. It is subject to cognitive processes of negotiation between various parties of users, consumers, producers, virtual navigators and policy makers. The communication with users is responsive and en masse, creating a cognitive web of responses, identities and opinions that resembles the model of social contract negotiation. Networks and services are built to elicit emotive and unconscious, spontaneous responses alongside consciously calculated decisions, user value processes, and consciously adopted user benefits. This aids both advertising and data collection management on user, audience or consumer thoughts and actions, depending on the role that a person may adopt at a given time of interactive engagement online. Interactive, by virtue of evidence shown elsewhere (Firefox Collusion app), includes the very act of browsing. The data thus collected may represent a 'high fidelity' or 'high resolution' image of manifold opinions, actions and connections across online communications, a hybrid of humans, discourses, networks and digital services, structures and stimuli.

The Kantian approach would require the understanding of innovation by creating new niches in product and/or service markets as connected to the modelling nature of mathematical thinking, that informs innovation in ICT-driven communications and media. Successes ranging from Google to Spotify cover a set of logical solutions going beyond disciplinary boundaries of natural and social science metaphors used to research and shape *by research*, the emerging digital societies and markets, models, tools and services. Tribal set analysis sits alongside classical statistics and forecasting concepts. Immersive communications continually exist between users, respondents, marketers, producers, entrepreneurs, artists, developers, media, retailers, distributors, services and increasingly intelligent software entities. This creates sets of Heisenbergian interactions which can be observed on the level of one unit, e.g. an immersive user, or on a grand scale resembling an electronic cloud, the chaotic movement of all the users and networks involved. This ability of contemporary online tools is truly novel and unique: to go from the singular (a human) to general (all users and networks), which too can be seen as singular (The internet) with all the correlations between levels and degrees of involvement, between the two ends of the analytical spectrum/continuum. Synergy and convergence can both be inferred, as the network is greater than the sum of all of its components both human and technological. This synergy is enabled through the way in which people, software, content and platforms, devices, discourses and channels are integrated through models which are referred to as convergent. There is no single convergence in this context. Benjamin analysed film as an inherently convergent form (and medium), while citing Valery in what appears like a precursor of the early twenty-first century utility models for music and other content. Therefore, the conceptual solutions were understood by theorists who would not witness an even greater complexity of the same principles they posited in the very early days of modern media. The complexity of contemporary convergent forms, formats and media is far beyond the one that characterized film or radio of their time. However, the mechanisms and logical principles behind formulating new convergent creative forms and formats remain the same. The speculative nature of the product or service, form or format, can be, and is negotiated through networked communications of multiple parties, from individual users to any number of major stakeholders. The idea that user, or creator empowerment would level the playing field appeared optimistically biased yet there are greater opportunities for entrepreneurs who do create new niches of value by building new models of communications, research or production – or a hybrid of those. In such cases, the first step of growth in influence may be knowledge and human capital rather than fixed assets; however, such assets would have to be attained to make a new model sustainable and influential, ranging from innovative entrepreneurs to emerging corporations.

Note

1 Even more so Rio Diamond, the ill-fated true innovator of portable mp3 players.

Archival and documentary data

www.agreenerfestival.com/2011/11/rhinekultur-cancelled-permanently/
www.bbc.co.uk/news/10469697
www.bonnaparte.de/tags/rheinkultur&prev=search
www.derelictlondon.com/central-london.html
http://edition.pagesuite-professional.co.uk/Launch.aspx?referral=other&pnum=3&refresh=X1e72S0wo9T0&EID=59771168-5369-4067-9906-52be7fa6798a&skip=true
https://en.wikipedia.org/wiki/Foundry_%28bar%29
www.festivalhopper.de/news/2014/05/08/rockaue-festival-rheinkulur-2015/&prev=search
http://festivalisten.de/12767-rheinkultur-2010-nachbericht&usg=ALkJrhhd0DnKsbI8NeBSSNSXpQg1xTr0Cw
http://festivalisten.de/12800-rheinkultur-vor-dem-aus&usg=ALkJrhgZbNP5OZs8PgTrW6vaevQeQm-Ojw
http://festivalisten.de/24535-rheinkultur-unruhen-und-polizeieinsatz-bei-der-mixery-raw-deluxe-stage&usg=ALkJrhjuhNlakv_qbXPf31n5YJs-8kEWHw
http://festivalisten.de/24785-rueckblick-so-wars-beim-rheinkultur-2011&usg=ALkJrhhnJb-eS72ceCtDVJy-i1jWTs5cKg
http://festivalisten.de/30961-rheinkultur-absage-fuer-2012&usg=ALkJrhhxkkpVW1SuGip6d-TTphDMwtkheA
www.foundry.tv/
www.foundry.tv/archive/
www.foundry.tv/archive/press/view/press_images/
www.foundry.tv/archive/radio/
www.konzertrocker.de/2014/05/08/rockaue-festival-will-in-bonn-in-die-fusstapfen-der-rheinkultur-steigen/&prev=search
LMU (London Metropolitan University)/UTT (University of Trinidad and Tobago) (2011), TING – *Transforming, Integrating, Engaging and Growing the Caribbean's Cultural Forms*: Helping Cultural Organizations Help Themselves (Project Notes, Unpublished)
www.metamute.org/editorial/articles/farewell-to-foundry
http://news.bbc.co.uk/1/hi/england/6665529.stm
www.pi-news.net/2011/07/bonn-eskalation-bei-musikfestival-rheinkultur/&prev=search
www.theguardian.com/lifeandstyle/2009/jun/14/pub-legendary-landlords
www.youtube.com/watch?v=R-2FTD1Oquk
www.zeit.de/news-072011/3/iptc-bdt-20110703-259-31225196xml&usg=ALkJrhig6aYW463WeX2oRmwYqkPNv-tKbA

References

Adhikari, V. K., Guo, Y., Hao, F., Varvello, M., Hilt, V., Steiner, M. and Zhang, Z. L. (2012), 'Unreeling netflix: Understanding and improving multi-cdn movie delivery', *INFOCOM, 2012 Proceedings of the IEEE*, pp. 1620–1628.

Adorno, T. W. and Bernstein, J. M. (1991) *The culture industry: Selected essays on mass culture*, London: Routledge.

Allen-Robertson, J. (2013), *Digital culture industry: A history of digital distribution*, Basingstoke: Palgrave Macmillan.

Anderson, C. (2009) *The long tail: How endless choice is creating unlimited demand*, London: Random House Business Books.

Anderson, J. (1996), 'The shifting stage of politics: New medieval and postmodern territorialities?' *Environment and Planning D: Society and Space*, 14(2): 133–153, doi: 10.1068/d140133.

Andrews, K. R. (1980), *The concept of corporate strategy*, Homewood, IL: Irwin.

Ansoff, H. I. (1988), *New corporate strategy*, New York: Wiley.

Ansoff, H. I. and McDonnell, E. (1990), *Implanting strategic management*, New York: Prentice Hall.

Armstrong, J. S. (1995), 'The devil's advocate responds to an MBA student's claim that research harms learning', *Journal of Marketing*, 59: 101–106.

Atkinson, P. and Hammersley, M. (1994), 'Ethnography and participant observation', *Handbook of Qualitative Research*, 1(23): 248–261.

Axelrod, R. and Cohen, M. (1999), *Harnessing complexity: Organizational implications of a scientific frontier*, New York: Free Press.

Bakir, A. and Bakir, V. (2006), 'Unpacking complexity, pinning down the "elusiveness" of strategy: A grounded theory study in leisure and cultural organizations', *Qualitative Research in Organizations and Management: An International Journal*, 1(3): 152–172.

Balogun, J., Jarzabkowski, P. and Seidl, D. (2007), 'Strategizing activity and practice', in Ambrosini, V. and Jenkins, M. (eds) *Advanced strategic management*, Basingstoke: Palgrave, 196–214.

Barney, J. (2001), 'The resource based view of a firm: Ten years after 1991', *Journal of Management*, 17(1): 99–120.

Barry, D. and Elmes, M. (1997), 'Strategy retold: Toward a narrative view of strategic discourse', *Academy of Management Review*, 22(2): 429–452.

Benjamin, W. (2008), *The work of art in the age of mechanical reproduction*, London: Penguin.

Bennett, A. (2001), *Cultures of popular music*, Buckingham: Open University Press.

Berniker, E. and McNabb, D. E. (2006), 'Dialectical inquiry: A structured qualitative research method', *Qualitative Report*, 11(4): 643–664, available at: www.nova.edu/ssss/QR/QR11-4/berniker.pdf (accessed 29 July 2008).

Bilton, C. (2007), *Management and creativity: From creative industries to creative management*, London: Blackwell Publishing.

Bilton, C. (2009), 'Relocating creativity in advertising: From aesthetic specialisation to strategic integration', in Pratt, A. C. and Jeffcutt, P. (eds), *Creativity, innovation and the cultural economy*, London: Routledge, 21–40.

Blakley, J. (2010), 'Lessons from fashion's free culture', TED Talk, available at: www.ted.com/talks/johanna_blakley_lessons_from_fashion_s_free_culture?language=en (accessed 19 November 2015).

Blakley, J. and Center, N. L. (2001), 'Entertainment goes global: Mass culture in a transforming world', University of Southern California at Annenburg, Norman Lear Center, Los Angeles, available at: http://learcenter.org/pdf/EntGlobal.pdf (accessed 5 June 2015).

Bloch, M. (2012), *Anthropology and the cognitive challenge*, Cambridge: Cambridge University Press.

Booth, C. (2002), 'The problems and possibilities of reflexivity in strategy', *Electronic Journal of Radical Organization Theory*, 8(1), available at: www.mngt.waikato.ac.nz/Research/ejrot/Vol. 8_1/Vol. 8_1articles/booth.asp.

Bourdieu, P. (1986), 'The forms of capital', repr. in Szeman, I. and Kaposy, T. (2010), *Cultural theory: An anthology*, New York: John Wiley and Sons, 81–93.

Bower, J. L. (2008), 'The teaching of strategy: From general manager to analyst and back again', *Journal of Management Inquiry*, 17(4): 269–275.

Bowman, E. H. and Hurry, D. (1993), 'Strategy through the open lens: An integrated view of resources investments and the incremental-choice process', *Academy of Management Review*, 18(4): 760–782.

Bowman, E. H., Singh, H. and Thomas, H. (2002), 'The domain of strategic management: History and evolution', in Pettigrew, A., Thomas, H. and Whittington R. (eds), *The handbook of strategy and management*, London: Sage, 31–54.

Braet, O., Spek, S. and Pauwels, C. (2013), 'Crowdfunding the movies: A business analysis of crowdfinanced moviemaking in small geographical markets', *Journal of Media Business Studies*, 10(1): 1–23, doi: 10.1080/16522354.2013.11073557.

Campbell, A. and Alexander, M. (1997), 'What's wrong with strategy?' *Harvard Business Review*, November–December: 42–51.

Casadesus-Masanell, R. and Ricart, J. E. (2010), 'From strategy to business models and onto tactics', *Long Range Planning*, 43(2–3): 195–215, doi: 10.1016/j.lrp. 2010.01.004.

Chaffee, E. (1985), 'Three models of strategy', *Academy of Management Review*, 10: 89–98.

Chandler, A. D. (1962), *Strategy and structure: Chapters in the history of the american industrial enterprise*, Cambridge, MA: MIT Press.

Chia, R. and Mackay, B. (2007), 'Post-processual challenges for the emerging strategy-as-practice perspective: Discovering strategy in the logic of practice', *Human Relations*, 60: 217–242.

Christensen, C. M. (2006), 'The ongoing process of building a theory of disruption', *Journal of Product Innovation Management*, 23(1): 39–55, doi: 10.1111/j.1540-5885.2005.00180.x.

Christensen, C. M. and Overdorf, M. (2000), 'Meeting the challenge of disruptive change', *Harvard Business Review*, 78(2): 66–77.

Christensen, C. M., Baumann, H., Ruggles, R. and Sadtler, T. M. (2006), 'Disruptive innovation for social change', *Harvard Business Review*, 84(12): 94.

Cohen, M. D., March, J. G. and Olsen, J. P. (1972), 'A garbage can model of organizational choice', *Administrative Science Quarterly*, 17: 1–25.

Cook, C. I. (2014), 'Netflix: A stepping stone in the evolution of television', project submitted for completion of MA in Journalism, University of South Florida St. Petersburg, August 2014, available at: http://dspace.nelson.usf.edu/xmlui/handle/10806/11681 (accessed 5 June 2015).

Cyert, R. M. and March, J. G. (1963), *A behavioral theory of the firm*, Englewood Cliffs, NJ: Prentice-Hall.

Daly, G. (2002), *Cannae: The experience of battle in the Second Punic War*, London: Routledge.

D'Aveni, R. A. (1994), *Hyper-competition*, New York: The Free Press.

de Certeau, M. (1984), *The practice of everyday life*. Berkeley: University of California Press.

Dillon, E. and Kallberg, J. (2002), *Medieval music-making and the Roman de Fauvel*, Cambridge: Cambridge University Press.

Dilthey, W. (1976), *Selected writings*, Cambridge: Cambridge University Press.

Doyle, G. (2013), *Understanding media economics*, 2nd edn, London: SAGE Publications.

Du Gay, P. (ed.) (1997), *Production of culture/cultures of production*, Thousand Oaks, CA: Sage in association with the Open University.

Eco, U. (1995), *Faith in fakes: Travels in hyperreality*, New York: Random House.

Eisenhardt, K. M. and Brown, S. L. (1999), 'Patching: Restitching business portfolios in dynamic markets', *Harvard Business Review*, 77: 72–82.

Eisenhardt, K. M. and Martin, J. A. (2000), 'Dynamic capabilities: What are they?' *Strategic Management Journal*, 21: 1105–1121.

Eisenhardt, K. M. and Sull, D. (2001), 'Strategy as simple rules', *Harvard Business Review*, 79: 106–119.

Epstein, S. A. (1991), *Wage labor and guilds in medieval Europe*, Durham, NC: University of North Carolina Press.

Epstein, S. R. (1998), 'Craft guilds, apprenticeship, and technological change in preindustrial Europe', *Journal of Economic History*, 58(03), 684–713, doi: 10.1017/s0022050700021124.

Epstein, S. R. (2002), *Freedom and growth: The rise of states and markets in Europe, 1300–1750*, London: Routledge.

Ezzamel, M. and Willmott, H. (2008), 'Strategy as discourse in a global retailer: A supplement to rationalist and interpretive accounts', *Organization Studies*, 29(2): 191–217.

Farr, J. R. (2000), *Artisans in Europe, 1300–1914*, Cambridge: Cambridge University Press.

Foals (2015), 'Mountain at my gates', music video, Foals YouTube channel, available at: www.youtube.com/watch?v=l_EIE5f2t6M&feature=youtu.be&app=desktop\ (accessed 30 July 2015] from: www.digitalmusicnews.com/permalink/2014/04/03/streamingstatements Accessed 5 June 2015).

Franklin, B. (2005), *Gonzo journalism*, doi: 10.4135/9781446215821.n80.

Fukuyama, F. (1989), 'Have we reached the end of history?' RAND Paper.

Gadamer, H. G. (1975), *Truth and method*, New York: Seabury.

Gadamer, H. G. (1989), *Truth and method*, 2nd edn, London: Sheed and Ward.

Gaddis, J. L. (2011), 'War, peace, and everything: Thoughts on Tolstoy', *Cliodynamics*, 2(1).

Garnham, N. (2005), 'From cultural to creative industries: An analysis of the implications of the "creative industries" approach to arts and media policy making in the United Kingdom', *International Journal of Cultural Policy*, 11(1): 15–29, doi: 10.1080/10286630500067606.

Geanellos, R. (2000), 'Exploring Ricoeur's hermeneutic theory of interpretation as a method of analysing research texts', *Nursing Inquiry*, 7: 112–119.

Geertz, C. (2000), *Local knowledge: Further essays in interpretive anthropology*, New York: Basic Books.

Gelder, K. and Thornton, S. (eds) (1997) *The subcultures reader*, London: Sage Publications.

Ghemawat, P. (1991), *Commitment: The dynamic of strategy*, New York: Free Press.

Gibson, L. (2008), 'In defence of instrumentality', *Cultural Trends*, 17(4): 247–257, doi: 10.1080/09548960802615380.

Gilbert, C., Alberti, L. B., Spencer, J. R., da Vinci, L. and McMahon, P. A. (1957), 'On painting', *Journal of Aesthetics and Art Criticism*, 15(4), doi: 10.2307/427164.

Goldsworthy, A. (2007), *Cannae: Hannibal's greatest victory*, London: Phoenix.

Goodwin, A. and Frith, S. (eds) (1990), *On record: Rock, pop, and the written word*, New York: Pantheon Books.

Graham, G. and Hardaker, G. (2000), Supply-chain management across the Internet. *International Journal of Physical Distribution and Logistics Management*, 30(3/4): 286–295.

Graham, G., Burnes, B., Lewis, G. J. and Langer, J. (2004), The transformation of the music industry supply chain: A major label perspective, *International Journal of Operations and Production Management*, 24(11): 1087–1103.

Grant, R. M. (1991), 'The resource-based theory of competitive advantage: Implications for strategy formulations', *California Management Review*, Spring: 119–135.

Grant, R. M. (1996), 'Toward a knowledge-based theory of the firm', *Strategic Management Journal*, 17: 109–122.

Grant, R. M. (2008), *Contemporary strategy analysis*, 6th edn, Maden, MA: Blackwell.

Hall, S. (1980a), *Race, articulation, and societies structured in dominance*, repr. in Baker, A. A. (ed.) (1996) *Black British cultural studies: A reader*, Chicago: University of Chicago Press, 16–60.

Hall, S. (1980b), 'Encoding/decoding', in Hall, S., Hobson, D., Lowe, A. and Willis, P. (eds) *Culture, media, language: Working papers in cultural studies, 1972–79*, London: Routledge.

Hall, S., Morley, D. and Chen, K. H. (1996), *Stuart Hall: Critical dialogues in cultural studies*, London: Routledge.

Hambrick, D. C. (2004), 'The disintegration of strategic management: It's time to consolidate our gains', *Strategic Organization*, 2(1): 91–98.

Hanlon, G. (2004), 'Institutional forms and organizational structures: Homology, trust and reputational capital in professional service firms', *Organization*, 11(2): 187–210, doi: 10.1177/1350508404041613.

Harris, R. J. J. and Sanborn, F. W. (2013), *A cognitive psychology of mass communication*, 5th edn, New York: Taylor and Francis.

Hartley, J. (2004). 'The "value chain of meaning" and the new economy', *International Journal of Cultural Studies*, 7(1): 129–141.

Hax, A. C. and Majluf, N. (1988), *The strategy concept and process: A pragmatic approach*, Englewood Cliffs, NJ: Prentice-Hall.

Heilman, K. M. (2005), *Creativity and the brain*, New York: Psychology Press.

Heisenberg, W. (1971), *Physics and beyond: Encounters and conversations* [*Der Teil und das Ganze*], trans. Pomerans, A. J., London: Allen and Unwin.

Heracleous, L. and Barrett, M. (2001), 'Organizational change as discourse: Communicative actions and deep structures in the context of information technology implementation', *Academy of Management Journal*, 44: 755–778.

Hewison, R. (2006), *What is the point of investing in cultural leadership, if cultural institutions remain unchanged?* London: DEMOS.

Hewison, R. and Holden, J. (2004), *The right to art: Making aspirations reality*, London: DEMOS.

Hirsch, P. M., Michaels, S. and Friedman, R. (1987), 'Dirty hands versus clean models: Is sociology in danger of being seduced by economics?' *Theory and Society*, 16(3): 317–336.

Holden, J. (2006), *Cultural value and the crisis of legitimacy: Why culture needs a democratic mandate*, London: Demos.

Holmes, G. (1995), *Art and politics in Renaissance Italy*, British Academy Lecture, May.

Holsinger, B. W. (2001), *Music, body, and desire in medieval culture: Hildegard of Bingen to Chaucer*, Stanford: Stanford University Press.

Hurst, D. K., Rush, J. C. and White, R. E. (1989), 'Top management teams and organizational renewal', *Strategic Management Journal*, 10(S1): 87–105.

Iivari, J. (2007), 'A paradigmatic analysis of information systems as a design science', *Scandinavian Journal of Information Systems*, 19(2): 5.

Imaz, M. and Benyon, D. (2007), *Designing with blends: Conceptual foundations of human-computer interaction and software engineering methods*, Cambridge, MA: MIT Press.

Jarzabkowski, P. and Fenton, E. (2006), 'Strategizing and organizing in pluralistic contexts', *Long Range Planning*, 39(6): 631–648.

Jarzabkowski, P. and Whittington, R. (2008a), 'Directions for a troubled discipline: Strategy research, teaching, and practice – Introduction to the dialogue', *Journal of Management Inquiry*, 17(4): 266–268.

Jarzabkowski, P. and Whittington, R. (2008b), 'A strategy-as-practice approach to strategy research and education', *Journal of Management Inquiry*, 17(4): 282–286.

Jarzabkowski, P. and Wilson, D. C. (2006), 'Actionable strategy knowledge: A practice perspective', *European Management Journal*, 24(5): 348–367.

Jenkins, H. (2006), *Convergence culture: Where old and new media collide*, New York: New York University Press.

Johnson, G., Scholes, K. and Whittington, R. (2008), *Exploring corporate strategy*, 8th edn, London: Prentice Hall.

Jones, S. G. (ed.) (1998), *Doing internet research: Critical issues and methods for examining the Net*, 4th edn, Thousand Oaks, CA: Sage Publications, Inc.

Jorgensen, D. L. (1989), *Participant observation*, New York: John Wiley and Sons.

Kant, I. and Meiklejohn, J. M. D. (2007), *The critique of pure reason*, El Paso, TX: El Paso Norte Press.

Kaplan, R. S. and Norton, D. P. (1993), 'Putting the balanced scorecard to work', *Harvard Business Review*, September–October: 134–147.

Kay, J. (1995), *Foundations of competitive success*, Oxford: Oxford University Press.

Kellner, D. (1997) 'Critical theory and cultural studies: The missed articulation', in McGuigan, J. (ed.) *Cultural methodologies*, London: Sage, 12–41.

Kelly, S. and Allison, M. A. (1999), *The complexity advantage*, New York: McGraw Hill

Kieser, A. (1989), 'Organizational, institutional, and societal evolution: Medieval craft guilds and the genesis of formal organizations', *Administrative Science Quarterly*, 34(4), doi: 10.2307/2393566.

Knights, D. and Morgan, D. (1991), 'Strategic discourse and subjectivity: Towards a critical analysis of corporate strategy in organizations', *Organization Studies*, 12(2): 251–273.

Knights, D. and Morgan, G. (1995), 'Strategy under the microscope: Strategic management and it in financial services', *Journal of Management Studies*, 32(2): 191–214.

Kononov, É. Y. and Koshelev, K. N. (1975), 'Inverse population of levels of multiply charged ions', *Soviet Journal of Quantum Electronics*, 4(11): 1340.

Krackhardt, D. and Hanson, J. R. (1993), 'Informal networks', *Harvard Business Review*, 71(4): 104–111.

Krackhardt, D. and Stern, R. N. (1988), 'Informal networks and organizational crises: An experimental simulation', *Social Psychology Quarterly*, 123–140.

Kreiner, K. and Schultz, M. (1993), 'Informal collaboration in R & D: The formation of networks across organizations', *Organization Studies*, 14(2): 189–209.

Kuhn, T. S. (1962), *The structure of scientific revolutions*, Chicago: University of Chicago Press.

Kuhn, T. S. and Hacking, I. (2012), *The structure of scientific revolutions: 50th anniversary edition*, Chicago: University of Chicago Press.

Langdridge, D. (2004), 'The hermeneutic phenomenology of Paul Ricoeur', *Existential Analysis*, 15(2): 243–255.

Lengnick-Hall, C. and Wolff, J. A. (1999), 'Similarities and contradictions in the core logic of three strategy research streams', *Strategic Management Journal*, 20: 1109–1132.

Leonard, A. (2013), 'How Netflix is turning viewers into puppets', *Salon*, available at: www.salon.com/2013/02/01/how_netflix_is_turning_viewers_into_puppets/ (accessed 6 May 2015).

Leppert, R. and McClary, S. (eds) (1989), *Music and society: The politics of composition, performance and reception*, New York: Cambridge University Press.

Lessig, L. (2007), 'The laws that choke creativity', available at: www.ted.com/talks/larry_lessig_says_the_law_is_strangling_creativity?language=en (accessed 5 June 2015).

Levy, D. L., Alvesson, M. and Willmott, H. (2003), 'Critical approaches to strategic management', in Alvesson, M. and Willmott, H. (eds) *Studying management critically*, London: SAGE, 92–110, doi: 10.4135/9781446220030.n5.

Lewis, M. W. and Kelemen, M. L. (2002), 'Multi-paradigm inquiry: Exploring organizational pluralism and paradox', *Human Relations*, 55(2): 251–275.

Lindblom, C. E. (1959), 'The science of muddling through', *Public Administration Review*, 19: 79–88.

Lyotard, J. F. (1984), *The postmodern condition: A report on knowledge*, Chicago: University of Minnesota Press.

MacCrimmon, K. R. (1993), 'Do firm strategies exist?' *Strategic Management Journal*, 14: 113–130.

Maffesoli, M. (1996), *The time of the tribes*, London: Sage Publications.

Mahoney, J. and McGahan, A. (2007), 'The field of strategic management within the evolving science of strategic organization', *Strategic Organization*, 5(1): 79–99.

Malhotra, Y. (1997), 'Knowledge management in inquiring organizations', *Proceedings of the 3rd Americas Conference on Information Systems* (Philosophy of Information Systems Mini-track), Indianapolis, 15–17 August: 293–295.

Malhotra, Y. (ed.) (2000), *Knowledge management and virtual organizations*, Hershey, PA: Idea Group Publishing.

March, J. G. and Olsen, J. P. (1976), *Ambiguity and choice in organizations*, Bergen: Universitetsforlaget Bergen.

Markides, C. (1997), 'Strategic innovation', *Sloan Management Review*, 38: 9–24.

Markides, C. C. (2000), *All the right moves: A guide to crafting breakthrough strategy*, Boston: Harvard Business School Press.

Markides, C. (2006), 'Disruptive innovation: In need of better theory', *Journal of Product Innovation Management*, 23(1): 19–25, doi: 10.1111/j.1540-5885.2005.00177.x.

Masters, R. D. (1996), *Machiavelli, Leonardo, and the science of power*, Notre Dame: University of Notre Dame Press.

McClellan, A. (1996), 'Watteau's dealer: Gersaint and the marketing of art in eighteenth-century Paris', *Art Bulletin*, 78(3), doi: 10.2307/3046194.

McMaster, M. (1996), 'Foresight: Exploring the structure of the future', *Long Range Planning*, 29(2): 149–155.

MIDEM (2013) 'Panel: How the Music Industry Manages Innovation – Midem Visionary Monday 2013'. Available from: https://www.youtube.com/watch?v=Hh3Ks4K xvtk> (accessed 5 June 2015).

Miller, C. C. and Cardinal, L. B. (1994), 'Strategic planning and firm performance: A synthesis of more than two decades of research', *Academy of Management Journal*, 37: 1649–1665.

Miller, K. D. and Waller, H. G. (2003), 'Scenarios, real options and integrated risk management', *Long Range Planning*, 36: 93–107.

Mintzberg, H. (1987), 'The strategy concept 1: Five Ps for strategy', *California Management Review*, 30(1): 11–24.

Mintzberg, H. (1989), *Mintzberg on management: Inside our strange world of organizations*, New York: Free Press.

Mintzberg, H. (1994), 'Rethinking strategic planning, Part I: Pitfalls and fallacies', *Long Range Planning*, 27(3): 12–21.

Mintzberg, H. and Waters, J. (1985), 'Of strategies, deliberate and emergent', *Strategic Management Journal*, 6: 257–272, doi: 10.1002/smj.4250060306.

Mintzberg, H., Lampel, J., Quinn, J. and Ghoshal, S. (2003), *The strategy process*, 4th edn, London: Pearson Education.

Misra, B. and Sudarshan, E. C. G. (1977) 'The Zeno's paradox in quantum theory', *Journal of Mathematical Physics*, 18: 756–763.

Mok, D., Wellman, B. and Carrasco, J. (2010), 'Does distance matter in the age of the Internet?' *Urban Studies*, 47(13): 2747–2783.

Mollick, E. (2014), 'The Dynamics of crowdfunding: An exploratory study', *Journal of Business Venturing*, 29(1): 1–16, doi: 10.1016/j.jbusvent.2013.06.005.

Montgomery, L. (2010), *China's creative industries: Copyright, social network markets and the business of culture in a digital age*, Cheltenham: Edward Elgar Publishing.

Moorman, C. and Miner, A. S. (1998), 'Organizational improvisation and organizational Memory', *Academy of Management Review*, 23(4): 698–723.

Moser, K., Muller, M. and Piller, F. T. (2006), 'Transforming mass customisation from a marketing instrument to a sustainable business model at Adidas', *International Journal of Mass Customisation*, 1(4): 463–479.

Muecke, F. (2007), 'Hannibal at the "Fields of Fire": A "wasteful excursion"? (Silius Italicus, Punica 12, 113–157)', *Materiali e discussioni per l'analisi dei testi classici*, 58: 73–91.

Müller-Prothmann, T. (2006), 'Knowledge communities, communities of practice and knowledge networks', in Cloakes, E. and Clark, S. (eds) *Encyclopedia of Communities of Practice in Information and Knowledge Management*, Hershey, PA: Information Science Reference, 264–271, doi: 10.4018/978-1-59140-556-6.ch046.

Mulvenna, C. M. (2007), 'Synaesthesia, the arts and creativity: A neurological connection', *Frontiers of Neurology and Neuroscience*, 22: 206–222, doi: 10.1159/000102882.

Mumby, D. K. and Stohl, C. (1991), 'Power and discourse in *Organization Studies*: Absence and the dialectic of control', *Discourse and Society*, 2(3): 313–332, doi: 10.1177/0957926591002003004.

Munro, R. (1995), 'Managing by ambiguity: An archaeology of the social in the absence of management accounting', *Critical Perspectives on Accounting*, 6(5): 433–482.

Murray, J. A., Markides, C. and Galavan, R. (2008), *Strategy, Innovation, and Change: Challenges for Management*, Oxford: Oxford University Press.

Music Week (2015), 'David Cameron applauds UK's "world-leading music industry"', *Music Week*, 3 June, available at: www.musicweek.com/news/read/david-cameron-applauds-uk-s-world-leading-music-industry/054948 (accessed 5 June 2015).

Mytelka, L. and Smith, K. (2001), 'Innovation theory and innovation policy, bridging the gap', paper presented at the Danish Research Unit for Industrial Dynamics Conference, Aalborg.

Nahapiet, J. and Ghoshal, S. (1998), 'Social capital, intellectual capital and the organizational advantage', *Academy of Management Review*, 23(2): 242–266.

Nakamoto, S. (2008), 'Bitcoin: A peer-to-peer electronic cash system', *Cryptography Mailing List*, metzdowd.com.

Negus, K. (1993), 'Plugging and programming: pop radio and record promotion in Britain and the United States', *Popular Music*, 12(1): 57–68.

Negus, K. (1999), *Music genres and corporate cultures*, London: Routledge.

Nemeth, C., Brown, K. and Rogers, J. (2001), 'Devil's advocate versus authentic dissent: Stimulating quantity and quality', *European Journal of Social Psychology*, 31(6): 707–720.

Neumann, E. (1992), *Neumann: The essays of Erich Neumann*, vol. 1: *Art and the creative unconscious*, transl. Manheim, R., 2nd edn, Princeton: Princeton University Press.

Nixon, N. W. and Blakley, J. (2012), 'Fashion thinking: Towards an actionable methodology', *Fashion Practice*, 4(2): 153–175.

Norris, C. (ed.) (1989), *Music and the politics of culture*, London: Lawrence & Wishart.

Obermaier, R. and Hofmann, J. (2012), 'Cost efficient mass customisation with a web-based manufacturing execution system', *International Journal of Mass Customisation*, 4(3–4): 195–207.

O'Brien, F. A. and Dyson, R. G. (2007), *Supporting strategy: Frameworks, methods and models*, Chichester: John Wiley and Sons.

Osterwalder, A. and Pigneur, Y. (2013), *Business model generation: A handbook for visionaries, game changers, and challengers*, New York: Wiley.

Ouchi, W. G. (1980), 'Markets, bureaucracies, and clans', *Administrative Science Quarterly*, 25(1), doi: 10.2307/2392231.

Overman, E. S. (1996), 'The new science of management: Chaos and quantum theory and method', *Journal of Public Administration Research and Theory*, 6(1): 75–89, doi: 10.1093/oxfordjournals.jpart.a024304.

Oxford Media Convention (2009) 'Parallel Panel 3: Whose responsibility? The role of ISPs in policing the net', www.ippr.org/files/uploadedFiles/events/OMC_09_programme.pdf?noredirect=1.

Palmer, R. E. (1969), *Hermeneutics: Interpretation theory in Schleiermacher, Dilthey, Heidegger, and Gadamer*, Evanston, IL: Northwestern University Press.

Partington, D. (2000), 'Building grounded theories of management action', *British Journal of Management*, 11(2): 91–102.

Pettigrew, A. (1992), 'On studying managerial elites', *Strategic Management Journal*, 13: 163–182.

Pine, B. J. and Gilmore, J. H. (1999), *The experience economy: Work is theatre and every business a stage*, Boston, MA: Harvard Business Press.

Porter, M. E. (1985), *Competitive advantage: Creating and sustaining superior performance*, New York: Free Press.

Porter, M. E. (1991), 'Towards a dynamic theory of strategy', *Strategic Management Journal*, 12: 95–117.

Pounds, N. J. G. (2014), *An economic history of medieval Europe*, London: Routledge.

Prahalad, C. K. and Hamel, G. (1990), 'The core competence of the organization', *Harvard Business Review*, 68: 79–91.

Prahalad, C. K. and Hamel, G. (1994), 'Strategy as a field of study: Why search for a new paradigm?' *Strategic Management Journal*, 15: 5–16.

Prasad, A. (2002), 'The contest over meaning: Hermeneutics as an interpretive methodology for understanding texts', *Organizational Research Methods*, 5(1): 12–33.

Prasad, A. and Prasad, P. (2002), 'The coming of age of interpretive organizational research', *Organizational Research Methods*, 5(1): 4–11.

Pratt, A. C. and Jeffcutt, P. (eds) (2009), *Creativity, innovation and the cultural economy*, London: Routledge.

Priem, R. L. and Butler, J. E. (2001), 'Is the resource-based "view" a useful perspective for strategic management research?' *Academy of Management Review*, 26(1): 22–40.

Quinn, J. B. (1981), 'Formulating strategy one step at a time', *Journal of Business Strategy*, 1(3): 42–63.

Rayna, T., Striukova, L. and Darlington, J. (2014), 'Open innovation, co-creation and mass customisation: What role for 3D printing platforms?' in Proceedings of the 7th World Conference on Mass Customization, Personalization, and Co-Creation (MCPC 2014), Aalborg, Denmark, 4–7 February, Springer International Publishing, 425–435.

Richardson, G. (2001), 'A tale of two theories: Monopolies and craft guilds in medieval England and modern imagination', *Journal of the History of Economic Thought*, 23(02): 217–242, doi: 10.1080/10427710120049237.

Ricoeur, P. (1981), *Hermeneutics and the human sciences: Essays on language, action and interpretation*, ed. J. B. Thompson, Cambridge: Cambridge University Press.

Ricoeur, P. (1990), 'Hermeneutics and the critique of ideology', in Ormiston, G. L. and Schrift, A. D. (eds), *The hermeneutic tradition*, Albany, NY: Suny Press, 298–334.

Ringland, G. (1998), *Scenario planning: Managing for the future*, New York: Wiley and Sons.

Robertson, A. (2012), 'How the art of "Angry Birds Star Wars" blended two pop-culture juggernauts', *The Verge*, 15 November, available at: www.theverge.com/2012/11/15/3649162/angry-birds-star-wars-art-blending-pop-culture-juggernauts (accessed 5 June 2015).

Schleiermacher, F. D. E. (1985), 'Selections from hermeneutics: The handwritten manuscripts of F. D. E. Schleiermacher', in Mueller-Vollmer, K. (ed.), *The hermeneutic reader*, New York: Continuum, 73–97.

Schön, D. (1983), *The reflective practitioner: How professionals think in action*, London: Temple Smith.

Schwandt, T. A. (1994), 'Constructivist, interpretivist approaches in human inquiry', in Denzin, N. K. and Lincoln, Y. S. (eds), *Handbook of qualitative research*, Thousand Oaks, CA: Sage, 118–138.

Schwartz, P. (1991), *The art of the long view*, New York: Doubleday.

Shaw, G. and Williams, A. (1998) 'Entrepreneurship, small business culture and tourism development', in Ioannides, D. and Debbage, K. (eds) *The economic geography of the tourist industry: A supply-side analysis*, London: Routledge, 235–255

Shneiderman, B. (2003), *Leonardo's laptop: Human needs and the new computing technologies*, Cambridge, MA: MIT Press.

Simon, H. A. (1960), *The new science of management decision*, New York: Harper and Row.

Skemp, R. R. (1976), 'Relational understanding and instrumental understanding', *Mathematics Teaching*, 77: 20–26.

Smythe, D. W. (1981), 'On the audience commodity and its work', *Media and Cultural Studies: Keyworks*, 230–256.

Sousa, J. P. (1906), 'The menace of mechanical music', *Appleton's Magazine*, 8(3): 278–284.

Stacey, R. D. (1992), *Managing the unknowable: Strategic boundaries between order and chaos in organizations*, San Francisco: Jossey-Bass.

Stacey, R. D. (1996), *Complexity and creativity in organizations*, San Francisco: Berrett-Koehler.

Stacey, R. D. (1996), *Strategic management and organizational dynamics*, 2nd edn, London, Pitman.

Stacey, R. D. (2007), *Strategic management and organizational dynamics*, 5th edn, Harlow: Prentice Hall.

Stacey, R. D. (2013), *The chaos frontier: Creative strategic control for business*, New York: Butterworth-Heinemann.

Staff, M. (2012), 'Angry Birds Star Wars interview with Rovio Entertainment's Ville Heijari', *Modojo*, available at: www.modojo.com/features/angry_birds_star_wars_interview_with_rovio_entertainments_ville_heijari (accessed 6 May 2015).

Starkey, K. and Madan, P. (2001), 'Bridging the relevance gap: Aligning stakeholders in the future of management research', *British Journal of Management*, 12(S1): 3–26.

Sternberg, R. J. (1981), 'The evolution of theories of intelligence', *Intelligence*, 5(3): 209–230, doi: 10.1016/s0160-2896(81)80009-8.

Sternberg, R. J. (1985), *Beyond IQ: A triarchic theory of human intelligence*, New York: Cambridge University Press.

Sternberg, R. J. (1997), 'The concept of intelligence and its role in lifelong learning and success', *American Psychologist*, 52(10): 1030.

Sternberg, R. J. (2003), 'WICS as a model of giftedness', *High Ability Studies*, 14(2): 109–137.

Stinger, C. L. (1998), *The Renaissance in Rome*, Bloomington: Indiana University Press.

Subotnik, R. F. and Jarvin, L. (2005), 'Beyond expertise', in Sternberg, R. J. and Davidson, J. E. (eds) *Conceptions of giftedness*, 2nd edn, Cambridge: Cambridge University Press, 343–357.

Swyngedouw, E. (1992), 'The Mammon quest – "Glocalisation", interspatial competition and the monetary order: The construction of new scales', in Dunford, M. and Kafkalis, G. (eds), *Cities and regions in the New Europe: The global-local interplay and spatial development strategies*, London: Belhaven Press, 39–68.

Teece, D. J., Pisano, G. and Shuen, A. (1997), 'Dynamic capabilities and strategic management', *Strategic Management Journal*, 18: 509–533.

Thornton, S. (1995), *Club cultures: Music, media and subcultural capital*, London: Polity.

Todorovic, M. (1999), *Love at first site: Music marketing on the internet, legal issues and the on-line community*, Master of Arts dissertation, Buckinghamshire Chilterns University College (unpublished).

Todorovic, M. (2003), *The underground music scene in Belgrade, Serbia: a multidisciplinary study*, Doctoral dissertation, Brunel University, available at: http://bura.brunel.ac.uk/handle/2438/5905.

Torenvlied, R. and Velner, G. (1998), 'Informal networks and resistance to organizational change: The introduction of quality standards in a transport company', *Computational and Mathematical Organization Theory*, 4(2): 165–188.

Tsoukas, H. (1998), 'The word and the world: A critique of representationalism in management research', *International Journal of Public Administration*, 21(5): 781–817.

Tsoukas, H. and Knudsen, C. (2002), 'The conduct of strategy research', in Pettigrew, A., Thomas, H. and Whittington, R. (eds), *The handbook of strategy and management*, London: Sage, 411–435.

Turchin, P. (2008), 'Arise "cliodynamics"', *Nature*, 454(7200): 34–35, doi: 10.1038/454034a.

Turchin, P. (2011), 'Toward cliodynamics: An analytical, predictive science of history', *Cliodynamics*, 2.

Turchin, P. (2014), 'Cultural evolution and cliodynamics', *Cliodynamics: The Journal of Quantitative History and Cultural Evolution*, 5(1).

Van der Heijden, K. (1996), *Scenarios: The art of strategic conversation*, Hoboken, NJ: Wiley and Sons.

Venkatraman, N. and Subramaniam, M. (2001), 'Theorizing the future of strategy: Questions for shaping strategy research in the knowledge economy', in Pettigrew, A., Thomas, H. and Whittington, R. (eds), *The handbook of strategy and management*, London: Sage, 461–474.

Volberda, H. W. and Elfring, T. (2001), *Rethinking strategy*, London: Sage.

Wallets, A. (2015), 'Netflix ratings revealed: New data sheds light on original series' audience levels', *Variety*, 24 April, available at: http://variety.com/2015/digital/news/netflix-originals-viewer-data-1201480234/ (accessed 5 July 2015).

Wang, Y. (2007), *Software engineering foundations: A software science perspective*, London: Auerbach.

Weber, M. (1968), *Economy and society: An outline of interpretive sociology*, ed. Roth, G. and Wittich, C., New York: Bedminster Press.

Wegman, R. C. (1995), 'Sense and sensibility in late-medieval music: Thoughts on aesthetics and "authenticity"', *Early Music*, 23(2): 298–314, doi: 10.1093/earlyj/xxiii.2.298.

Weick, K. E. (2002), 'Puzzles in organizational learning: An exercise in disciplined imagination', *British Journal of Management*, 13(2): 7–15.

Wernerfelt, B. (1984), 'A resource-based view of the firm', *Strategic Management Journal*, 5(2): 171–180.

West, G. B. (2011), 'Can there be a quantitative theory for the history of life and society?', *Cliodynamics*, 2(1).

Whittington, R. (2001), *What is strategy, and does it matter?* London: Cengage Learning.

Whittington, R. (2003), 'The work of strategizing and organizing: For a practice perspective', *Strategic Organization*, 1(1): 117–125.

Wilhelms, E. A. and Reyna, V. F. (eds) (2014), *Neuroeconomics, Judgment, and Decision Making*, New York: Psychology Press.

Williamson, O.E. (1991), 'Comparative economic organization: The analysis of discrete structural alternatives', *Administrative Science Quarterly*, 36: 269–296.

Worren, N., Moore, K. and Elliot, R. (2002), 'When theories become tools: Toward a framework for pragmatic validity', *Human Relations*, 55(10): 1227–1250.

Yin, H., Cui, B., Li, J., Yao, J. and Chen, C. (2012), 'Challenging the long tail recommendation', *Proceedings of the VLDB Endowment*, 5(9): 896–907, doi: 10.14778/2311906.2311916.

Yin, R. (1994), *Case study research: Design and methods*. Thousand Oaks, CA: Sage.

YouTube (2013), 'The first-ever YouTube Music Awards (YTMA)', available at: https://www.youtube.com/watch?v=yXBPbnv1H-U (accessed 5 June 2015).

Further reading

The breadth, depth, variety and complexity of creative industry strategies may require further exploration of literature. A spectrum of subjects may need to be covered for further reading, including the full diversity of disciplines and fields such as psychology, technology, creative practice or cultural change, together with specific cases and analyses of concrete, practical examples. Thus the indicative list of further reading presented below is long yet by no means exhaustive. The proliferation, fragmentation and convergent nature of new sub-sectors and modes of practice may require consulting a literature beyond what is covered at present.

Abbott, J. L. and Geddie, M. W. (2000), 'Event and venue management: Minimizing liability through effective crowd management techniques', *Event Management*, 6(4): 259–270, doi: 10.3727/152599500108751417.

Accardi-Petersen, M. (2011), *Agile marketing*, New York: Springer Science + Business Media.

Accardi-Petersen, M. (2011), 'Agile: Marketing's new method', *Agile Marketing*: 1–44, doi: 10.1007/978-1-4302-3316-9_1.

Accardi-Petersen, M. (2011), 'Crowdsourcing or once again formalizing my practice', *Agile Marketing*: 189–215, doi: 10.1007/978-1-4302-3316-9_6.

Accardi-Petersen, M. (2011), 'How to get moving in Agile', *Agile Marketing*: 171–187, doi: 10.1007/978-1-4302-3316-9_5.

Acquisti, A. and Gross, R. (2006), 'Imagined communities: Awareness, information sharing, and privacy on the Facebook', *Lecture Notes in Computer Science*, 4258: 36–58, doi: 10.1007/11957454_3.

Adderio, L. D' (2001), 'Crafting the virtual prototype: How firms integrate knowledge and capabilities across organisational boundaries', *Research Policy*, 30(9): 1409–1424, doi: 10.1016/s0048-7333(01)00159–7.

Adnan, M., Leak, A. and Longley, P. (2014), 'A geocomputational analysis of Twitter activity around different world cities', *Geo-spatial Information Science*, 17(3): 145–152, doi: 10.1080/10095020.2014.941316.

Adorno, T. W., Lenhardt, C., Adorno, G. and Tiedemann, R. (1982), *Aesthetic theory*, London: Routledge and Kegan Paul.

Afuah, A. (2014), *Business model innovation: Concepts, analysis, and cases*, London: Routledge.

Agins, T. (2000), *The end of fashion: How marketing changed the clothing business forever*, New York: Harper Paperbacks.

Alexandrov, H. (2009), 'Experiencing knowledge: The vicissitudes of a research journey – Researching beneath the surface', in Clarks, H. and Hodgett, P., *Psycho-social research methods in practice*, London: Karnac, 29–51.

Allen, J., Harris, R. and Bowdin, G. A. J. (2010), *Events management*, 3rd edn, London: Taylor and Francis.

Allen, J., O'Toole, W., McDonnell, I. and Harris, R. (2008), *Festival and special event management*, 4th edn, London: John Wiley and Sons.

Allen, T. J. and Henn, G. (2007), *The organization and architecture of innovation: Managing the flow of technology*, Amsterdam: Butterworth-Heinemann.

Alvesson, M. and Skoldberg, K. (2009), *Reflexive methodology: New vistas for qualitative research*, London: SAGE Publications.

Alvesson, M. and Willmott, H. (eds) (2003), *Studying Management Critically*, London: Sage Publications.

Amabile, T. M. (1988), 'A model of creativity and innovation in organizations', *Research in Organizational Behavior*, 10 (1): 123–167.

Amabile, T. M. (1993), 'What does a theory of creativity require?', *Psychological Inquiry*, 4(3): 179–181, doi: 10.1207/s15327965pli0403_2.

Amabile, T. M., Conti, R., Coon, H., Lazenby, J. and Herron, M. (1996), 'Assessing the work environment for creativity', *Academy of Management Journal*, 39(5): 1154–1184, doi: 10.2307/256995.

Amit, R. and Zott, C. (2012), 'Creating value through business model innovation', *Sloan Management Review*, 53.

Anderson, B., Fagan, P., Woodnutt, T. and Chamorro-Premuzic, T. (2012), 'Facebook psychology: Popular questions answered by research', *Psychology of Popular Media Culture*, 1(1): 23.

Anderson, C. (2009), *The long tail: How endless choice is creating unlimited demand*, London: Random House Business Books.

Anderton, C. (2008), 'Commercializing the carnivalesque: The V Festival and image/risk management', *Event Management*, 12(1): 39–51, doi: 10.3727/152599509787992616.

Andreessen, M. (2011), 'Why software is eating the world', *Wall Street Journal*, 20 August, available at: www.wsj.com/articles/SB10001424053111903480904576512250915629460 (accessed 6 July 2015).

Andrejevic, M. (2009), *iSpy: Surveillance and power in the interactive era*, Lawrence, KS: University Press of Kansas.

Androulaki, E., Karame, G. O., Roeschlin, M., Scherer, T. and Capkun, S. (2013), 'Evaluating user privacy in Bitcoin', *Financial Cryptography and Data Security Conference 2013*, Berlin: Springer, 34–51.

Ang, S. and Van Dyne, L. (2008), *Handbook of cultural intelligence: Theory, measurement, and applications*, New York: M. E. Sharpe.

Apitzsch, B. (2010), 'Informal networks and risk coping strategies in temporary organizations: The case of media production in Germany', *Forum Qualitative Sozialforschung/Forum: Qualitative Social Research*, 11(1).

Argenti, P. A. and Druckenmiller, B. (2004), 'Reputation and the corporate brand', *Corporate Reputation Review*, 6(4): 368–374, doi: 10.1057/palgrave.crr.1540005.

Arthur, C. (2014), 'Facebook emotion study breached ethical guidelines, researchers say', *Guardian*, 30 June, available at: www.theguardian.com/technology/2014/jun/30/facebook-emotion-study-breached-ethical-guidelines-researchers-say (accessed 15 July 2015).

Aspers, P. (2007), 'Theory, reality, and performativity in markets', *American Journal of Economics and Sociology*, 66(2): 379–398, doi: 10.1111/j.1536-7150.2007.00515.x.

Astrachan, J. B. (2010), 'Transparency in the new media', *SSRN Electronic Journal*, doi: 10.2139/ssrn.1619506.

Audretsch, D. B. and Keilbach, M. (2013), 'The theory of knowledge spillover entrepreneurship', *Public Policy in the Entrepreneurial Society*, doi: 10.4337/9781783476923.00013.

Aycock, A. (1995), '"Technologies of the self": Foucault and internet discourse', *Journal of Computer-Mediated Communication*, 1(2), doi: 10.1111/j.1083-6101.1995.tb00328.x.

Baase, S. (2008), *A gift of fire: Social, legal, and ethical issues for computing and the Internet*, Chicago: Prentice Hall.

Babaioff, M., Dobzinski, S., Oren, S. and Zohar, A. (2012). 'On bitcoin and red balloons', *Proceedings of the 13th ACM conference on electronic commerce*, 56–73.

Baden-Fuller, C. and Haefliger, S. (2013), 'Business models and technological innovation', *Long Range Planning*, 46(6): 419–426.

Baden-Fuller, C. and Mangematin, V. (2013), 'Business models: A challenging agenda', *Strategic Organization*, 11(4): 418–427, doi: 10.1177/1476127013510112.

Badenhausen, K. (2015), 'The world's most valuable brands', *Forbes Online*, available at: www.forbes.com/powerful-brands/ (accessed 5 June 2015).

Bainbridge, C. and Yates, C. (eds) (2014), *Media and the inner world: Psycho-cultural approaches to emotion, media and popular culture*, London: Palgrave Macmillan.

Baker, T. and Nelson, R. E. (2005), 'Creating something from nothing: Resource construction through entrepreneurial bricolage', *Administrative Science Quarterly*, 50(3): 329–366, doi: 10.2189/asqu.2005.50.3.329.

Bakhshi, H., Hargreaves, I. and Mateos-Garcia, J. (2013), *A manifesto for the creative economy*, available at: http://orca.cf.ac.uk/49323/ (accessed 5 June 2015).

Banksy (2005), *Wall and Piece*, London: Random House UK.

Barbican (2014), 'Robert Henke: Lumière + Robin Fox: RGB: Two audiovisual laser performances which promise to blow your mind', music event notes, available at: www.barbican.org.uk/music/event-detail.asp?ID=16283 (accessed 5 June 2015).

Bargh, J. A. (ed.) (2014), *Social psychology and the unconscious: The automaticity of higher mental processes*, New York: Psychology Press.

Barnes, L. and Lea-Greenwood, G. (2006), 'Fast fashioning the supply chain: Shaping the research agenda', *Journal of Fashion Marketing and Management: An International Journal*, 10(3): 259–271, doi: 10.1108/13612020610679259.

Barney, J. B. (1986), 'Organizational culture: Can it be a source of sustained competitive advantage?' *Academy of Management Review*, 11(3), doi: 10.2307/258317.

Baron-Cohen, S., Harrison, J., Goldstein, L. H. and Wyke, M. (1993), 'Coloured speech perception: Is synaesthesia what happens when modularity breaks down?' *Perception*, 22(4): 419–426, doi: 10.1068/p220419.

Barron, F. X. (1969), *Creative person and creative process*, New York: Holt, Rinehart & Winston.

Bass, R. and Bass, B. M. (2008), *The Bass handbook of leadership: Theory, research, and managerial applications*, 4th edn, New York: Simon and Schuster Adult Publishing Group.

Bateman, A. and Holmes, J. (1995), *An introduction to psychoanalysis: Contemporary theory and practice*, London: Taylor and Francis.

Bateman, A. and Wood, M. (2009), 'Cloud computing', *Bioinformatics*, 25(12): 1475–1475, doi: 10.1093/bioinformatics/btp274.

Baudrillard, J. and Levin, C. (1981), *For a critique of the political economy of the sign*, New York: Telos Press.

Baym, N. K. (2013), 'Data not seen: The uses and shortcomings of social media metrics', *First Monday*, 18(10).

BBC (2015), 'Imagine ... – Summer 2015: 3. Beware of Mr Baker', dir. J Bulger, available at: www.bbc.co.uk/iplayer/episode/b061y4qk/imagine-summer-2015-3-beware-of-mr-baker.

BBC News (2014), 'Banksy's Mobile Lovers artwork raises £400k for boys' club', BBC Technology News Online, 27 August, available at: http://m.bbc.co.uk/news/uk-england-bristol-28950398 (accessed 15 July 2015).

BBC News (2014), 'Facebook privacy challenge attracts 25,000 users', BBC Technology News Online, 6 August, available at: http://m.bbc.co.uk/news/technology-28677667 (accessed 15 July 2015).

BBC News (2014), 'FBI investigates "Cloud" celebrity picture leaks', BBC Technology News, 2 September, available at: http://m.bbc.co.uk/news/technology-29011850 (accessed 15 July 2015).

BBC News (2014), 'Google Glass hack allows brainwave control', BBC Technology News, 10 July, available at: http://m.bbc.co.uk/news/technology-28237582 (accessed 15 July 2015).

BBC News (2014), 'Google launches new venture fund for European start-ups', BBC Technology News, 10 August, available at: www.bbc.com/news/business-28242004 (accessed 15 July 2015).

BBC News (2014), 'Google revenue helped by ads as business boss leaves', BBC Technology News, 18 July, available at: http://m.bbc.co.uk/news/business-28359349 (accessed 15 July 2015).

BBC News (2014), 'Google takes on top hacker George Hotz for Project Zero', BBC Technology News, 16 July, available at: http://m.bbc.co.uk/news/technology-28327117 (accessed 15 July 2015).

BBC News (2014), 'Jersey approves first regulated Bitcoin fund', BBC Technology News, 10 July, available at: http://m.bbc.co.uk/news/world-europe-jersey-28247796 (accessed 14 July 2015).

Beattie, V. and Smith, S. J. (2013), 'Value creation and business models: Refocusing the intellectual capital debate', *British Accounting Review*, 45(4): 243–254, doi: 10.1016/j.bar.2013.06.001.

Becker, D., Riedel, M., Streit, A. and Wolf, F. (2009), 'Grid-based workflow management', *Grid and Services Evolution*, doi: 10.1007/978-0-387-85966-8_8.

Beech, N. and Gilmore, C. (2015) *Organising music: Theory, practice, performance*, Cambridge: Cambridge University Press.

Beggs, A. and Graddy, K. (1997), 'Declining values and the afternoon effect: Evidence from art auctions', *RAND Journal of Economics*, 28(3), doi: 10.2307/2556028.

Belfiore, E. (2002), 'Art as a means of alleviating social exclusion: Does it really work? A critique of instrumental cultural policies and social impact studies in the UK', *International Journal of Cultural Policy*, 8(1): 91–106, doi: 10.1080/102866302900324658.

Belk, R. (2014), 'You are what you can access: Sharing and collaborative consumption online', *Journal of Business Research*, 67(8): 1595–1600, doi: 10.1016/j.jbusres.2013.10.001.

Bennett, L. (2011), 'Music fandom online: R.E.M. fans in pursuit of the ultimate first listen', *New Media and Society*, 14(5): 748–763, doi: 10.1177/1461444811422895.

Bennett, L. (2012), 'Patterns of listening through social media: Online fan engagement with the live music experience', *Social Semiotics*, 22(5): 545–557, doi: 10.1080/10350330.2012.731897.

Bennett, L. (2014), 'Tracing textual poachers: Reflections on the development of fan studies and digital fandom', *Journal of Fandom Studies*, 2(1): 5–20, doi: 10.1386/jfs.2.1.5_1.

Bennett, W. L. and Segerberg, A. (2013), *The logic of connective action: Digital media and the personalization of contentious politics*, Cambridge: Cambridge University Press.

Bently, L. and Maniatis, S. M. (eds) (1998), *Intellectual property and ethics*, London: Sweet and Maxwell.

Bently, L. and Sherman, B. (2001), *Intellectual property law*, New York: Oxford University Press.

Berg, M. C., Amit, N. and Powell, J. D. (1988), 'Multirate digital control system design: Automatic control', *IEEE Transactions*, 33(12): 1139–1150.

Bergvall-Forsberg, J. and Towers, N. (2007), 'Creating agile supply networks in the fashion industry: A pilot study of the European textile and clothing industry', *Journal of the Textile Institute*, 98(4): 377–386, doi: 10.1080/00405000701502925.

Bernabei, R. and Power, J. (2012), 'Differentiating co-design and mass customisation from a user completion model within the realm of product design', *In 2nd International Conference on Design Creativity*, 2: 227–233.

Bernardo, F. and Martins, L. G. (2014), 'Disintermediation effects on independent approaches to music business', *International Journal of Music Business Research*, 3(2).

Bernays, E. L. (ed.) (1956), *The engineering of consent*, Norman, OK: University of Oklahoma Press. (1956): 50(02), doi: 10.1017/s0003055400230311.

Bernays, E. L. and Miller, M. C. (2004), *Propaganda*, New York: Ig Publishing.

Berthold-Bond, D. (1991), 'A Kierkegaardian critique of Heidegger's concept of authenticity', *Man and World*, 24(2): 119–142.

Beslay, L. and Hakana, H. (2011), 'Digital territory: Bubbles', in Kidd, P. T. (ed.), *European visions for the knowledge age: A quest for new horizons in the information age*, London: Cheshire Henbury: 69–79.

Bharadwaj, A., El Sawy, O. A., Pavlou, P. A. and Venkatraman, N. (2013), 'Digital business strategy: Toward a next generation of insights', *MIS Quarterly*, 37(2): 471–482.

Bidney, D. (1968), *Theoretical anthropology*, New York: Transaction Publishers.

Biey, M. L. and Zanola, R. (2005), 'The market for Picasso prints: A hybrid model approach', *Journal of Cultural Economics*, 29(2): 127–136.

Bigné, E. (2014), *The Routledge companion to the future of marketing*, London: Routledge.

Bik, H. M. and Goldstein, M. C. (2013), 'An introduction to social media for scientists', *PLoS Biology*, 11(4), doi: 10.1371/journal.pbio.1001535.

Billau, D. and Graczyk, D. (2003), 'Hannibal: The father of strategy reconsidered', *Comparative Strategy*, 22(4): 335–353, doi: 10.1080/01495930390236970.

Billieux, J., Deleuze, J., Griffiths, M. D. and Kuss, D. J. (2014), 'Internet gaming addiction: The case of massively multiplayer online role-playing games', *Textbook of Addiction Treatment: International Perspectives*: 1515–1525, doi: 10.1007/978-88-470-5322-9_105.

Bing, L., Chan, K. C. C. and Ou, C. (2014), 'Public sentiment analysis in twitter data for prediction of a company's stock price movements', *2014 IEEE 11th International Conference on e-Business Engineering*, doi: 10.1109/icebe.2014.47.

Bird, J., Curtis, B. and Putnam, T. (eds) (1992), *Mapping the futures: Local cultures, global change*, New York: Routledge.

Bivens, H. P. (2001), 'Grid workflow', Grid Computing Environments Working Group, Global Grid Forum.

Blaszczyk, R. L. (2009), *Producing fashion commerce, culture, and consumers*. Philadelphia: University of Pennsylvania Press.

Bleak v. Spotify USA Inc. (N.D. Cal. Apr. 16, 2014) (CV 13–5653 CRB), San Francisco, CA.

Blumenthal, M. S. and Clark, D. D. (2001), 'Rethinking the design of the Internet: The end-to-end arguments vs. the brave new world', *ACM Transactions on Internet Technology*, 1(1): 70–109, doi: 10.1145/383034.383037.

Boar, B. (1995), 'Planning theory: Sun Tzu and Machiavelli on strategy', *Journal of Business Strategy*, 16(1), doi: 10.1108/eb039675.

Boden, M. (ed.) (1994), *Dimensions of Creativity*, Cambridge, MA: MIT Press.

Boland, R. J., Lyytinen, K. and Yoo, Y. (2007), 'Wakes of innovation in project networks: The case of digital 3-D representations in architecture, engineering, and construction', *Organization Science*, 18(4): 631–647, doi: 10.1287/orsc.1070.0304.

Bontis, N. (1998), 'Intellectual capital: An exploratory study that develops measures and models', *Management Decision*, 36(2): 63–76, doi: 10.1108/00251749810204142.

Boons, F. and Lüdeke-Freund, F. (2013), 'Business models for sustainable innovation: State-of-the-art and steps towards a research agenda', *Journal of Cleaner Production*, 45: 9–19, doi: 10.1016/j.jclepro.2012.07.007.

Bose, P. (2004), *Alexander the Great's art of strategy: The timeless leadership lessons of history's greatest empire builder*, New York: Gotham Books.

Boudreau, K. J. (2012), 'Let a thousand flowers bloom? An early look at large numbers of software app developers and patterns of innovation', *Organization Science*, 23(5): 1409–1427, doi: 10.1287/orsc.1110.0678.

Bourdieu, P. and Nice, R. (1984), *Bourdieu: Distinction: A social critique of the judgement of taste*, Cambridge, MA: Harvard University Press.

Bozeman, B. and Rogers, J. D. (2002), 'A churn model of scientific knowledge value: Internet researchers as a knowledge value collective', *Research Policy*, 31(5): 769–794, doi: 10.1016/s0048-7333(01)00146-9.

Brabazon, T. (2009), 'Fundamentalism of the mind or wagging the long tail? Google and the future of thinking', *Libri*, 59, doi: 10.1515/libr.2009.007.

Brady, T., Rush, H., Hobday, M., Davies, A., Probert, D. and Banerjee, S. (1997), 'Tools for technology management: An academic perspective', *Technovation*, 17(8): 417–426, doi: 10.1016/s0166-4972(97)00017-5.

Bragdon, A., Reiss, S. P., Zeleznik, R., Karumuri, S., Cheung, W., Kaplan, J., Coleman, C., Adeputra, F. and LaViola, J. J. (2010), 'Code bubbles', *Proceedings of the 32nd ACM/IEEE International Conference on Software Engineering – ICSE '10*, doi: 10.1145/1806799.1806866.

Braun, P. (2002), 'Digital knowledge networks: Linking communities of practice with innovation', *Journal of Business Strategies*, 19(1): 43.

Bridgstock, R. and Cunningham, S. (2015), 'Creative labour and graduate outcomes: Implications for higher education and cultural policy', *International Journal of Cultural Policy*.

British Fashion Council (2010), *The value of the UK fashion industry*, London: British Fashion council, available at: www.britishfashioncouncil.com/uploads/media/62/16356. pdf (accessed 5 June 2015).

Brockhoff, K., Chakrabarti, A. K. and Hauschildt, J. (eds) (1999), *The dynamics of innovation: Strategic and managerial implications*, Berlin: Springer-Verlag.

Brookes, A. J. and Poole, D. (eds) (2003), *Innovation in architecture: A path to the future*, New York: Taylor and Francis.

Brousseau, E. and Penard, T. (2007), 'The economics of digital business models: A framework for analyzing the economics of platforms', *Review of Network Economics*, 6, doi: 10.2202/1446-9022.1112.

Brown, S. and Hutton, A. (2013), 'Developments in the real-time evaluation of audience behaviour at planned events', *International Journal of Event and Festival Management*, 4(1): 43–55, doi: 10.1108/17582951311307502.

Bruce-Novoa, J. (1979), 'Fear and loathing on the Buffalo trail', *MELUS*, 6(4), doi: 10.2307/467055.

Brunsting, S. and Postmes, T. (2002), 'Social movement participation in the digital age: Predicting offline and online collective action', *Small Group Research*, 33(5): 525–554, doi: 10.1177/104649602237169.

Bruzzi, S. and Gibson, P. C. (eds) (2013), *Fashion cultures revisited: Theories, explorations and analysis*, 2nd edn, New York: Routledge.

Bulhof, I. N. and Weinsheimer, J. C. (1986), 'Gadamer's hermeneutics: A reading of truth and method', *American Historical Review*, 91(5), doi: 10.2307/1864382.

Bums, J. S. (2002), 'Chaos theory and leadership studies: Exploring uncharted seas', *Journal of Leadership and Organizational Studies*, 9(2): 42–56, doi: 10.1177/107179190200900204.

Burgess, J. and Green, J. (2013), *YouTube: Online video and participatory culture*, London: Polity Press.

Burk, D. L. (2007), 'Intellectual property in the context of e-science', *Journal of Computer-Mediated Communication*, 12(2): 600–617, doi: 10.1111/j.1083-6101.2007.00340.x.

Burkart, P. (2013), 'Music in the cloud and the digital sublime', *Popular Music and Society*, 37(4): 393–407, doi: 10.1080/03007766.2013.810853.

Burrows, P. (2010), 'Apple vs Google', *Bloomberg Business Week*, 25 (28).

Burton, G. (2004), *Media and society: Critical perspectives*, Maidenhead: Open University Press.

Bustinza, O. F., Parry, G. C. and Vendrell-Herrero, F. (2013), 'Supply and demand chain management: The effect of adding services to product offerings', *Supply Chain Management: An International Journal*, 18(6): 618–629, doi: 10.1108/scm-05-2013-0149.

Bustinza, O. F., Vendrell-Herrero, F., Parry, G. and Myrthianos, V. (2013), 'Music business models and piracy', *Industrial Management and Data Systems*, 113(1): 4–22, doi: 10.1108/02635571311289638.

Cabaroglu, N. (2014), 'Re-visiting the theory and practice gap through the lens of student teacher dilemmas', *Australian Journal of Teacher Education*, 39, doi: 10.14221/ajte.2014v39n2.10.

Cambria, E., Schuller, B., Xia, Y. and Havasi, C. (2013), 'New avenues in opinion mining and sentiment analysis', *IEEE Intelligent Systems*, 28(2): 15–21, doi: 10.1109/mis.2013.30.

Carlsen, J., Andersson, T. D., Ali-Knight, J., Jaeger, K. and Taylor, R. (2010), 'Festival management innovation and failure', *International Journal of Event and Festival Management*, 1(2): 120–131, doi: 10.1108/17852951011056900.

Carman, T. (2003), *Heidegger's analytic: Interpretation, discourse and authenticity in being and time*, Cambridge: Cambridge University Press.

Carr, D. (2013), 'Giving viewers what they want', *New York Times*, 24 February, available at: www.nytimes.com/2013/02/25/business/media/for-house-of-cards-using-big-data-to-guarantee-its-popularity.html?_r=1 (accessed 5 June 2015).

Casper, S. and van Waarden, F. (eds) (2005), *Innovation and institutions: A multidisciplinary review of the study of innovation systems*, Cheltenham: Edward Elgar Publishing.

Cavalcante, S., Kesting, P. and Ulhøi, J. (2011), 'Business model dynamics and innovation: (Re)establishing the missing linkages', *Management Decision*, 49(8): 1327–1342, doi: 10.1108/00251741111163142.

Caves, R. E. (2002), *Creative industries: Contracts between art and commerce*, Cambridge, MA: Harvard University Press.

Chakmakin, A. (2014), 'A Grammy nominated artist shares his royalty statements', *Digital Music News*, 3 April, available at: www.digitalmusicnews.com/permalink/2014/04/03/streamingstatements (accessed 5 June 2015).

Chalaby, J. K. (2012), 'Producing TV content in a globalized intellectual property market: The emergence of the international production model', *Journal of Media Business Studies*, 9(3): 19–39, doi: 10.1080/16522354.2012.11073550.

Chang, P. L. and Chieng, M. H. (2006), 'Building consumer–brand relationship: A cross-cultural experiential view', *Psychology and Marketing*, 23(11): 927–959.

Chapman, L. and Sadd, D. (2014), 'Events as strategic marketing tools in shopping centers', *Event Management*, 18(3): 357–367, doi: 10.3727/152599514x13989500765925.

Charitou, C. D. and Markides, C. C. (2013), 'Responses to disruptive strategic innovation', *Sloan Management Review*, 1.

Chemers, M. (2014), *An integrative theory of leadership*, London: Taylor and Francis.

Chesbrough, H. and Press, H. B. S. (2006), *Open business models: How to thrive in the new innovation landscape*, Boston: Harvard Business School Press.

Chillingworth, M. (2004), 'Creative commons attracts BBC's attention', *Information World Review*, 11.

Chin, B. (2013), 'The fan-media producer collaboration', *Science Fiction Film and Television*, 6(1): 87–99, doi: 10.3828/sfftv.2013.8.

Choo, C. W. and Bontis, N. (eds) (2002), *The strategic management of intellectual capital and organizational knowledge*, New York: Oxford University Press.

Chow, R., Golle, P., Jakobsson, M., Shi, E., Staddon, J., Masuoka, R. and Molina, J. (2009), 'Controlling data in the cloud', *Proceedings of the 2009 ACM workshop on Cloud computing security – CCSW '09*, doi: 10.1145/1655008.1655020.

Christofides, E., Muise, A. and Desmarais, S. (2009), 'Information disclosure and control on Facebook: Are They two sides of the same coin or two different processes?' *CyberPsychology and Behavior*, 12(3): 341–345, doi: 10.1089/cpb.2008.0226.

Christopher, M. (2000), 'The agile supply chain', *Industrial Marketing Management*, 29(1): 37–44, doi: 10.1016/s0019-8501(99)00110-8.

Christopher, M., Lowson, R. and Peck, H. (2004), 'Creating agile supply chains in the fashion industry', *International Journal of Retail and Distribution Management*, 32(8): 367–376, doi: 10.1108/09590550410546188.

Christopherson, S. and van Jaarsveld, D. (2005), 'New media after the Dot.com bust: The persistent influence of political institutions on work in cultural industries', *International Journal of Cultural Policy*, 11(1): 77–93, doi: 10.1080/10286630500067846.

Chu, W. W. (2014), *Data mining and knowledge discovery for big data methodologies, challenge and opportunities*, Berlin: Springer.

Ciulla, J. B. (2008), 'Leadership studies and "the fusion of horizons"', *Leadership Quarterly*, 19(4): 393–395, doi: 10.1016/j.leaqua.2008.05.001.

Clarke, R., Grampp, W. D., Frey, B. S., Pommerehne, W. W. and Wilson, D. M. (1992), 'Pricing the priceless: Art, artists, and economics', *Economic Journal*, 102(412), doi: 10.2307/2234323.

Clausewitz, C. von (2000), *On war*, London: NTC/Contemporary Publishing Company.

Clausewitz, C. von (2001), *Clausewitz on strategy : Inspiration and insight from a master strategist*, ed. Von Ghyczy, T., von Oetinger, B. and Bassford, C., New York: John Wiley and Sons.

Clement, M., Wu, S., Völckner, F. and Burmester, A. B. (2014), 'The positive and negative effects of licenses on sales-an analysis of the games industry', EMMA Conference, May.

Click, M. A., Lee, H. and Holladay, H. W. (2013), 'Making monsters: Lady Gaga, fan identification, and social media', *Popular Music and Society*, 36(3): 360–379, doi: 10.1080/03007766.2013.798546.

Cobley, P. (ed.) (2009), *The Routledge companion to semiotics*, London: Taylor and Francis.

Cohen v. Facebook, Inc. (2011), (N.D. Cal. 2011): 798 F. Supp. 2d 1090.

Cohen, S. (2013), 'Musical memory, heritage and local identity: Remembering the popular music past in a European Capital of Culture', *International Journal of Cultural Policy*, 19(5): 576–594, doi: 10.1080/10286632.2012.676641.

Cohen, S. (2012), *Why won't they pay for music*, Keynote Address, 6 November presented as part of the Orchard Lab Module, London Metropolitan University.

Cohen, S. and Nielsen, E. (2015), 5th Orchard Lab Grand Plenary, Expert Panel Discussion, presented as part of The Orchard Lab Module, London Metropolitan University, 28 April.

Coleman, G. E. (2012), *Coding freedom: The ethics and aesthetics of hacking*, Princeton: Princeton University Press.

Collins, F. S. (2003), 'The Human Genome Project: Lessons from large-scale biology', *Science*, 300(5617): 286–290, doi: 10.1126/science.1084564.

Condon, S. L. and Cech, C. G. (1996), 'Discourse management strategies in face-to-face and computer-mediated decision making interactions', *Electronic Journal of Communication/Revue électronique de communication*, 6(3).

Coombes, P. H. and Nicholson, J. D. (2013), 'Business models and their relationship with marketing: A systematic literature review', *Industrial Marketing Management*, 42(5): 656–664, doi: 10.1016/j.indmarman.2013.05.005.

Copeland, P. (2010), 'Google's innovation factory: Testing, culture, and infrastructure', *2010 Third International Conference on Software Testing, Verification and Validation*, doi: 10.1109/icst.2010.65.

Couldry, N. (2012), *Media, society, world: Social theory and digital media practice*, Cambridge: Polity Press.

Craig, R. T. (1999), 'Communication theory as a field', *Communication Theory*, 9(2): 119–161, doi: 10.1111/j.1468-2885.1999.tb00355.x.

Crawford, G., Gosling, V. K. and Light, B. (eds) (2013), *Gamers: The social and cultural significance of online games*, New York: Routledge.

Creative Industries Federation (2015), 'How public investment in arts contributes to growth in the creative industries', available at: www.creativeindustriesfederation.com/assets/userfiles/files/CIF_Arts%20and%20Growth%5B3%5D.pdf (accessed 6 May 2015).

Creative Industries Federation (2015), 'The Creative Industries Federation's Creative Education Agenda: How and why the next government should support cultural and creative learning in the UK', available at: www.creativeindustriesfederation.com/assets/userfiles/files/CIF_EduAgenda_spreads.pdf (accessed 5 June 2015).

Cristiano, A. (ed.) (2008), *The economics of innovation*, New York: Routledge.

Crowther, P., Bostock, J. and Perry, J. (2015), 'Review of established methods in event research', *Event Management*, 19(1): 93–107, doi: 10.3727/152599515x14229071393061.

Cummings, S. (1993), 'Brief case: The first strategists', *Long Range Planning*, 26(3): 133–135.

Danescu-Niculescu-Mizil, C., Kossinets, G., Kleinberg, J. and Lee, L. (2009), 'How opinions are received by online communities: A case study on Amazon.com', *Proceedings of the 18th International Conference on the World Wide Web – WWW '09*, doi: 10.1145/1526709.1526729.

Danesi, M. (2002), *Understanding media semiotics*, London: Bloomsbury.

Danielsen, A. (1997), 'His name was Prince: A study of diamonds and pearls', *Popular Music*, 16(03), doi: 10.1017/s0261143000008412.

Dann, K. T. (1998), *Bright colors falsely seen: Synaesthesia and the search for transcendental knowledge*, New Haven, CT: Yale University Press.

DaSilva, C. M., Trkman, P., Desouza, K. and Lindič, J. (2013), 'Disruptive technologies: A business model perspective on cloud computing', *Technology Analysis and Strategic Management*, 25(10): 1161–1173.

Davidson, A. (2015), 'Foals team up with GroPro for groundbreaking "Mountain at My Gates" video', *Digital Spy*, 30 July, available at: www.digitalspy.co.uk/music/news/a660913/foals-team-up-with-gropro-for-groundbreaking-mountain-at-my-gates-video.html#ixzz3hYoJcDB0(accessed 30 July 2015).

Davies, W. (2011), 'Knowing the unknowable: The epistemological authority of innovation policy experts', *Social Epistemology*, 25(4): 401–421, doi: 10.1080/02691728.2011.605479.

Day, G. S. (1994), 'The capabilities of market-driven organizations', *Journal of Marketing*, 58(4), doi: 10.2307/1251915.

Debatin, B., Lovejoy, J. P., Horn, A.-K. and Hughes, B. N. (2009), 'Facebook and online privacy: Attitudes, behaviors, and unintended consequences', *Journal of Computer-Mediated Communication*, 15(1): 83–108, doi: 10.1111/j.1083-6101.2009.01494.x.

Deitrick, W. and Hu, W. (2013), 'Mutually enhancing community detection and sentiment analysis on Twitter networks', *Journal of Data Analysis and Information Processing*, 1(03): 19–29, doi: 10.4236/jdaip. 2013.13004.

DeLong, K. and Norris, C. (1992), 'Music and the politics of culture', *Notes*, 48(4), doi: 10.2307/942129.

Del Real, P. (2009), '"Ye shall receive"', *Journal of Architectural Education*, 62(4): 122–126, doi: 10.1111/j.1531-314x.2009.01013.x.

De-Miguel-Molina, B., Hervas-Oliver, J.-L., Boix, R. and De-Miguel-Molina, M. (2012), 'The importance of creative industry agglomerations in explaining the wealth of European regions', *European Planning Studies*, 20(8): 1263–1280, doi: 10.1080/09654313.2012.680579.

Denzin, N. K. and Lincoln, Y. S. (2000), *Handbook of qualitative research*, 2nd edn, Thousand Oaks, CA: Sage Publications.

De Vries, E. and Huizing, A. (eds) (2007), *Information management: Setting the scene*, Amsterdam: Elsevier Science.

Dickens, L. (2010), 'Pictures on walls? Producing, pricing and collecting the street art screen print', *City*, 14(1–2): 63–81.

Diehl, S. and Karmasin, M. (2013), 'Media and convergence management', Berlin: Springer.

Dignan, A. (2011), *Game frame: Unlocking the power of game dynamics in business and in life*, New York: Free Press.

Dinh, J. E., Lord, R. G., Gardner, W. L., Meuser, J. D., Liden, R. C. and Hu, J. (2014), 'Leadership theory and research in the new millennium: Current theoretical trends and changing perspectives', *Leadership Quarterly*, 25(1): 36–62, doi: 10.1016/j.leaqua.2013.11.005.

Dipple, J. (2014), 'Public policy recommendations for the sustainable growth of the UK music industry', *UK Music*, September, available at: www.ukmusic.org/assets/general/UK_MUSIC_Policy_Recommendations.pdf (accessed 15 July 2015).

Doctorow, C. (2014), 'The slow death of Silicon Roundabout', *Guardian*, 10 March, available at: www.theguardian.com/cities/2014/mar/10/slow-death-of-silicon-roundabout (accessed 15 July 2015).

Donson, T. B. (1978), *Prints and the print market: A handbook for buyers, collectors, and connoisseurs*, New York: Crowell.

Dorfman, B. (ed.) (2004), *Culture, media, theory, practice: Perspectives*, Aalborg: Aalborg Universitetsforlag.

Dredge, S. (2013), 'UK's £1bn recorded music revenues in 2013 included £103m from streaming subscriptions', *MusicAlly*, 1 January, available at: http://musically.com/2014/01/01/uks-1bn-recorded-music-revenues-in-2013-included-103m-from-streaming-subscriptions/ (accessed 6 May 2015).

Dror, Y. (1964), 'Muddling Through – "Science" or Inertia?', *Public Administration Review*, 24(3), doi: 10.2307/973640.

Drucker, P. (2014), *Innovation and entrepreneurship*, London: Routledge.

Du Gay, P., Madsen, A. K. and Hall, S. (2013), *Doing cultural studies: The story of the Sony Walkman*, London: SAGE Publications.

Duits, L., Zwaan, K. and Reijnders, S. (eds) (2014), *The Ashgate research companion to fan cultures*, London: Ashgate Publishing.

Dumas, M., Van der Aalst, W. M. and Ter Hofstede, A. H. (2005), 'Process-aware information systems: Bridging people and software through process technology', New York: John Wiley and Sons.

Dushnitsky, G. and Marom, D. (2013), 'Crowd monogamy', *Business Strategy Review*, 24(4): 24–26, doi: 10.1111/j.1467-8616.2013.00990.x.

Dwyer, T. (2010), *Media convergence*, Maidenhead: McGraw Hill/Open University Press.

Eckstein, J. and Young, A. M. (2015), 'Cooking, celebrity chefs, and public chef intellectuals', *Communication and Critical/Cultural Studies*, 12(2): 205–208, doi: 10.1080/14791420.2015.1014155.

Eco, U. (1976), *A theory of semiotics*, Bloomington: Indiana University Press.

Edmonds, E. and Candy, L. (2002), 'Creativity, art practice, and knowledge', *Communications of the ACM*, 45, doi: 10.1145/570907.570939.

Edquist, C. and Hommen, L. (1999), 'Systems of innovation: Theory and policy for the demand side', *Technology in Society*, 21(1): 63–79, doi: 10.1016/s0160–791x(98)00037-2.

Ellsworth-Jones, W. (2013), *Banksy: The man behind the wall*, New York: St. Martin's Press.

Elmer, G. (2003), 'A diagram of panoptic surveillance', *New Media and Society*, 5(2): 231–247, doi: 10.1177/1461444803005002005.

Elmer, G. (2004), *Profiling machines: Mapping the personal information economy*, Cambridge, MA: MIT Press.

Elmquist, M., Fredberg, T. and Ollila, S. (2009), 'Exploring the field of open innovation', *European Journal of Innovation Management*, 12(3): 326–345, doi: 10.1108/14601060910974219.

Eltham, B. (2013), 'Three arguments against "soft innovation": Towards a richer understanding of cultural innovation', *International Journal of Cultural Policy*, 19(5): 537–556, doi: 10.1080/10286632.2012.658044.

Ely, P. and Campbell, F. (2011), 'Higher education stimulating creative enterprise', available at: www.research.ucreative.ac.uk/1185/1/HE-CreativeEnterprise_Digital_LowRes.pdf (accessed 5 June 2015).

Engels, D. W. (1978), *Alexander the Great and the logistics of the Macedonian army*, Berkeley: University of California Press.

Engholm, I. and Hansen-Hansen, E. (2013), 'The fashion blog as genre – between user-driven bricolage design and the reproduction of established fashion system', *Digital Creativity*, 25(2): 140–154, doi: 10.1080/14626268.2013.814148.

Epstein, S. R. (2006), *Freedom and growth: The rise of states and markets in Europe, 1300–1750*, London: Routledge.

Erdős, P. and Ormos, M. (2010), 'Random walk theory and the weak-form efficiency of the US art auction prices', *Journal of Banking and Finance*, 34(5): 1062–1076, doi: 10.1016/j.jbankfin.2009.11.001.

Erickson, I. (2010), 'Documentary with ephemeral media: Curation practices in online social spaces', *Bulletin of Science, Technology and Society*, 30(6): 387–397, doi: 10.1177/0270467610380007.

Esser, A. (2013), 'The format business: Franchising television content', *International Journal of Digital Televison*, 4(2): 141–158, doi: 10.1386/jdtv.4.2.141_1.

Evans, D. S., Hagiu, A. and Schmalensee, R. L. (2006), *Invisible engines: How software platforms drive innovation and transform industries*, Cambridge, MA: MIT Press.

Even, Y. and Holmes, G. (1995), 'Art and politics in Renaissance Italy: British Academy Lectures', *Sixteenth Century Journal*, 26(1), doi: 10.2307/2541580.

Everett, M. G. and Krackhardt, D. (2012), 'A second look at Krackhardt's graph theoretical dimensions of informal organizations', *Social Networks*, 34(2): 159–163, doi: 10.1016/j.socnet.2011.10.006.

Ezell, S. J. and Atkinson, R. D. (2012), *Innovation economics: The race for global advantage*, New Haven: Yale University Press.

Fairholm, M. R. and Fairholm, G. W. (2008), 'The leadership perspectives model', *Understanding Leadership Perspectives*, doi: 10.1007/978-0-387-84902-7_2.

Fardal, H. and Sørnes, J. O. (2008), 'IS strategic decision-making: A garbage can view', *Issues in Informing Science and Information Technology*, 5: 553–569.

Feldman, R. (2013), 'Techniques and applications for sentiment analysis', *Communications of the ACM*, 56(4), doi: 10.1145/2436256.2436274.

Ferguson, C. (2014), Technology left behind – the temptations of Netflix', *Against the Grain*, 22(6): 43.

Festinger, L. (1962), *A theory of cognitive dissonance*, Stanford: Stanford University Press.

Filson, D. (2004), 'The impact of e-commerce strategies on firm value: Lessons from Amazon.com and its early competitors', *Journal of Business*, 77(S2): 135–154, doi: 10.1086/381640.

Findlay, J. N. (1981), *Kant and the transcendental object: A hermeneutic study*, New York: Oxford University Press.

Finkle, T. A. (2011), 'Corporate entrepreneurship and innovation in Silicon Valley: The case of Google, Inc', *Entrepreneurship Theory and Practice*, 36(4): 863–884, doi: 1 0.1111/j.1540-6520.2010.00434.x.

Finney, A. (2010), *The international film business: A market guide beyond Hollywood*, London: Taylor and Francis.

Firstenberg, A. and Salas, J. (2014), *Designing and developing for Google Glass: Thinking differently for a new platform*, Los Angeles: O'Reilly Media, Inc.

Fitzgerald, B. F. and Oi, I. (2004), 'Free culture: Cultivating the creative commons', *Media and Arts Law Review*, 9(2).

Flaxman, S. R., Goel, S. and Rao, J. M. 'Filter bubbles, echo chambers, and online news consumption', available at: https://m.5harad.com/papers/bubbles.pdf (accessed 5 June 2015).

Fromme, J. and Unger, A. (2012), *Computer games and new media cultures: A handbook of digital games studies*, New York: Springer Science and Business Media.

Fuchs, C. (2008), *Internet and society: Social theory in the information age*, New York: Taylor and Francis.

Fujita, Y. (2014), 'Optimizing fashion branding strategies: Management of variety of items and length of lifecycles in a stochastically fluctuating market', *International Series on Consumer Science*: 49–61, doi: 10.1007/978-1-4939-0277-4_4.

Fukuyama, F. (2006), *The end of history and the last man*, Chicago: Simon and Schuster.

Fuller, G., Hamilton, C. and Seale, K. (2013), 'Working with amateur labour: Between culture and economy', *Cultural Studies Review*, 19(1), p. 143.

Gackenbach, J. (ed.) (2007), *Psychology and the internet: Intrapersonal, interpersonal, and transpersonal implications*, 2nd edn, Amsterdam: Elsevier/Academic Press.

Gaffney, M. and Rafferty, P. (2009), 'Making the long tail visible: Social networking sites and independent music discovery', *Program: Electronic Library And Information Systems*, 43(4): 375–391, doi: 10.1108/00330330910998039.

Gagliardi, G. and Tzu, S. (2006), *Sun Tzu's 'The art of war' for the business warrior: Strategy for entrepreneurs*, Seattle: Clearbridge Publishing.

Garud, R. and Karnøe, P. (2003), 'Bricolage versus breakthrough: Distributed and embedded agency in technology entrepreneurship', *Research Policy*, 32(2): 277–300, doi: 10.1016/s0048-7333(02)00100-2.

Gauch, H. G. (2002), *Scientific method in practice*, New York: Cambridge University Press.

Gaudesi (2015), *The contribution of artist management processes to success/failure in the music industry – a case study*. Submitted in partial fulfilment of the requirements of the London Metropolitan University for the Degree of Master of Philosophy, LMU (unpublished).

Gawer, A. and Cusumano, M. A. (2013), 'Industry platforms and ecosystem innovation', *Journal of Product Innovation Management*, 31(3): 417–433, doi: 10.1111/jpim.12105.

Gendlin, E. T. (1978), 'Heidegger and the philosophy of psychology', *Review of Existential Psychology and Psychiatry*, 16(1–3): 43–71.

George, G. and Bock, A. J. (2011), 'The business model in practice and its implications for entrepreneurship research', *Entrepreneurship Theory and Practice*, 35(1): 83–111, doi: 10.1111/j.1540–6520.2010.00424.x.

Gerlitz, C. and Helmond, A. (2013), 'The like economy: Social buttons and the data-intensive web', *New Media and Society*, 15(8): 1348–1365, doi: 10.1177/1461444812472322.

Getz, D. (1991), *Festivals, special events and tours*, New York: Van Nostrand Reinhold.

Getz, D. (2005), *Event management and event tourism*, 2nd edn, Putnam Valley, NY: Cognizant Communication Corporation.

Getz, D. (2010), 'The nature and scope of festival studies', *International Journal of Event Management Research*, 5(1): 1–47.

Getz, D. and Andersson, T. D. (2008), 'Sustainable festivals: On becoming an institution', *Event Management*, 12(1): 1–17, doi: 10.3727/152599509787992625.

Getz, D., Andersson, T. and Carlsen, J. (2010), 'Festival management studies', *International Journal of Event and Festival Management*, 1(1): 29–59, doi: 10.1108/17852951011029298.

Giaccardi, E. (ed.) (2012), *Heritage and social media: understanding heritage in a participatory culture*, New York: Taylor and Francis.

Gibson, R. (2010), 'The "art" of creative teaching: Implications for higher education', *Teaching in Higher Education*, 15(5): 607–613, doi: 10.1080/13562517.2010.493349.

Giles, D. (2002), *Media Psychology*, Mahwah, NJ: Lawrence Erlbaum Associates Publishers.

Gold, A. H. and Arvind Malhotra, A. H. S. (2001), 'Knowledge management: An organizational capabilities perspective', *Journal of Management Information Systems*, 18(1): 185–214.

Goldsmith, J. L. and Wu, T. (2006), *Who controls the internet? Illusions of a borderless world*, New York: Oxford University Press.

Gomes, C., Schneider, D., Moraes, K. and de Souza, J. (2012), 'Crowdsourcing for music: Survey and taxonomy', *2012 IEEE International Conference on Systems, Man, and Cybernetics (SMC)*, doi: 10.1109/icsmc.2012.6377831.

Gomide, J., Veloso, A., Meira, W., Almeida, V., Benevenuto, F., Ferraz, F. and Teixeira, M. (2011), 'Dengue surveillance based on a computational model of spatio-temporal locality of Twitter', *Proceedings of the 3rd International Web Science Conference on – WebSci '11*, doi: 10.1145/2527031.2527049.

Gough, P. (ed.) (2012), *Banksy: The Bristol legacy*, London: Redcliffe Press.

Goumagias, N., Devlin, S. and Nucciarelli, A. (2014), 'The evolution of organisational forms in the digital games industry', available at: www.nemog.org/sites/default/files/The%20Evolution%20of%20Organisational%20Forms%20in%20the%20Digital%20Games%20Industry-DE2014-Submission.pdf (accessed 15 July 2015).

Graham-Dixon, A. (2009), *Michelangelo and the Sistine Chapel*, New York: Skyhorse Publishing.

Greisch, J. (1993), 'Creating a hermeneutic of the self – the short route (Heidegger) and the long route (Ricoeur)', *Revue de Métaphysique et de Morale*, 98(3): 413–427.

Griffiths, G. (2012), *Internet and surveillance: The challenges of Web 2.0 and social media*, London: Routledge.

Grubbs, J. B., Sessoms, J., Wheeler, D. M. and Volk, F. (2010), 'The cyber-pornography use inventory: The development of a new assessment instrument', *Sexual Addiction and Compulsivity*, 17(2): 106–126, doi: 10.1080/10720161003776166.

Grunwell, S. and Ha, I. (2007), 'Film festivals: An empirical study of factors for success', *Event Management*, 11(4): 201–210, doi: 10.3727/152599508785899893.

Grupp, H. and Freeman, C. (1998), *Foundations of the economics of innovation: Theory, Measurement and practice*, Cheltenham: Edward Elgar.

Guazzini, A., Yoneki, E. and Gronchi, G. (2015), 'Cognitive dissonance and social influence effects on preference judgments: An eye tracking based system for their automatic assessment', *International Journal of Human-Computer Studies*, 73: 12–18, doi: 10.1016/j.ijhcs.2014.08.003.

Guercini, S., and Tunisini, A. (2015), 'Competitive supply chains: An insight into the luxury industry', *Global Fashion Management Conference*, University of Florence, 283–287, doi: 10.15444/gfmc2015.02.08.02.

Guignon, C. B. (1984), 'Heidegger's "authenticity" revisited', *Review of Metaphysics*, 321–339.

Guilbault, J. and Lipsitz, G. (1997), 'Dangerous crossroads: Popular music, postmodernism, and the poetics of place', *American Music*, 15(2), doi: 10.2307/3052734.

Gustafsson, B. (1987), 'The rise and economic behaviour of medieval craft guilds an economic-theoretical interpretation', *Scandinavian Economic History Review*, 35(1): 1–40, doi: 10.1080/03585522.1987.10408080.

Gustafsson, V. and Schwarz, E. J. (2013), 'Business modelling and convergence', *Media and Convergence Management*, doi: 10.1007/978-3-642-36163-0_2.

Hacklin, F. (2007), *Management of convergence in innovation: Strategies and capabilities for value creation beyond blurring industry boundaries*, Heidelberg: Physica-Verlag.

Hadjiminas, N. and Child, C. (2012), 'Be the controller: A Kinect tool kit for video game control recognition of human motion using skeletal relational angles', *2nd Annual International Conference on Computer Games, Multimedia and Allied Technology (CGAT 2012)*, doi: 10.5176/2251-1679_cgat23.

Hallinan, B. and Striphas, T. (2014), 'Recommended for you: The Netflix Prize and the production of algorithmic culture', *New Media and Society*, doi: 10.1177/1461444814538646.

Hamilton, C. (2012), 'Symbolic amateurs: On the discourse of amateurism in contemporary media culture', *Cultural Studies Review*, 19(1), doi: 10.5130/csr.v19i1.2679.

Handel, M. I. (1986), *Clausewitz and modern strategy*, London: Frank Cass Publishers.

Hanna, R., Rohm, A. and Crittenden, V. L. (2011), 'We're all connected: The power of the social media ecosystem', *Business Horizons*, 54(3): 265–273, doi: 10.1016/j.bushor.2011.01.007.

Hardy, C., Palmer, I. and Phillips, N. (2000), 'Discourse as a strategic resource', *Human Relations*, 53(9): 1227–1248, doi: 10.1177/0018726700539006.

Hardy, S. (2008), 'The pornography of reality', *Sexualities*, 11(1–2): 60–64, doi: 10.1177/13634607080110010209.

Hargreaves, D. J. and North, A. C. (eds) (2004), *The social psychology of music*, Oxford: Oxford University Press.

Harrington, H. J. (1991), *Business process improvement: The breakthrough strategy for total quality, productivity, and competitiveness*, New York: McGraw-Hill.

Harris, A. (2012), 'Art and gentrification: Pursuing the urban pastoral in Hoxton, London', *Transactions of the Institute of British Geographers*, 37(2): 226–241.

Harris, R., Edwards, D. and Homel, P. (2014), 'Managing alcohol and drugs in event and venue settings: The Australian case', *Event Management*, 18(4): 457–470, doi: 10.3727/152599514x14143427352238.

Harrison, J. E. and Baron-Cohen, S. (eds) (1997), *Synaesthesia: Classic and contemporary readings*, Cambridge, MA: Blackwell Publishers.

Hartley, J. (2012), *Communication, cultural and media studies: The key concepts*, New York: Routledge.

Hasbro, Inc. (2013), 'Hasbro and Rovio Enter into expanded Angry Birds licensing agreement', *Business Wire*, available at: www.businesswire.com/multimedia/home/20130617006348/en/#.Vbpub3jMayc (accessed 6 May 2015).

Haucap, J. and Heimeshoff, U. (2014), 'Google, Facebook, Amazon, eBay: Is the internet driving competition or market monopolization?' *International Economics and Economic Policy*, 11(1–2): 49–61, doi: 10.1007/s10368-013-0247-6.

Hauser, J. (2011), 'A marketing science perspective on recognition-based heuristics (and the fast-and-frugal paradigm)', *Judgment and Decision Making*, 6(5): 396–408.

Hayles, N. K. (2012), *How we think: Digital media and contemporary technogenesis*, Chicago: University of Chicago Press.

Hayward, D. (2006), 'Creative Clusters: A critical examination of the processes behind and implications of the emergence of a creative cluster in Shoreditch, London', BA dissertation, University of Portsmouth, available at: http://eprints.port.ac.uk/200/ (accessed 5 June 2015).

Hazard, P. D. and Klapper, J. T. (1962), 'The effects of mass communication', *American Quarterly*, 14(1), doi: 10.2307/2710239.

Heidegger, M. (1996), *Being and time* [*Sein und Zeit*], transl. Stambaugh, J., New York: SUNY Press.

Heidegger, M. (2008), *Ontology: The hermeneutics of facticity*, Bloomington: Indiana University Press.

Heidegger, M. and Hofstadter, A. (1988), *The basic problems of phenomenology*, rev. edn, Bloomington: Indiana University Press.

Heisenberg, W. and Northrop, F. S. C. (1999), *Physics and philosophy: The revolution in modern science*, Prometheus Books.

Helfat, C. E. and Peteraf, M. A. (2003), 'The dynamic resource-based view: Capability lifecycles', *Strategic Management Journal*, 24(10): 997–1010, doi: 10.1002/smj.332.

Hemphill, C. S. and Suk, J. (2009), 'The law, culture, and economics of fashion', *Stanford Law Review*, 61(5): 1147–1199.

Henderson, J. C. (2011), 'Celebrity chefs: Expanding empires', *British Food Journal*, 113(5): 613–624, doi: 10.1108/00070701111131728.

Hendrix, P. E. (2014), 'How digital technologies are enabling consumers and transforming the practice of marketing', *Journal of Marketing Theory and Practice*, 22(2): 149–150, doi: 10.2753/mtp1069-6679220209.

Hennig-Thurau, T., Gwinner, K. P., Walsh, G. and Gremler, D. D. (2004), 'Electronic word-of-mouth via consumer-opinion platforms: What motivates consumers to articulate themselves on the Internet?', *Journal of Interactive Marketing*, 18(1): 38–52, doi: 10.1002/dir.10073.

Hertog, P. D. (2000), 'Knowledge-intensive business services as co-producers of innovation', *International Journal of Innovation Management*, 4(4): 491–528, doi: 10.1142/s136391960000024x.

Hesmondhalgh, D. (2005), 'Media and cultural policy as public policy', *International Journal of Cultural Policy*, 11(1): 95–109, doi: 10.1080/10286630500067861.

Hesmondhalgh, D. (2012), *The cultural industries*, 3rd edn, London: SAGE Publications.

Hesmondhalgh, D. (2013), *Why music matters*, London: Wiley-Blackwell.

Hesmondhalgh, D., Pratt, A. C., Hall, S., McRobbie, A. and Butler, J. (2006), 'Cultural industries and cultural policy', *International Journal of Cultural Policy*.

Heuer, M. (2011), 'Ecosystem cross-sector collaboration: Conceptualizing an adaptive approach to sustainability governance', *Business Strategy and the Environment*, 20(4): 211–221, doi: 10.1002/bse.673.

Hewison, R. (2004), 'The crisis of cultural leadership in Britain', *International Journal of Cultural Policy*, 10(2): 157–166, doi: 10.1080/1028663042000255781.

Hewison, R. H. and Holden, J. (2011), *The cultural leadership handbook: How to run a creative organization*, London: Gower Publishing.

Hill, A. (2014), 'Big Brother is watching you, London', *Time Out*, 8 July, available at: http://now-here-this.timeout.com/2014/07/08/big-brother-is-watching-you-london/ (accessed 15 July 2015).

Hill, R. (2014), 'Online programming realities: A case study of *House of Cards* and the perceived advantages over traditional television', project submitted for completion of MA at University of Stockholm, available at: www.diva-portal.org/smash/record.jsf?pid=diva2%3A725183&dswid=-6957 (accessed 5 June 2015).

Hill, R. and Johnson, L. W. (2003), 'When creativity is a must: Professional "applied creative" services', *Creativity and Innovation Management*, 12(4): 221–229, doi: 10.1111/j.0963-1690.2003.00285.x.

Hillis, K., Petit, M. and Jarrett, K. (2012), *Google and the culture of search*, New York: Taylor and Francis.

Hobbs, M. and Masters, R. D. (1999), 'Fortune is a river: Leonardo da Vinci and Niccolo Machiavelli's magnificent dream to change the course of Florentine history', *Sixteenth Century Journal*, 30(3), doi: 10.2307/2544846.

Hochel, M. and Milán, E. G. (2008), 'Synaesthesia: The existing state of affairs', *Cognitive Neuropsychology*, 25(1): 93–117, doi: 10.1080/02643290701822815.

Home, S. (2004), 'Down and out in Shoreditch and Hoxton', London: Do-Not Press Ltd.

Homer, J. M. (2006), 'Integrating architecture and structural design in the comprehensive design studio', *Building Integration Solutions*, doi: 10.1061/40798(190)48.

Höök, K. and Löwgren, J. (2012), 'Strong concepts: Intermediate-level knowledge in interaction design research', *ACM Transactions on Computer–Human Interaction*, 19(3): 1–18, doi: 10.1145/2362364.2362371.

Hopkins, D. H. and Swift, T. (2008), 'Business leaders speak out: Their real strategic problems', *Journal of Business Strategy*, 29(5): 32–37, doi: 10.1108/02756660810902305.

Horkheimer, M., Adorno, T. W. and McCumber, J. (2009), 'The twilight of Enlightenment: Theodor W. Adorno and Max Horkheimer', *A History of Continental Thought*, 225–250, doi: 10.1017/upo9781844652778.010.

Hossain, S. (2012), 'The internet as a tool for studying the collective unconscious', *Jung Journal*, 6(2): 103–109, doi: 10.1525/jung.2012.6.2.103.

Hotho, S. and McGregor, N. (eds) (2013), *Changing the rules of the game: Economic, management and emerging issues in the computer games industry*, London: Palgrave Macmillan.

Hoyer, V., Stanoesvka-Slabeva, K., Janner, T. and Schroth, C. (2008), 'Enterprise mashups: Design principles towards the long tail of user needs', *2008 IEEE International Conference on Services Computing*, doi: 10.1109/scc.2008.88.

Huang, E., Davison, K., Shreve, S., Davis, T., Bettendorf, E. and Nair, A. (2006), 'Facing the challenges of convergence: Media professionals' concerns of working across media platforms', *Convergence: The International Journal of Research into New Media Technologies*, 12(1): 83–98, doi: 10.1177/1354856506061557.

Hudson, S. and Hudson, R. (2013), 'Engaging with consumers using social media: A case study of music festivals', *International Journal of Event and Festival Management*, 4(3): 206–223, doi: 10.1108/ijefm-06-2013-0012.

Hudson, T. (2014), 'Messaging apps offer brands extended global reach and deeper engagement', *Guardian*, 23 July, available at: www.theguardian.com/media-network/media-network-blog/2014/jul/23/messaing-apps-marketing-kik-snapchat (accessed 15 July 2015).

Hugos, M. (2012), 'Enterprise games: Using game mechanics to build a better business', Los Angeles: O'Reilly Media, Inc.

Hunt, H. (2005), 'Synaesthesia, metaphor and consciousness: A cognitive-developmental perspective', *Journal of Consciousness Studies*, 12(12): 26–45.

Hyder, D. (2009), 'Foucault, Cavaillès, and Husserl on the historical epistemology of the sciences', *Essays on Husserl's Crisis of European Sciences*, 177–198, doi: 10.11126/stanford/9780804756044.003.0011.

Iansiti, M. and Levien, R. (2004), 'Strategies as ecology', *Harvard Business Review*, 4; 68–78.

Ione, A. (2006), 'Neurology, synaesthesia, and painting', *International Review of Neurobiology*: 69–78, doi: 10.1016/s0074-7742(06)74006–5.

Ip, B. (2008), 'Technological, content, and market convergence in the games industry', *Games and Culture*, 3(2): 199–224, doi: 10.1177/1555412008314128.

Jackson, K. M. (2013), *The influence of television and film on interest in space and science*, doctoral dissertation, University of North Dakota.

Jansen, J. J. P., Volberda, H. W. and Van Den Bosch, F. A. J. (2006), 'Exploratory innovation, exploitative innovation, and performance: Effects of organizational antecedents and environmental moderators', *Management Science*, 52(11): 1661–1674, doi: 10.1287/mnsc.1060.0576.

Jarl, O. and Huse, M. (1993), 'Informal strategic networks and the board of directors', *Entrepreneurship: Theory and Practice (Impact Factor: 2.54)*, 18(1): 23–36.

Jarzabkowski, P. and Whittington, R. (2008), 'A strategy-as-practice approach to strategy research and education', *Journal of Management Inquiry*, 17(4): 282–286, doi: 10.1177/1056492608318150.

Jarzabkowski, P. and Whittington, R. (2008), 'Directions for a troubled discipline: Strategy research, teaching, and practice – Introduction to the dialogue', *Journal of Management Inquiry*, 17(4): 266–268, doi: 10.1177/1056492608318148.

Jarzabkowski, P. and Wilson, D. C. (2006), 'Actionable strategy knowledge: A practice perspective', *European Management Journal*, 24.3: 348–367.

Jarzabkowski, P., Balogun, J. and Seidl, D. (2007), 'Strategizing: The challenges of a practice perspective', *Human Relations*, 2007, 60(1): 5–27.

Jarzabkowski, P., Smets, M. and Spee, P. (2010), 'Trading risks: The value of relationships, models and face-to-face interaction in the global reinsurance market', Insurance Intellectual Capital Initiative Executive Briefing.

Javehery, H. (2003), *Multiple user interfaces: Cross-platform applications and context-aware interfaces*, London: Wiley, John and Sons.

Jenkins, H. (2002), 'Interactive audiences? The collective intelligence of media fans', *The new media book*, 157–170.

Jenkins, H. (2006), *Fans, bloggers, and gamers: Media consumers in a digital age*, New York: New York University Press.

Jenkins, H. (2006), *The wow climax: Tracing the emotional impact of popular culture*, New York: New York University Press.

Jenkinson, A. and Bishop, K. (2012), 'The IBM brand system: An interview with Kevin Bishop', *Journal of Brand Strategy*, 1(3): 223–233.

Jensen, R. (2007), *Getting off: Pornography and the end of masculinity*, Cambridge, MA: South End Press.

Jewels, T. and Underwood, A. (2004), *The impact of informal networks on knowledge management strategy*, Hershey, PA: Idea Group, doi: 10.4018/978-1-59140-281-7.ch001.

Johannessen, J.-A., Olsen, B. and Olaisen, J. (1999), 'Aspects of innovation theory based on knowledge-management', *International Journal of Information Management*, 19(2): 121–139, doi: 10.1016/s0268–4012(99)00004–3.

Johnson, J. and Tellis, G. J. (2005), 'Blowing bubbles: Heuristics and biases in the run-up of stock prices', *Journal of the Academy of Marketing Science*, 33(4), p. 486, doi: 10.1177/0092070305277381.

Johnson, M. W., Christensen, C. M. and Kagermann, H. (2008), 'Reinventing your business model', *Harvard Business Review*, 86(12): 57–68.

Johnson, T. (2014), 'Disney defends effort to halt Deadmau5's mouse ears trademark', *Variety*, available at: http://variety.com/2014/biz/news/disney-defends-effort-to-halt-deadmau5s-mouse-ears-trademark-1201299168/ (accessed 5 June 2015).

Jones, G. R. (2010), *Organizational theory, design, and change*, Upper Saddle River, NJ: Pearson.

Jones, S. G. (ed.) (1998), *Doing internet research: Critical issues and methods for examining the Net*, 4th edn, Thousand Oaks, CA: Sage Publications, Inc.

Jørgensen, K. A. (2009), 'Customisation design: Levels of customisation', 5th World Conference on Mass Customization and Personalization, October.

Jowitt, T. (2014), 'Apple grows profit ahead of iPhone 6 launch', *Tech Week Europe*, 23 July, available at: www.techweekeurope.co.uk/workspace/apple-profits-ahead-iphone-6-149626?utm_source=2014-07-24&utm_medium=email&utm_campaign=uk_techweekeurope&id_prob=37090_239552&t=0f3c1d7d311ec2b5ee e397f43bc6bb941307309 (accessed 15 July 2015).

Kagermann, H., Osterle, H. and Jordan, J. M. (2010), *IT-driven business models: Global case studies in transformation*, New York: John Wiley and Sons.

Kant, I. and Popović, N. M. (1932), *Kritika Čistoga Uma*, Belgrade: Geca Kon.

Kaplan, A. M. and Haenlein, M. (2012), 'The Britney Spears universe: Social media and viral marketing at its best', *Business Horizons*, 55(1): 27–31, doi: 10.1016/j.bushor.2011.08.009.

Kaplan, A. M. and Haenlein, M. (2006), 'Toward a parsimonious definition of traditional and electronic mass customization', *Journal of Product Innovation Management*, 23(2): 168–182, doi: 10.1111/j.1540-5885.2006.00190.x.

Kaplan, K. (2013), 'Crowd-funding: Cash on demand', *Nature*, 497(7447): 147–149, doi: 10.1038/nj7447-147a.

Karakas, F. (2009), 'Welcome to World 2.0: The new digital ecosystem', *Journal of Business Strategy*, 30(4): 23–30, doi: 10.1108/02756660910972622.

Karakas, F. (2010), 'Positive management education: Creating creative minds, passionate hearts, and kindred spirits', *Journal of Management Education*, 35(2): 198–226, doi: 10.1177/1052562910372806.

Karakas, F. and Manisaligil, A. (2012), 'Reorienting self-directed learning for the creative digital era', *European Journal of Training and Development*, 36(7): 712–731.

Kashef, T. E. (2015), 'What is the value of event management education? The views of six industry practitioners', *Event Management*, 19(1): 1–13, doi: 10.3727/1525995 15x14229071392828.

Kaye, J. (1991), 'Apple vs. Apple: Name at core of Beatles lawsuit', *Los Angeles Times*, 7 April, available at: http://articles.latimes.com/1991-08-04/business/fi-351_1_apple-corps (accessed 5 June 2015).

Kemp, P., Dreyfus, H. L., Rabinow, P. and Foucault, M. (1984), 'Michel Foucault. beyond structuralism and hermeneutics', *History and Theory*, 23(1), doi: 10.2307/2504973.

Kerr, A. and Kelleher, J. D. (2015), 'The recruitment of passion and community in the service of capital: Community managers in the digital games industry', *Critical Studies in Media Communication*: 1–16, doi: 10.1080/15295036.2015.1045005.

Kevles, D. J. and Hood, L. (1992), *The code of codes: Scientific and social issues in the human genome project*, 8th edn, Cambridge, MA: Harvard University Press.

Khan, F. H., Bashir, S. and Qamar, U. (2014), 'TOM: Twitter opinion mining framework using hybrid classification scheme', *Decision Support Systems*, 57: 245–257, doi: 10.1016/j.dss.2013.09.004.

Kiernan, M. J. (1993), 'The new strategic architecture: Learning to compete in the twenty-first century', *Academy of Management Perspectives*, 7(1): 7–21, doi: 10.5465/ame.1993.9409142055.

Kim, C. and Mauborgne, R. (2004), *Blue ocean strategy: How to create uncontested market space and make the competition irrelevant*, Boston: Harvard Business School Press.

Kim, J. (2001), 'Phenomenology of digital-being', *Human Studies*, 24(1–2): 87–111, doi: 10.1023/a:1010763028785.

Kincheloe, J. L. (2001), 'Describing the bricolage: Conceptualizing a new rigor in qualitative research', *Qualitative Inquiry*, 7(6): 679–692, doi: 10.1177/107780040100700601.

Kjus, Y. (2015), 'Reclaiming the music: The power of local and physical music distribution in the age of global online services', *New Media and Society*, doi: 10.1177/1461444815580414.

Klarer, M. (2014), 'Putting television "aside": Novel narration in *House of Cards*', *New Review of Film and Television Studies*, 12(2): 203–220, doi: 10.1080/17400309.2014.885818.

Klaus, P. (2013), 'The case of Amazon.com: Towards a conceptual framework of online customer service experience (OCSE) using the emerging consensus technique (ECT)', *Journal of Services Marketing*, 27(6): 443–457, doi: 10.1108/jsm-02-2012-0030.

Klimmt, C. and Vorderer, P. (2003), 'Media Psychology "is not yet there": Introducing theories on media entertainment to the presence debate', *Presence: Teleoperators and Virtual Environments*, 12(4): 346–359, doi: 10.1162/105474603322391596.

Knoppers, B. M. and Chadwick, R. (2006), 'Human genetic research: Emerging trends in ethics', *Focus*, 4(3): 416–422.

Knott, P. (2008), 'Strategy tools: Who really uses them?' *Journal of Business Strategy*, 29(5): 26–31, doi: 10.1108/02756660810902297.

Ko, H. T. and Lau, H. (2013), 'A pricing equilibrium model for digital music market', *7th IFAC Conference on Manufacturing Modelling, Management, and Control, 2013*, doi: 10.3182/20130619-3-ru-3018.00398.

Kocher, D. (2008), 'Convergence culture: Where old and new media collide by Henry Jenkins', *First Monday*, 13(5).

Kogler, H. H. (1999), *The power of dialogue: Critical hermeneutics after Gadamer and Foucault*, Cambridge, MA: MIT Press.

Kong, L. (2005), 'The sociality of cultural industries: Hong Kong's cultural policy and film industry', *International Journal of Cultural Policy*, 11(1): 61–76, doi: 10.1080/10286630500067812.

Kornberger, M. (2013), 'Clausewitz: On strategy', *Business History*, 55(7): 1058–1073, doi: 10.1080/00076791.2013.838035.

Kozinets, R. V. (2010), *Netnography: Doing ethnographic research online*, London: Sage Publications Ltd.

Krackhardt, D. and Hanson, J. R. (2006), 'Informal networks: The company behind the chart', *Creative Management and Development*, doi: 10.4135/9781446213704.n15.

Krackhardt, D. and Stern, R. N. (1988), 'Informal networks and organizational crises: An experimental simulation', *Social Psychology Quarterly*, 51(2), doi: 10.2307/2786835.

Krasnova, H., Spiekermann, S., Koroleva, K. and Hildebrand, T. (2010), 'Online social networks: Why we disclose', *Journal of Information Technology*, 25(2): 109–125, doi: 10.1057/jit.2010.6.

Kress, G. and Van Leeuwen, T. J. (2001), *Multimodal discourse: The modes and media of contemporary communication*, London: Bloomsbury.
Kuss, D. J. and Griffiths, M. D. (2011), 'Online social networking and addiction – A review of the psychological literature', *International Journal of Environmental Research and Public Health*, 8(12): 3528–3552, doi: 10.3390/ijerph8093528.
Kuss, D. J. and Griffiths, M. D. (2012), 'Internet gaming addiction: A systematic review of empirical research', *International Journal of Mental Health and Addiction*, 10(2): 278–296, doi: 10.1007/s11469-011-9318-5.
Lammers, J. C. and Barbour, J. B. (2006), 'An institutional theory of organizational communication', *Communication Theory*, 16(3): 356–377, doi: 10.1111/j.1468-2885.2006.00274.x.
Langvardt, A. W. (2012), 'Business ethics and intellectual property in the global marketplace', *Business Horizons*, 55(4): 325–327, doi: 10.1016/j.bushor.2012.02.002.
Laporte, G. (1992), 'The traveling salesman problem: An overview of exact and approximate algorithms', *European Journal of Operational Research*, 59(2): 231–247, doi: 10.1016/0377-2217(92)90138-y.
Lashinsky, A. (2013), 'Amazon's Jeff Bezos: The ultimate disrupter', CNN, available at: http://management.fortune.cnn.com/2012/11/16/jeff-bezos-amazon/ (accessed 15 June 2015).
Lastowka, G. (2007), 'Google's law', *SSRN Electronic Journal*, doi: 10.2139/ssrn.1017536.
Latonero, M. and Sinnreich, A. (2013), 'The hidden demography of new media ethics', *Information, Communication and Society*, 17(5): 572–593, doi: 10.1080/1369118x.2013.808364.
Lawton, K. and Marom, D. (2012), 'The crowdfunding revolution: How to raise venture capital using social media', New York: McGraw Hill Professional.
Lee, D. (2014), 'Google faces data watchdogs over "right to be forgotten"', BBC News, 24 July, available at: http://m.bbc.co.uk/news/technology-28458194 (accessed 15 July 2015).
Lee, L.-H., Juan, Y.-C., Tseng, W.-L., Chen, H.-H. and Tseng, Y.-H. (2014), 'Mining browsing behaviors for objectionable content filtering', *Journal of the Association for Information Science and Technology*, 66(5): 930–942, doi: 10.1002/asi.23217.
Lee, M. J. and Lee, S. (2014), 'Subject areas and future research agendas in exhibition research: Visitors' and organizers' perspectives', *Event Management*, 18(3): 377–386, doi: 10.3727/152599514x14038805493392.
Lee, N. (2014), 'Food culture and chefs', *Encyclopedia of Food and Agricultural Ethics*: 868–874, doi: 10.1007/978-94-007-0929-4_460.
Lee, N. and Drever, E. (2013), 'The creative industries, creative occupations and innovation in London', *European Planning Studies*, 21(12): 1977–1997, doi: 10.1080/09654313.2012.722969.
Leeflang, P. S. H., Verhoef, P. C., Dahlström, P. and Freundt, T. (2014), 'Challenges and solutions for marketing in a digital era', *European Management Journal*, 32(1): 1–12, doi: 10.1016/j.emj.2013.12.001.
Leigh, W., Modani, N., Purvis, R. and Roberts, T. (2002), 'Stock market trading rule discovery using technical charting heuristics', *Expert Systems with Applications*, 23(2): 155–159, doi: 10.1016/s0957-4174(02)00034-9.
Leonhard, G., Kusek, D. and Lindsay, S. G. (2005), *The future of music: Manifesto for the digital music revolution*, Boston: Berklee Press Publications.
Lessig, L. (2000), *Code: And other laws of cyberspace*, New York: Basic Books.
Lessig, L. (2001), *The future of ideas: The fate of the commons in a connected world*, New York: Random House.

Lessig, L. (2004), *Free culture: How big media uses technology and the law to lock down culture and control creativity*, New York: Penguin Press.

Lessig, L. (2006), '(Re)creativity: How creativity lives', *Copyright and other fairy tales*, doi: 10.4337/9781781951019.00006.

Lessig, L. (2009), 'Remix: Making art and commerce thrive in the hybrid economy', *Choice Reviews Online*, 46(09): 46–5102, doi: 10.5860/choice.46-5102.

Lessig, L. (2010), 'Getting our values around copyright right', *Educause Review*, 45(2): 26–42.

Levina, N. and Arriaga, M. (2014), 'Distinction and status production on user-generated content platforms: Using Bourdieu's theory of cultural production to understand social dynamics in online fields', *Information Systems Research*, 25(3): 468–488, doi: 10.1287/isre.2014.0535.

Levinson, J. (ed.) (2003), *The Oxford handbook of aesthetics*, New York: Oxford University Press, USA.

Lewis, T. (2011), '"You've put yourselves on a plate": The labours of selfhood on MasterChef Australia', in Skeggs, B. and Wood, H. (eds) *Reality Television and Class*, London: British Film Institute, 104–116.

Li, G., Chang, K. and Hoi, S. C. H. (2014), 'Twitter microblog sentiment analysis', *Encyclopedia of Social Network Analysis and Mining*: 2253–2259, doi: 10.1007/978-1-4614-6170-8_265.

Liberman, L. (2013), 'Garbage can model of decision making', *Encyclopedia of Management Theory*, doi: 10.4135/9781452276090.n92.

Lin, K.-C., Wu, S.-H., Chen, L.-P., Ku, T. and Chen, G.-D. (2014), 'Mining the user clusters on Facebook fan pages based on topic and sentiment analysis', *Proceedings of the 2014 IEEE 15th International Conference on Information Reuse and Integration (IEEE IRI 2014)*, doi: 10.1109/iri.2014.7051948.

Lindblom, P. C. E. (1989), *The Science of 'Muddling Through'*, Stratford, NH: Irvington Publishers.

Lingel, J. and Naaman, M. (2011), 'You should have been there, man: Live music, DIY content and online communities', *New Media and Society*, 14(2): 332–349, doi: 10.1177/1461444811417284.

Liu, B. (2011), 'Opinion mining and sentiment analysis', *Web Data Mining*: 459–526, doi: 10.1007/978-3-642-19460-3_11.

Llorens, C. and Costache, A. M. (2013), 'Media pluralism and media governance: Convergent or divergent roads in a digital scenario?' *Communication and Media Policy in the Era of the Internet*: 57–69, doi: 10.5771/9783845243214–57.

Locatelli, G. and Mancini, M. (2014), 'Controlling the delivering of projects in mega-events: An Application on Expo 2015', *Event Management*, 18(3): 285–301, doi: 10. 3727/152599514x13989500765763.

Lord, B. W. and Velez, R. (2013), *Converge: Transforming business at the intersection of marketing and technology*, New York: John Wiley and Sons.

Low, K. C. P. and Ang, S.-L. (2013), 'Blue ocean strategy and CSR', *Encyclopedia of Corporate Social Responsibility*: 179–188, doi: 10.1007/978-3-642-28036-8_633.

Lowe, S., Carr, A. N., Thomas, M. and Watkins-Mathys, L. (2005), 'The fourth hermeneutic in marketing theory', *Marketing Theory*, 5(2): 185–203.

Lueck, A. F. and Auna, R. A. (2007), 'Information disclosure on internet social networking sites: MySpace and Facebook', *PsycEXTRA Dataset*, doi: 10.1037/e659052007-001.

Luxford, A. and Dickinson, J. E. (2015), 'The role of mobile applications in the consumer experience at music festivals', *Event Management*, 19(1): 33–46, doi: 10.3727/152599515x14229071392909.

Lyotard, J. F. (1993), *The postmodern condition: A report on knowledge*, Minneapolis: University of Minnesota Press.

Lopez, M. M., Heymann, E. and Senar, M. A. (2009), 'Analysis of dynamic heuristics for workflow scheduling on grid systems', *IEEE Xplore*, p. 199.

MacCaskill, S. (2014), 'Dropbox adds business security and collaboration tools ahead of UK office opening', *Tech Week Europe*, 23 July, available at: www.techweekeurope.co.uk/workspace/dropbox-for-business-smb-privacy-149650?utm_source=2014-07-24&utm_medium=email&utm_campaign=uk_techweekeurope&id_prob=37090_239552&t=0f3c1d7d311ec2b5eee397f43bc6bb941307309 (accessed 15 July 2015).

MacCaskill, S. (2014), 'Researcher disputes Apple's explanation for iOS backdoor', *Tech Week Europe*, 23 July, available at: www.techweekeurope.co.uk/news/ios-backdoor-apple-security-149635?utm_source=2014-07-24&utm_medium=email&utm_campaign=uk_techweekeurope&id_prob=37090_239552&t=0f3c1d7d311ec2b5eee397f43bc6bb941307309 (accessed 15 July 2015).

MacCaskill, S. (2014), 'Silent Circle and Geeksphone create privacy-focused Blackphone', *Tech Week Europe*, 15 January, available at: www.techweekeurope.co.uk/news/blackphone-geeksphone-silent-circle-135968 (accessed 15 July 2015).

MacCaskill, S. (2014), 'Silent Circle and Geeksphone start Blackphone shipments', *Tech Week Europe*, 30 June, available at: www.techweekeurope.co.uk/news/blackphone-silent-circle-geeksphone-shipments-148256?utm_source=2014-07-01&utm_medium=email&utm_campaign=uk_techweekeurope&id_prob=34585_239552&t=0f3c1d7d311ec2b5eee397f43bc6bb941307309 (accessed 15 July 2015).

Macek, J. (2013), 'More than a desire for text: Online participation and the social curation of content', *Convergence: The International Journal of Research into New Media Technologies*, 19(3): 295–302, doi: 10.1177/1354856513486530.

Machiavelli, N., Detmold, C. E. and Kekewich, L. M. (1993), *The Prince*, London: Wordsworth Editions Ltd.

Mackay, H. (ed.) (1997), *Consumption and everyday life*, London: SAGE Publications.

Madden, S. (2012), 'From databases to big data', *IEEE Internet Computing*, 16(3): 4–6, doi: 10.1109/mic.2012.50.

Maglio, P. P., Nusser, S. and Bishop, K. (2010), 'A service perspective on IBM's brand', *Marketing Review St. Gallen*, 27(6): 44–48, doi: 10.1007/s11621-010-0098-2.

Malheiro, B., Foss, J., Burguillo, J. C., Peleteiro, A. and Mikic, F. (2011), 'Dynamic personalisation of media content', in *Semantic Media Adaptation and Personalization (SMAP): 2011 Sixth International Workshop*, 21–26.

Malone, T. W. (1982), 'Heuristics for designing enjoyable user interfaces', *Proceedings of the 1982 Conference on Human Factors In Computing Systems – CHI '82*, doi: 10.1145/800049.801756.

Mamlouk, L. and Segard, O. (2015), 'Big data and intrusiveness: Marketing issues', *Indian Journal of Science and Technology*, 8(S4), doi: 10.17485/ijst/2015/v8is4/71219.

Maneker, M. (2015), 'Danh Vo stirs the pot on Artnet', *Art Market Monitor*, 16 July, available at: www.artmarketmonitor.com/2015/07/16/danh-vo-stirs-the-pot-on-artnet/ (accessed 20 July 2015).

Mang, P. Y. (2000), 'Strategic innovation: Constantinos Markides on strategy and management', *Academy of Management Perspectives*, 14(3): 43–45, doi: 10.5465/ame.2000.4468064.

Manovich, L. (2001), *The language of new media*, Cambridge, MA: MIT Press.

Manovich, L. (2010), *Software culture*, 2nd edn, Milan: Edizioni Olivares.

Manyika, J. (2011), *Big data: The next frontier for innovation, competition and productivity*, New York: McKinsey and Company.

Manyika, J. (2011), 'Google's CFO on growth, capital structure, and leadership', *Treasury Management International*, 200: 44.

Marchand, A. and Hennig-Thurau, T. (2013), 'Value creation in the video game industry: Industry economics, consumer benefits, and research opportunities', *Journal of Interactive Marketing*, 27(3): 141–157, doi: 10.1016/j.intmar.2013.05.001.

Mardani, A., Akhgar, B., Andrews, S., Yates, S. and Hassanzadeh, M. (2012), 'Investigating the unofficial factors in Google ranking', Sheffield Hallam University research archive, available at: http://shura.shu.ac.uk/6332/1/Akhgar_investigating_the_unofficial_factors.pdf.

Marinescu, D. C. (2013), *Cloud computing: Theory and practice*, Burlington, MA: Morgan Kaufmann Publishers.

Marjanovic, S., Fry, C. and Chataway, J. (2012), 'Crowdsourcing based business models: In search of evidence for innovation 2.0', *Science and Public Policy*, 39(3): 318–332, doi: 10.1093/scipol/scs009.

Markham, A. N. (2005), 'Disciplining the future: A critical organizational analysis of internet studies', *Information Society*, 21(4): 257–267, doi: 10.1080/0197224059 1007571.

Marsden, C. T. (2005), 'Free, open or closed – approaches to the information ecology', *Info*, 7(5): 6–19, doi: 10.1108/14636690510618248.

Marshall, P. D. (2014), 'Seriality and persona', *M/C Journal*, 17(3).

Martin, J. (1981), 'A garbage can model of the psychological research process', *American Behavioral Scientist*, 25(2): 131–151, doi: 10.1177/000276428102500203.

Marwick, A. E. (2008), 'To catch a predator? The MySpace moral panic', *First Monday*, 13 June.

Matheson, B. (2006), 'A culture of creativity: Design education and the creative industries', *Journal of Management Development*, 25(1): 55–64, doi: 10.1108/026217 10610637963.

Mathiesen, K. (2004), 'What is information ethics?' *ACM SIGCAS Computers and Society*, 34(1), doi: 10.1145/1050305.1050312.

May, A., Chaintreau, A., Korula, N. and Lattanzi, S. (2014), 'Filter and follow', *ACM SIGMETRICS Performance Evaluation Review*, 42(1): 43–55, doi: 10.1145/26373 64.2592010.

Mayer-Schönberger, V., Cukier, K. and Mayer-Schonberger, V. (2014), *Big data: A revolution that will transform how we live, work, and think*. New York: Eamon Dolan/Houghton Mifflin Harcourt.

McBride, N. (2005), 'Chaos theory as a model for interpreting information systems in organizations', *Information Systems Journal*, 15(3): 233–254, doi: 10.1111/j.1365-2575.2005.00192.x.

McCleary, K. W. (1995), 'Applying internal marketing techniques for better festival organisation and management', *Festival Management and Event Tourism*, 3(1): 1–7.

McGuigan, J. (2004), *Rethinking cultural policy*, London: Open University Press.

McIntosh, D. (1984), 'The modernity of Machiavelli', *Political Theory*, 12(2): 184–203, doi: 10.1177/0090591784012002003.

McKay, P. (2011), 'Culture of the future: Adapting copyright law to accommodate fan-made derivative works in the twenty-first century', *Regent University Law Review*, 24, 117.

McLuhan, M. (1965), *Understanding media: The extensions of man*, New York: McGraw-Hill.

McPhillips, S. and Merlo, O. (2008), 'Media convergence and the evolving media business model: An overview and strategic opportunities', *Marketing Review*, 8(3): 237–253, doi: 10.1362/146934708x337663.

McQuail, D. (2010), *McQuail's Mass Communication Theory*, 6th edn, London: SAGE Publications.

McRobbie, A. (1998), *British fashion design: Rag trade or image industry?* New York: Routledge.

McRobbie, A. (2002), 'Clubs to companies: Notes on the decline of political culture in speeded up creative worlds', *Cultural Studies*, 16(4): 516–531, doi: 10.1080/09502380210139098.

McRobbie, A. (2004), 'A mixed economy of fashion design', *Blackwell Cultural Economy Reader*: 1–14, doi: 10.1002/9780470774274.ch1.

McWane, S. H. (2001), 'Hollywood vs. Silicon Valley: DeCSS down, Napster to go', *CommLaw Conspectus*, 9: 87.

Meghabghab, G. (2001), 'Google's Web page ranking applied to different topological Web graph structures', *Journal of the American Society for Information Science and Technology*, 52(9): 736–747.

Meizel, K. (2010), *Idolized: Music, media, and identity in American idol*, Bloomington: Indiana University Press.

Menzies, H. (1995), *Whose brave new world? The information highway and the new economy*, Toronto: Between the Lines.

Merli, P. (2013), 'Creating the cultures of the future: Cultural strategy, policy and institutions in Gramsci', *International Journal of Cultural Policy*, 19(4): 399–420, doi: 10.1080/10286632.2011.643872.

Merlo, O., Merlo, O., Lukas, B. A. and Whitwell, G. J. (2008), 'Heuristics revisited: Implications for marketing research and practice', *Marketing Theory*, 8(2): 189–204.

Michael, S. (2011) 'The rise and inglorious fall of MySpace', *Bloomberg Business Week*, 22 June, available at: www.bloomberg.com/bw/magazine/content/11_27/b423505 3917570.htm (accessed 5 June 2015).

Miller, G. (2014), 'Using smartphones to track our everyday moral judgments', *Wired*, 9 November, available at: www.wired.com/2014/09/smartphone-study-moral-psychology (accessed 7 July 2015).

Miller, J. (2011), *Fashion and music*, Oxford: Berg Publishers.

Miller, K. W. and Voas, J. (2010), 'Ethics and the cloud', *IT Professional*, 12(5): 4–5, doi: 10.1109/mitp. 2010.129.

Minazzi, R. (2015), 'Social media metrics and analysis', *Social Media Marketing in Tourism and Hospitality*: 137–163, doi: 10.1007/978-3-319-05182-6_6.

Mintzberg, H., Ahlstrand, B. W. and Lampel, J. (2005), *Strategy safari: A guided tour through the wilds of strategic management*, New York: Free Press.

Mjos, O. J. (2013), *Music, social media and global mobility: MySpace, Facebook, YouTube*, London: Taylor and Francis.

Möller, K. E. K. and Törrönen, P. (2003), 'Business suppliers' value creation potential', *Industrial Marketing Management*, 32(2): 109–118, doi: 10.1016/s0019-8501 (02)00225-0.

Moore, T. and Christin, N. (2013), 'Beware the middleman: Empirical analysis of bitcoin-exchange risk', *Financial Cryptography and Data Security 2013*, Berlin: Springer, 25–33

Morozov, E. (2011), 'From internet freedom to oppression', *New Scientist*, 209(2802): 30–31, doi: 10.1016/s0262-4079(11)60501-0.

Morozov, E. (2011), *The net delusion: The dark side of internet freedom*, New York: PublicAffairs.

Mortensen, D. C. (ed.) (2008), *Communication theory*, 2nd edn, New Brunswick, NJ: Transaction Publishers.

Neisser, U., Boodoo, G., Bouchard, T. J., Boykin, A. W., Brody, N., Ceci, S. J., Halpern, D. F., Loehlin, J. C., Perloff, R., Sternberg, R. J. and Urbina, S. (1996), 'Intelligence: Knowns and unknowns', *American Psychologist*, 51(2): 77–101, doi: 10.1037//0003-066x.51.2.77.

Neri, F., Aliprandi, C., Capeci, F., Cuadros, M. and By, T. (2012), 'Sentiment analysis on social media', *2012 IEEE/ACM International Conference on Advances in Social Networks Analysis and Mining*, doi: 10.1109/asonam.2012.164.

Ng, B. D. and Wiemer-Hastings, P. (2005), 'Addiction to the internet and online gaming', *CyberPsychology and Behavior*, 8(2): 110–113, doi: 10.1089/cpb.2005.8.110.

Nielsen, E. (2013), Inaugural Professorial Lecture, 16 April, presented at London Metropolitan University.

Nielsen, E. (2015), Erik Nielsen Master Class, Keynote Speech with question-and-answer session, 28 April, presented at London Metropolitan University.

Nisbett, M. (2013), 'New perspectives on instrumentalism An empirical study of cultural diplomacy', *International Journal of Cultural Policy*, 19(5): 557–575, doi: 10.1080/10286632.2012.704628.

Nixon, B. (2015), 'The old media business in the new: 'the Googlization of everything' as the capitalization of digital consumption', *Media, Culture and Society*, doi: 10.1177/0163443715594036.

Nonaka, I., Kodama, M., Hirose, A. and Kohlbacher, F. (2014), 'Dynamic fractal organizations for promoting knowledge-based transformation – A new paradigm for organizational theory', *European Management Journal*, 32(1): 137–146, doi: 10.1016/j.emj.2013.02.003.

Nordenflycht, A. von (2010), 'What is a professional service firm? Toward a theory and taxonomy of knowledge-intensive firms', *Academy of Management Review*, 35(1): 155–174, doi: 10.5465/amr.2010.45577926.

Norman, D. A. and Verganti, R. (2014), 'Incremental and radical innovation: Design research vs. technology and meaning change', *Design Issues*, 30(1): 78–96, doi: 10.1162/desi_a_00250.

Nosko, A., Wood, E. and Molema, S. (2010), 'All about me: Disclosure in online social networking profiles: The case of Facebook', *Computers in Human Behavior*, 26(3): 406–418, doi: 10.1016/j.chb.2009.11.012.

Nurse, K. (2004), 'Trinidad carnival: Festival tourism and cultural industry', *Event Management*, 8(4): 223–230, doi: 10.3727/1525995031436854.

Nyström, H. (1979), *Creativity and innovation*, New York John Wiley and Sons.

Obeyesekere, G. (1990), *The work of culture: Symbolic transformation in psychoanalysis and anthropology*, Chicago: University of Chicago Press.

O'Brien, M. (2014), 'The internet, child pornography and cloud computing: The dark side of the web?' *Information and Communications Technology Law*, 23(3): 238–255, doi: 10.1080/13600834.2014.970376.

O'Connor, J. (2005), 'Creative exports: Taking cultural industries to St Petersburg', *International Journal of Cultural Policy*, 11(1): 45–60, doi: 10.1080/102866305 00067747.

Odio, M. A., Wells, J. and Kerwin, S. (2014), 'Full-time student, part-time employee: Capturing the effects of socialization influences on affective commitment for student employees', *Event Management*, 18(3): 325–336, doi: 10.3727/152599514x13989500765844.

Oh, I. and Lee, H. J. (2013), 'Mass media technologies and popular music', *Korea Journal*, 53(4): 34–58.

Ortigosa, A., Martín, J. M. and Carro, R. M. (2014), 'Sentiment analysis in Facebook and its application to e-learning', *Computers in Human Behavior*, 31: 527–541, doi: 10.1016/j.chb.2013.05.024.

O'Sullivan, D. and Jackson, M. J. (2002), 'Festival tourism: A contributor to sustainable local economic development?' *Journal of Sustainable Tourism*, 10(4): 325–342, doi: 10.1080/09669580208667171.

Otteman, T. and Janes, P. (2014), 'It is time? Ending a long-term event', *Event Management*, 18(3): 369–376, doi: 10.3727/152599514x13989500765961.

Padgett, J. F. (1980), 'Managing garbage can hierarchies', *Administrative Science Quarterly*, 25(4), doi: 10.2307/2392282.

Pak, A. and Paroubek, P. (2010), 'Twitter as a corpus for sentiment analysis and opinion mining', *Proceedings of LREC*, 10(May): 1320–1326.

Pak, A. and Paroubek, P. (2011), 'Twitter as a corpus for sentiment analysis and opinion mining', *Database and Expert Systems Applications, DEXA, International Workshops, Toulouse, France, August 29 – Sept. 2 2011.*

Pallares-Barbera, M., Dot, E. and Casellas, A. (2012), 'Artists, cultural gentrification and public policy', *Urbani izziv*, 23(s 1): 104–114.

Paltoglou, G. and Thelwall, M. (2012), 'Twitter, MySpace, Digg', *ACM Transactions on Intelligent Systems and Technology*, 3(4): 1–19, doi: 10.1145/2337542.2337551.

Pang, Z. (2011), 'Optimal dynamic pricing and inventory control with stock deterioration and partial backordering', *Operations Research Letters*, 39(5): 375–379, doi: 10.1016/j.orl.2011.06.009.

Pariser, E. (2011), *The filter bubble: What the internet is hiding from you*, New York: Penguin.

Park, H.-J. and Rabolt, N. J. (2009), 'Cultural value, consumption value, and global brand image: A cross-national study', *Psychology and Marketing*, 26(8): 714–735, doi: 10.1002/mar.20296.

Parker, D. and Stacey, R. D. (1994), *Chaos, management and economics: The implications of non-linear thinking*, 2nd edn, London: Institute of Economic Affairs.

Parker, R., Cox, S. and Thompson, P. (2014), 'How technological change affects power relations in global markets: Remote developers in the console and mobile games industry', *Environment and Planning A*, 46(1): 168–185, doi: 10.1068/a45663.

Parks, B., Pharr, S. W. and Lockeman, B. D. (1994), 'A marketer's guide to Clausewitz: Lessons for winning market share', *Business Horizons*, 37(4): 68–73, doi: 10.1016/0007-6813(94)90051-5.

Paton, G. (2009), 'CSI fuels forensic science degree rise', *The Telegraph*, 16 October, available at: www.telegraph.co.uk/education/6348107/CSI-fuels-forensic-science-degree-rise.html (accessed 6 May 2015).

Pavlik, J. V. (2008), *Media in the digital age*, New York: Columbia University Press.

Pavlik, J. V. (ed.). (2015), 'Digital technology and the future of broadcasting: Global perspectives', New York: Routledge.

Pearce, P. L. and Moscardo, G. M. (1986), 'The concept of authenticity in tourist experiences', *Journal of Sociology*, 22(1): 121–132.

Pearson, S. (2013), *Privacy and security for cloud computing*, London: Springer.

Pedersen, E. R. G. and Gwozdz, W. (2014), 'From resistance to opportunity-seeking: Strategic responses to institutional pressures for corporate social responsibility in the Nordic fashion industry', *Journal of Business Ethics*, 119(2): 245–264, doi: 10.1007/s10551-013-1630-5.

Peters, A. E. and Peters, E. E. (1994), *Fractal market analysis: Applying chaos theory to investment and economics*, New York: Wiley, John and Sons.

Peters, M. A. (2011), 'Greening the knowledge economy: Ecosophy, ecology and economy', *Economics, Management, and Financial Markets*, 2: 11–38, doi: 10.4324/9780203813331.ch46.

Petry, N. M. and O'Brien, C. P. (2013), 'Internet gaming disorder and the DSM-5', *Addiction*, 108(7): 1186–1187, doi: 10.1111/add.12162.

Petz, G., Karpowicz, M., Fürschuß, H., Auinger, A., Stříteský, V. and Holzinger, A. (2013), 'Opinion mining on the Web 2.0 – Characteristics of user generated content and their impacts', *Lecture Notes in Computer Science*: 35–46, doi: 10.1007/978-3-642-39146-0_4.

Phan, M., Thomas, R. and Heine, K. (2011), 'Social media and luxury brand management: The case of Burberry', *Journal of Global Fashion Marketing*, 2(4): 213–222, doi: 10.1080/20932685.2011.10593099.

Phillips, F. (2011), 'The Star Wars franchise, fan edits, and Lucasfilm', *Transformative Works and Cultures*, 9.

Picon, A. (2013), 'Architecture, innovation and tradition', *Architectural Design*, 83(1): 128–133, doi: 10.1002/ad.1535.

Pisano, G. (2006), 'Profiting from innovation and the intellectual property revolution', *Research Policy*, 35(8): 1122–1130, doi: 10.1016/j.respol.2006.09.008.

Poel, M., Renda, A. and Ballon, P. (2007), 'Business model analysis as a new tool for policy evaluation: Policies for digital content platforms', *Info*, 9(5): 86–100, doi: 10.1108/14636690710816471.

Poisot, T., Mounce, R. and Gravel, D. (2013), 'Moving toward a sustainable ecological science: Don't let data go to waste!' *Ideas in Ecology and Evolution*, 6, doi: 10.4033/iee.2013.6b.14.f.

Polkinghorne, B. G., Massey, P. D., Durrheim, D. N., Byrnes, T. and MacIntyre, C. R. (2013), 'Prevention and surveillance of public health risks during extended mass gatherings in rural areas: The experience of the Tamworth Country Music Festival, Australia', *Public Health*, 127(1): 32–38, doi: 10.1016/j.puhe.2012.09.014.

Postigo, H. (2014), 'The socio-technical architecture of digital labor: Converting play into YouTube money', *New Media and Society*, doi: 10.1177/1461444814541527.

Potschka, C. (2013), 'Broadcasting and market-driven politics in the UK and Germany: The Peacock Committee in comparative perspective', *International Journal of Cultural Policy*, 19(5): 595–609, doi: 10.1080/10286632.2012.704629.

Potts, J., Cunningham, S., Hartley, J. and Ormerod, P. (2008), 'Social network markets: A new definition of the creative industries', *Journal of Cultural Economics*, 32(3): 167–185, doi: 10.1007/s10824-008-9066-y.

Pratt, A. C. (2005), 'Cultural industries and public policy: An oxymoron?' *International Journal of Cultural Policy*, 11(1): 31–44, doi: 10.1080/10286630500067739.

Preston, P. and Rogers, J. (2013), 'Convergence, crisis and the digital music economy', *Media and Convergence Management*: 247–260, doi: 10.1007/978-3-642-36163-0_17.

Prevas, J. (2001), *Hannibal crosses the Alps: The invasion of Italy and the Second Punic War*, Cambridge, MA: Da Capo Press.

Psomakelis, E., Tserpes, K., Anagnostopoulos, D. and Varvarigou, T. (2014), 'Comparing methods for Twitter sentiment analysis', *Proceedings of the International Conference on Knowledge Discovery and Information Retrieval*, doi: 10.5220/0005075302250232.

Pugh, C. and Wood, E. H. (2004), 'The strategic use of events within local government: A study of London Borough Councils', *Event Management*, 9(1): 61–71, doi: 10.3727/1525995042781093.

Puisa, R., Murphy, A., Mohamed, K. and Vassalos, D. (2012), 'Design customisation and optimisation through effective design space exploration', *11th International Marine Design Conference*.

Quinn, M. J. (2014), *Ethics for the information age*, 5th edn, Boston: Pearson Education.

Rae-Hunter, C. (2012), 'Better mousetraps: Licensing, access, and innovation in the new music marketplace', *Journal of Business and Technology Law*, 7: 35.

Ramachandran, V. S. and Hubbard, E. M. (2001), 'Psychophysical investigations into the neural basis of synaesthesia', *Proceedings of the Royal Society B: Biological Sciences*, 268(1470): 979–983, doi: 10.1098/rspb.2000.1576.

Ramsey, P. and White, A. (2014), 'Art for art's sake? A critique of the instrumentalist turn in the teaching of media and communications in UK universities', *International Journal of Cultural Policy*: 1–19, doi: 10.1080/10286632.2013.878338.

Rashid, T., Raj, R. and Walters, P. (2011), *Events management: An integrated and practical approach*, London: SAGE Publications.

Rastogi, S., Singhal, R. and Kumar, R. (2014), 'A sentiment analysis based approach to Facebook user recommendation', *International Journal of Computer Applications*, 90(16): 21–25, doi: 10.5120/15805-4670.

Ratten, V. (2013), 'Cloud computing: A social cognitive perspective of ethics, entrepreneurship, technology marketing, computer self-efficacy and outcome expectancy on behavioural intentions', *Australasian Marketing Journal*, 21(3): 137–146.

Reid, F. and Harrigan, M. (2013), *An analysis of anonymity in the bitcoin system*, New York: Springer.

Reimers, I. and Waldfogel, J. (2014), 'Throwing the books at them: Amazon's puzzling long run pricing strategy', *SSRN Electronic Journal*, doi: 10.2139/ssrn.2442747.

Reimsbach-Kounatze, C. and Wunsch-Vincent, S. (2010), 'Online games and virtual worlds: Business and policy developments', *Governance of Digital Game Environments and Cultural Diversity*, doi: 10.4337/9781849806350.00008.

Reinish, L. (2011), 'Media consolidation: The illusion of choice', *Free Press*, 22 November, available at: www.freepress.net/blog/11/11/22/media-consolidation-illusion-choice (accessed 15 July 2015).

Reist, M. T. and Bray, A. (eds) (2012), *Big Porn Inc: Exposing the harms of the global pornography industry*, Australia: Independent Pub Group.

Rennings, K. (2000), 'Redefining innovation – eco-innovation research and the contribution from ecological economics', *Ecological Economics*, 32(2): 319–332, doi: 10.1016/s0921-8009(99)00112-3.

Renzulli, J. S. (2005), 'The three-ring conception of giftedness: A developmental model for promoting creative productivity', *Conceptions of Giftedness*: 246–279, doi: 10.1017/cbo9780511610455.015.

Resca, A., Za, S. and Spagnoletti, P. (2013), 'Digital platforms as sources for organizational and strategic transformation: A case study of the midblue project', *Journal of Theoretical and Applied Electronic Commerce Research*, 8(2): 11–12, doi: 10.4067/s0718-18762013000200006.

Resnick, P., Garrett, K. R., Kriplean, T., Munson, S. A. and Stroud, N. J. (2013), 'Bursting your (filter) bubble', *Proceedings of the 2013 Conference on Computer Supported Cooperative Work Companion – CSCW '13*, doi: 10.1145/2441955.2441981.

Reynolds, C. F. (2013), 'Expanding visions of creative intelligence: An interdisciplinary exploration', *Roeper Review*, 35(3): 206–207, doi: 10.1080/02783193.2013.795480.

Reynolds, N. (2001), 'Turner Prize won by man who turns lights off', *The Telegraph*, 10 December, available at: www.telegraph.co.uk/news/uknews/1364860/Turner-Prize-won-by-man-who-turns-lights-off.html (accessed 15 July 2015).

Reynolds, N. (2003), 'Art rivals in a row about nothing', *The Telegraph*, 29 April, available at: www.telegraph.co.uk/news/uknews/1364860/Turner-Prize-won-by-man-who-turns-lights-off.html (accessed 15 July 2015).

Richardson, B. (1994), 'Comprehensive approach to strategic management', *Management Decision*, 32(8): 27–41, doi: 10.1108/eum0000000004314.

Rindfleisch, A. (1996), 'Marketing as warfare: Reassessing a dominant metaphor', *Business Horizons*, 39(5): 3–10, doi: 10.1016/s0007-6813(96)90060-9.

Ritala, P., Golnam, A. and Wegmann, A. (2014), 'Coopetition-based business models: The case of Amazon.com', *Industrial Marketing Management*, 43(2): 236–249, doi: 10.1016/j.indmarman.2013.11.005.

Ritala, S. (2013), 'Pandora and Spotify: Legal issues and licensing requirements for interactive and non-interactive internet radio broadcasters', *IDEA*, 54, 23.

Robards, B. (2012), 'Leaving MySpace, joining Facebook: "Growing up" on social network sites', *Continuum*, 26(3): 385–398, doi: 10.1080/10304312.2012.665836.

Robson, L. M. (2008), 'Event management body of knowledge (EMBOK): The future of event industry research', *Event Management*, 12(1): 19–25, doi: 10.3727/152599509787992607.

Rogers, E. M. and Kincaid, L. D. (1980), *Communication networks: Towards a new paradigm for research*, New York: Collier Macmillan.

Rogers, E. M., Hagerstrand, T. and Pred, A. (1969), 'Innovation Diffusion as a spatial process', *Technology and Culture*, 10(3), doi: 10.2307/3101713.

Rollings, A. and Morris, D. (2003), *Game architecture and design*, Indianapolis, IN: New Riders Publishing.

Ron, D. and Shamir, A. (2013), 'Quantitative analysis of the full bitcoin transaction graph', *Financial Cryptography and Data Security 2013*, Berling: Springer, 6–24.

Rosenkrantz, D. J., Stearns, R. E. and Lewis, P. M. (1977), 'An analysis of several heuristics for the traveling salesman problem', *SIAM Journal on Computing*, 6(3): 563–581, doi: 10.1137/0206041.

Rothen, N. and Meier, B. (2010), 'Higher prevalence of synaesthesia in art students', *Perception*, 39(5): 718–720, doi: 10.1068/p6680.

Rouleau, L. and Séguin, F. (1995), 'Strategy and organization theories: Common forms of discourse', *Journal of Management Studies*, 32(1): 101–117, doi: 10.1111/j.1467-6486.1995.tb00647.x.

Rousseau, S. (2012), *Food media: Celebrity chefs and the politics of everyday interference*, New York: Bloomsbury USA Academic.

Rousseau, S. (2014), 'Food "porn" in media', *Encyclopedia of Food and Agricultural Ethics*: 748–754, doi: 10.1007/978-94-007-0929-4_395.

Rubinstein, I. and Good, N. (2012) 'Privacy by design: A Counterfactual analysis of Google and Facebook privacy incidents', *SSRN Electronic Journal*, doi: 10.2139/ssrn.2128146.

Rumbold, K. (2010), 'From "access" to "creativity": Shakespeare institutions, new media, and the language of cultural value', *Shakespeare Quarterly*, 61(3): 313–336, doi: 10.1353/shq.2010.0009.

Rushdi, Y. A. K. and Kamal, A. N. (2014), 'An evaluation of Google's organisational and recruitment culture', *Management*, 4(4): 98–101.

Rutter, P. (2011), *The music industry handbook*, New York: Taylor and Francis.

Rutter, R. N. (2014), 'A retailer perspective of e-commerce brand management', *E-commerce Platform Acceptance*: 101–128, doi: 10.1007/978-3-319-06121-4_6.

Ryan, L. (2013), 'Leading change through creative destruction: How Netflix's self-destruction strategy created its own market', *International Journal of Business Innovation and Research*, 7(4), doi: 10.1504/ijbir.2013.054868.

Sabin, P. (1996), 'The mechanics of battle in the Second Punic War', *Bulletin of the Institute of Classical Studies*, 41(S67): 59–79, doi: 10.1111/j.2041-5370.1996.tb01914.x.

Sahgal, A. and Elfering, A. (2011), 'Relevance of cognitive dissonance, activation and involvement to branding: An overview', *Escritos de Psycología/Psychological Writings*, 4(3): 15–26, doi: 10.5231/psy.writ.2011.0809.

Sako, M. (2012), 'Business models for strategy and innovation', *Communications of the ACM*, 55(7), doi: 10.1145/2209249.2209259.

Salama, A. M. and Wilkinson, N. (2007), *Design studio pedagogy: Horizons for the future*, Gateshead: Urban International Press.

Salmon, E. T. (1960), 'The strategy of the Second Punic War', *Greece and Rome (Second Series)*, 7(2): 131, doi: 10.1017/S0017383500014571.

Salo, J., Lankinen, M. and Mäntymäki, M. (2013), 'The use of social media for artist marketing: Music industry perspectives and consumer motivations', *International Journal on Media Management*, 15(1): 23–41, doi: 10.1080/14241277.2012.755682.

Salomon, G. (1979), *Interaction of media, cognition, and learning: An exploration of how symbolic forms cultivate mental skills and affect knowledge acquisition*, 2nd edn, San Francisco: Jossey-Bass.

Satell, G. (2013), 'What Netflix's *House of Cards* means for the future of TV', *Forbes Online*, available at: www.forbes.com/sites/gregsatell/2013/03/04/what-netflixs-house-of-cards-means-for-the-future-of-tv/ (accessed 5 June 2015).

Scanlon, L. (1994/2007), *Narrative, authority, and power: The medieval exemplum and the Chaucerian tradition*, New York: Cambridge University Press.

Schau, H. J., Muñiz Jr, A. M. and Arnould, E. J. (2009), 'How brand community practices create value', *Journal of Marketing*, 73(5): 30–51.

Schelling, T. C. (1980), *The strategy of conflict*, Cambridge, MA: Harvard University Press.

Schmidt, G. M. and Druehl, C. T. (2008), 'When is a disruptive innovation disruptive?' *Journal of Product Innovation Management*, 25(4): 347–369, doi: 10.1111/j.1540-5885.2008.00306.x.

Scholz, T. (2013), *Digital labor: The internet as playground and factory*, New York: Routledge.

Schott, G. and Burn, A. (2004), 'Art (re) production as an expression of collective agency within Oddworld Fan-culture', *Works and Days, Capitalizing on Play: Politicized Readings of the Computer Game Industry*, 22(1): 251–274.

Schott, G. and Burn, A. (2007), 'Fan-art as a function of agency in Oddworld fan-culture', *Videogames and Art*, Bristol: Intellect Books, 238–254.

Schultz, N., Zarnekow, R., Wulf, J. and Nguyen, Q. T. (2011), 'The new role of developers in the mobile ecosystem: An Apple and Google case study', *Intelligence in Next Generation Networks (ICIN): 2011 15th International Conference*, October, 103–108.

Schumpeter, J. A. (1949), *Theory of economic development*, London: Oxford University Press.

Scott, D. M. (2007), *The new rules of marketing and PR: How to use news releases, blogs, podcasting, viral marketing and online media to reach buyers directly*, New York: John Wiley and Sons.

Sedigh, A. K. and Roudaki, M. (2003), 'Identification of the dynamics of Google's ranking algorithm', *13th IFAC Symposium on System Identification.*

Shalley, C., Hitt, M. A., Zhou, J., Rigolizzo, M. and Amabile, T. (2015), 'Entrepreneurial creativity', *The Oxford handbook of creativity, innovation, and entrepreneurship*, doi: 10.1093/oxfordhb/9780199927678.013.0018.

Shannon, C. E. (1949), 'Communication theory of secrecy systems', *Bell System Technical Journal*, 28(4): 656–715, doi: 10.1002/j.1538-7305.1949.tb00928.x.

Shannon, C., E. (1993), *A mathematical theory of communication*, doi: 10.1109/978047 0544242.ch1.

Sharifi, S. S. and Esfidani, M. R. (2014), 'The impacts of relationship marketing on cognitive dissonance, satisfaction, and loyalty', *International Journal of Retail and Distribution Management*, 42(6): 553–575, doi: 10.1108/ijrdm-05–2013–0109.

Sharma, R. S., Tan, M. and Pereira, F. (eds) (2012), *Understanding the interactive digital media marketplace: Frameworks, platforms, communities and issues*, Information Science Reference.

Shaw, K. (2013), 'Independent creative subcultures and why they matter', *International Journal of Cultural Policy*, 19(3): 333–352, doi: 10.1080/10286632.2013.788162.

Shaw, M. and Black, D. W. (2008), 'Internet addiction', *CNS Drugs*, 22(5): 353–365, doi: 10.2165/00023210-200822050-00001.

Shefrin, E. (2004), 'Lord of the Rings, Star Wars, and participatory fandom: Mapping new congruencies between the internet and media entertainment culture', *Critical Studies in Media Communication*, 21(3): 261–281, doi: 10.1080/0739318042 000212729.

Shen, B., Jung, J., Chow, P.-S. and Wong, S. (2014), 'Co-branding in fast fashion: The impact of consumers' need for uniqueness on purchase perception', *International Series on Consumer Science*: 101–112, doi: 10.1007/978-1-4939-0277-4_7.

Shields, R. (ed.) (1996), *Cultures of internet: Virtual spaces, real histories, living bodies*, Thousand Oaks, CA: Sage Publications.

Shrum, L. J. (2004), *The psychology of entertainment media: Blurring the lines between entertainment and persuasion*, Mahwah, NJ: Lawrence Erlbaum Associates.

Siau, K., Nah, F. F.-H., Mennecke, B. E. and Schiller, S. Z. (2010), 'Co-creation and collaboration in a virtual world', *Journal of Database Management*, 21(4): 1–13, doi: 10.4018/jdm.2010100101.

Sidawi, B. (2012), 'The impact of social interaction and communications on innovation in the architectural design studio', *Buildings*, 2(4): 203–217, doi: 10.3390/ buildings2030203.

Silberholz, J., Raiconi, A., Cerulli, R., Gentili, M., Golden, B. and Chen, S. (2013), 'Comparison of heuristics for the colourful travelling salesman problem', *International Journal of Metaheuristics*, 2(2): 141–173.

Simmel, G. (1957), 'Fashion', *American Journal of Sociology*, 62(6), doi: 10.1086/ 222102.

Simpson, S. (2004), 'Explaining the commercialization of the internet', *Information, Communication and Society*, 7(1): 50–68, doi: 10.1080/1369118042000208898.

Singh, J. V. (2006), 'Ecology, strategy and organizational change', *Advances in Strategic Management*: 177–214, doi: 10.1016/s0742-3322(06)23006-7.

Singh, S. and Lyon, D. (2012), 'Surveilling consumers: The social consequences of data processing on Amazon. com', *The Routledge companion to digital consumption*, London: Routledge, doi: 10.4324/9780203105306.ch28.

Sirianni, J. M. and Vishwanath, A. (2015), 'Problematic online pornography use: A media attendance perspective', *Journal of Sex Research*, 1–14, doi: 10.1080/0022 4499.2014.980496.

Skoric, M. M. and Kwan, G. C. E. (2011), 'Platforms for mediated sociability and online social capital: The role of Facebook and massively multiplayer online games', *Asian Journal of Communication*, 21(5): 467–484, doi: 10.1080/01292986.2011.587014.

Skinner, Q. (1983), 'Machiavelli on the maintenance of liberty', *Politics*, 18(2): 3–15.

Smith, R. R. (2010), *Breakfast with Socrates*, New York: Free Press.

Smith, R. R. (2010), *Death-drive: Freudian hauntings in literature and art*, Edinburgh: Edinburgh University Press.

Smith, R. R. (2013), *The reality test: Still relying on strategy?* London: Profile Books.

Snickars, P. (2010), *The YouTube reader*, Stockholm: Statens Ljud-och Bildarkiv.

Somit, A. and Masters, R. D. (1998), 'Machiavelli, Leonardo, and the science of power', *American Political Science Review*, 92(1), doi: 10.2307/2585946.

Souza, C. D' and Prentice, D. (2002), 'Auctioneer strategy and pricing: Evidence from an art auction', *Marketing Intelligence and Planning*, 20(7): 417–427, doi: 10.1108/02634500210450855.

Spagnoletti, P., Resca, A. and Lee, G. (2015), 'A design theory for digital platforms supporting online communities: A multiple case study', *Journal of Information Technology*, doi: 10.1057/jit.2014.37.

Spee, A. P. and Jarzabkowski, P. (2009), 'Strategy tools as boundary objects', *Strategic Organization*, 7(2): 223–232, doi: 10.1177/1476127009102674.

Speh, T. W. and Hutt, M. D. (2010), *Business marketing management b2b*, 10th edn, Mason, OH: South-Western Cengage Learning.

Stacey, R. D. (1995), 'The science of complexity: An alternative perspective for strategic change processes', *Strategic Management Journal*, 16(6): 477–495, doi: 10.1002/smj.4250160606.

Stacey, R. D. (2002), 'An alternative perspective for strategic change processes', *Strategy: Critical Perspectives on Business and Management*, 4(1995): 3.

Stallabrass, J. (2001), *High art lite: British art in the 1990s*, London: Verso Books.

Stanoevska-Slabeva, K. and Schmid, B. F. (2001), 'A typology of online communities and community supporting platforms', *Proceedings of the 34th Annual Hawaii International Conference on System Sciences*, doi: 10.1109/hicss.2001.927041.

Stechow, W. and Clark, K. (1953), 'Leonardo da Vinci, an account of His Development as an artist', *Journal of Aesthetics and Art Criticism*, 11(3), doi: 10.2307/426775.

Steiber, A. and Alänge, S. (2013), 'A corporate system for continuous innovation: The case of Google Inc', *European Journal of Innovation Management*, 16(2): 243–264, doi: 10.1108/14601061311324566.

Stelter, B. (2011), 'News corporation sells MySpace for $35 Million', *New York Times*, 29 June, available at: http://mediadecoder.blogs.nytimes.com/2011/06/29/news-corp-sells-myspace-to-specific-media-for-35-million/ (accessed 15 July 2015).

Stern, D. B. (2003), 'The fusion of horizons: Dissociation, enactment, and understanding', *Psychoanalytic Dialogues*, 13(6): 843–873, doi: 10.1080/10481881309348770.

Sternberg, R. J. and Lubart, T. I. (1995), 'Defying the crowd: Cultivating creativity in a culture of conformity', *Choice Reviews Online*, 33(03): 33–1835, doi: 10.5860/choice.33-1835.

Sternberg, R. J. and Lubart, T. I. (1998), 'The concept of creativity: Prospects and paradigms', *Handbook of Creativity*: 3–15, doi: 10.1017/cbo9780511807916.003.

Stewart, N. (2012), 'What comes after the Elsevier boycott? The answer might be found by following the "green'road to open access"', Impact of Social Sciences Blog.

Stinger, C. L. (1985), *The Renaissance in Rome*, Bloomington: Indiana University Press.

Storz, C., Riboldazzi, F. and John, M. (2015), 'Mobility and innovation: A cross-country comparison in the video games industry', *Research Policy*, 44(1): 121–137, doi: 10.1016/j.respol.2014.07.015.

Strategic Direction (2013), 'Sony, Spotify and the statistical symphony: How data can save the music industry', *Strategic Direction*, 29(7): 25–27

Sultan, N. and van de Bunt-Kokhuis, S. (2012), 'Organisational culture and cloud computing: Coping with a disruptive innovation', *Technology Analysis and Strategic Management*, 24(2): 167–179, doi: 10.1080/09537325.2012.647644.

Summer, L. (2010), 'Music: The aesthetic elixir', *Voices: A World Forum for Music Therapy*, 10, doi: 10.15845/voices.v10i3.558.

Sun, Y. S. and Guo, S. (2013), 'Media use, social comparison, cognitive dissonance and peer pressure as antecedents of fashion involvement', *Intercultural Communication Studies*, 22(1).

Sutton, B. (2015), 'Poll: Who is the bigger baby, Artist Danh Võ or Collector Bert Kreuk?' *Hyper Allergic*, 17 July, available at: http://hyperallergic.com/223014/poll-who-is-the-bigger-baby-artist-danh-vo-or-collector-bert-kreuk/ (accessed 20 July 2015).

Swan, J., Robertson, M. and Newell, S. (2014), 'Managing the "unknowable" in complex innovation projects', *Academy of Management Proceedings*, 2014(1): 13549–13549, doi: 10.5465/ambpp. 2014.13549abstract.

Tamony, P. (1983), 'Gonzo', *American Speech*, 58(1), doi: 10.2307/454762.

Taneja, H., Webster, J. G., Malthouse, E. C. and Ksiazek, T. B. (2012), 'Media consumption across platforms: Identifying user-defined repertoires', *New Media and Society*, 14(6): 951–968, doi: 10.1177/1461444811436146.

Tanford, S. and Montgomery, R. (2014), 'The effects of social influence and cognitive dissonance on travel purchase decisions', *Journal of Travel Research*, doi: 10.1177/0047287514528287.

Tarlton, C. D. (1999) 'Fortuna and the landscape of action in Machiavelli's *Prince*', *New Literary History*, 30(4): 737–755.

Teece, D. J. (2010), 'Business models, business strategy and innovation', *Long Range Planning*, 43(2–3): 172–194, doi: 10.1016/j.lrp. 2009.07.003.

Teipen, C. (2008), 'Work and employment in creative industries: The video games industry in Germany, Sweden and Poland', *Economic and Industrial Democracy*, 29(3): 309–335, doi: 10.1177/0143831x08092459.

Telci, E. E., Maden, C. and Kantur, D. (2011), 'The theory of cognitive dissonance: A marketing and management perspective', *Procedia – Social and Behavioral Sciences*, 24: 378–386, doi: 10.1016/j.sbspro.2011.09.120.

Terra, L. A. A. and Passador, J. L. (2015), 'A phenomenological approach to the study of social systems', *Systemic Practice and Action Research*, doi: 10.1007/s11213-015-9350-7.

Thomas, J. (2014), 'Beware bubbles and echo chambers', *Hastings Center Report*, 44(S5): 43–45, doi: 10.1002/hast.400.

Thompson, C. (2008), 'Brave new world of digital intimacy', *New York Times*, 9 July, available at: www.nytimes.com/2008/09/07/magazine/07awareness-t.html?pagewanted=all&_r=0 (accessed 5 June 2015).

Thompson, D. (2014), 'Is *House of Cards* really a hit?' *The Atlantic*, 24 February, available at: www.theatlantic.com/business/archive/2014/02/is-i-house-of-cards-i-really-a-hit/284035/ (accessed 5 June 2015).

Timmermans, J., Stahl, B. C., Ikonen, V. and Bozdag, E. (2010), 'The ethics of cloud computing: A conceptual review', *2010 IEEE Second International Conference on Cloud Computing Technology and Science*, doi: 10.1109/cloudcom.2010.59.

Tompkins, J. (2013), 'Horror 2.0 (on demand): The digital convergence of horror film culture', *Television and New Media*, 15(5): 413–432, doi: 10.1177/1527476412470493.

Townley, B., Beech, N. and McKinlay, A. (2009). *Managing in the creative industries*, London: Sage Publications.

Trice, H. M. and Beyer, J. M. (1991), 'Cultural leadership in organizations', *Organization Science*, 2(2): 149–169, doi: 10.1287/orsc.2.2.149.

Tsai, M. H., Lin, Y. D. and Su, Y. H. (2011), 'A grounded theory study on the business model structure of Google', *International Journal of Electronic Business Management*, 9(3): 231.

Tsang, D. (2015), *Entrepreneurial creativity in a virtual world*, Cheltenham: Edward Elgar Publishing.

Tschang, T. F. (2007), 'Balancing the tensions between rationalization and creativity in the video games industry', *Organization Science*, 18(6): 989–1005, doi: 10.1287/orsc.1070.0299.

Tsou, M.-H., Jung, C.-T., Allen, C., Yang, J.-A., Gawron, J.-M., Spitzberg, B. H. and Han, S. (2015), 'Social media analytics and research test-bed (SMART dashboard)', p. 2.

Tungate, M. (2009), *Fashion brands: Branding style from Armani to Zara*, 2nd edn, London: Kogan Page Publishers.

Tyson, G., Elkhatib, Y., Sastry, N. and Uhlig, S. (2013), 'Demystifying porn 2.0', *Proceedings of the 2013 conference on Internet measurement conference – IMC '13*, doi: 10.1145/2504730.2504739.

Tzu, S., Group, D. T. and Sun, T. (2002), *The art of war: The Denma translation*, Boston: Shambhala Publications.

Udwadia, F. E. (1990), 'Creativity and innovation in organizations: Two models and managerial implications', *Technological Forecasting and Social Change*, 38(1): 65–80, doi: 10.1016/0040-1625(90)90018-q.

United States Copyright Office (2015), 'Copyright and the music marketplace – a report of the register of copyrights', February, available at: http://copyright.gov/policy/musiclicensingstudy/copyright-and-the-music-marketplace.pdf (accessed 5 June 2015).

Valencia, J. C. N. (2011), 'Organizational culture as determinant of product innovation', *Strategic Direction*, 27, doi: 10.1108/sd.2011.05627dad.006.

Van Cuilenburg, J. and McQuail, D. (2003), 'Media policy paradigm shifts: Towards a new communications policy paradigm', *European Journal of Communication*, 18(2): 181–207, doi: 10.1177/0267323103018002002.

Van Dam, J.-W. and van de Velden, M. (2015), 'Online profiling and clustering of Facebook users', *Decision Support Systems*, 70: 60–72, doi: 10.1016/j.dss.2014.12.001.

Van den Berg, I., Admiraal, W. and Pilot, A. (2006), 'Design principles and outcomes of peer assessment in higher education', *Studies in Higher Education*, 31(3): 341–356.

VanderBurgh, J. (2010), 'New media in the white cube and beyond: Curatorial models for digital art', *Visual Studies*, 25(1): 107–108, doi: 10.1080/14725861003607124.

Van Dijck, J. (2012), 'Facebook and the engineering of connectivity: A multi-layered approach to social media platforms', *Convergence: The International Journal of Research into New Media Technologies*, 19(2): 141–155, doi: 10.1177/1354856512457548.

Van Noorden, R. (2012), 'Journal offers flat fee for "all you can publish"', Nature, 486(7402): 166.

Van Winkle, C. M. and Falk, J. H. (2015), 'Personal meaning mapping at festivals: A useful tool for a challenging context', *Event Management*, 19(1): 143–150, doi: 10.3727/152599515x14229071393223.

Veit, D., Clemons, E., Benlian, A., Buxmann, P., Hess, T., Kundisch, D., Leimeister, J. M., Loos, P. and Spann, M. (2014), 'Business models', *Business and Information Systems Engineering*, 6(1): 45–53, doi: 10.1007/s12599-013-0308-y.

Velthuis, O. and Troy, G. (2005), *Talking prices: Symbolic meanings of prices on the market for contemporary art*, Princeton: Princeton University Press.

Verstraete, G. (2014), 'Mapping the rise of the iPhone: Between phones and mobile media', *NECSUS European Journal of Media Studies*, 3(1): 21–41.

Villi, M. (2012), 'Social curation in audience communities: UDC (user-distributed content) in the networked media ecosystem', *Participations: The International Journal of Audience and Reception Studies*, 9(2): 614–632.

Vise, D. (2007), 'The Google story', *Strategic Direction*, 23, doi: 10.1108/sd.2007.05623jae.001.

Viswanath, B., Mislove, A., Cha, M. and Gummadi, K. P. (2009), 'On the evolution of user interaction in Facebook', *Proceedings of the 2nd ACM Workshop on Online Social Networks – WOSN '09*, doi: 10.1145/1592665.1592675.

Wakefield, J. (2014), 'UK broadband not fit for purpose, says business group', BBC News, 14 July, available at: http://m.bbc.co.uk/news/technology-28232142 (accessed 14 July 2015).

Wall, T. and Dubber, A. (2010), 'Experimenting with fandom, live music, and the internet: Applying insights from music fan culture to new media production', *Journal of New Music Research*, 39(2): 159–169, doi: 10.1080/09298215.2010.489645.

Walton, N. (2012), '"Four-closure": How Amazon, Apple, Facebook and Google are driving business model innovation', *2012 International Conference on Innovation Management and Technology Research*, doi: 10.1109/icimtr.2012.6236368.

Wan, C.-S. and Chiou, W.-B. (2006), 'Psychological motives and online games addiction: A test of flow theory and humanistic needs theory for Taiwanese adolescents', *CyberPsychology and Behavior*, 9(3): 317–324, doi: 10.1089/cpb.2006.9.317.

Ward, J., Huckstep, B. and Tsakanikos, E. (2006), 'Sound-colour synaesthesia: To what extent does it use cross-modal mechanisms common to us all?' *Cortex*, 42(2): 264–280, doi: 10.1016/s0010-9452(08)70352-6.

Ward, J., Thompson-Lake, D., Ely, R. and Kaminski, F. (2008), 'Synaesthesia, creativity and art: What is the link?' *British Journal of Psychology*, 99(1): 127–141, doi: 10.1348/000712607x204164.

Wardrop, K. (2010), 'Festivals management studies: Developing a framework and priorities for comparative and cross cultural research', *International Journal of Event and Festival Management*, 1, doi: 10.1108/ijefm.2010.43401aae.002.

Water, R. (2012), 'Angry Birds billionaires in the making? Rovio ownership structure laid bare', *The Next Web*, available at: http://thenextweb.com/insider/2012/02/23/angry-birds-billionaires-in-the-making-rovio-ownership-structure-laid-bare/ (accessed 5 June 2015).

Waterworth, J. A. (1997), 'Creativity and sensation: The Case for synaesthetic media', *Leonardo*, 30(4), doi: 10.2307/1576481.

Watts, C. and Hilton, D. (2011), 'Pornography addiction: A neuroscience perspective', *Surgical Neurology International*, 2(1), doi: 10.4103/2152-7806.76977.

Weckert, J. and Henschke, A. (2009), 'Computer ethics and applied contexts', *Cambridge handbook of information and computer ethics*: 181–198, doi: 10.1017/cbo9780511845239.012.

Weichselbraun, A., Gindl, S. and Scharl, A. (2014), 'Enriching semantic knowledge bases for opinion mining in big data applications', *Knowledge-Based Systems*, 69: 78–85, doi: 10.1016/j.knosys.2014.04.039.

Weick, K. E. (1996), 'Drop your tools: An allegory for organizational studies', *Administrative Science Quarterly*, 301–313.

Weick, K. E. and Mintzberg, H. (1974), 'The nature of managerial work', *Administrative Science Quarterly*, 19(1), doi: 10.2307/2391793.

Weijters, B., Goedertier, F. and Verstreken, S. (2014), 'Online music consumption in today's technological context: Putting the influence of ethics in perspective', *Journal of Business Ethics*, 124(4): 537–550, doi: 10.1007/s10551-013-1892-y.

Weinstein, A. and Lejoyeux, M. (2010), 'Internet addiction or excessive internet use', *American Journal of Drug and Alcohol Abuse*, 36(5): 277–283, doi: 10.3109/00952990.2010.491880.

While, A. (2003), 'Locating art worlds: London and the making of young British art', *Area*, 35(3): 251–263, doi: 10.1111/1475-4762.00174.

Whitfield, J. (2012), 'Elsevier boycott gathers pace: Rebel academics ponder how to break free of commercial publishers', *Nature News*, 2(9).

Whittington, R. (2006), 'Completing the practice turn in strategy research', *Organization Studies*, 27(5): 613–634, doi: 10.1177/0170840606064101.

Wicklund, R. A. and Brehm, J. W. (2013), *Perspectives on cognitive dissonance*, New York: Psychology Press.

Wikstrom, P. (2014), *The music industry: Music in the cloud*, London: Polity Press.

Wilden, A. (1987), *The rules are no game: The strategy of communication*, New York: Routledge and Keegan Paul.

Wilding, R. D. (1998), 'Chaos theory: Implications for supply chain management', *International Journal of Logistics Management*, 9(1): 43–56, doi: 10.1108/09574099810805735.

Wilkins, A. L. and Ouchi, W. G. (1983), 'Efficient cultures: Exploring the relationship between culture and organizational performance', *Administrative Science Quarterly*, 28(3), doi: 10.2307/2392253.

Williams, H. L. (2013), 'Intellectual property rights and innovation: Evidence from the human genome', *Journal of Political Economy*, 121(1): 1–27, doi: 10.1086/669706.

Wilson, M. C. (2012), 'The Elsevier boycott and beyond', available at: mcw.wordpress.fos.auckland.ac.nz (accessed 5 June 2015).

Winter, C. (2013), 'Media development and convergence in the music industry', *Media and Convergence Management*: 261–281, doi: 10.1007/978-3-642-36163-0_18.

Wiseman, A., Zilczer, J., Brougher, K. and Mattis, O. (2005), *Visual music synaesthesia in art and music since 1900*, London: Thames and Hudson.

Wolf, M. J. P. and Perron, B. (eds) (2014), *The Routledge companion to video game studies*, London: Routledge.

Wood, H. and Skeggs, B. (eds) (2011), *Reality television and class*, New York: Palgrave Macmillan / British Film Institute.

Woodman, R. W., Sawyer, J. E. and Griffin, R. W. (1993), 'Toward a theory of organizational creativity', *Academy of Management Review*, 18(2): 293–321, doi: 10.5465/amr.1993.3997517.

Woodside, A. G., Megehee, C. M. and Sood, S. (2012), 'Conversations with(in) the collective unconscious by consumers, brands, and relevant others', *Journal of Business Research*, 65(5): 594–602, doi: 10.1016/j.jbusres.2011.02.016.

Yeoman, I., Robertson, M., Ali-Knight, J., Drummond, S. and McMahon-Beattie, U. (eds) (2003), *Festival and Events Management: An International Arts and Culture Perspective*, Amsterdam: Elsevier Butterworth-Heinemann.

Yoo, Y., Boland, R. J., Lyytinen, K. and Majchrzak, A. (2012), 'Organizing for innovation in the digitized world', *Organization Science*, 23(5): 1398–1408, doi: 10.1287/orsc.1120.0771.

Yoo, Y., Henfridsson, O. and Lyytinen, K. (2010), 'Research commentary – The new organizing logic of digital innovation: An agenda for information systems research', *Information Systems Research*, 21(4): 724–735, doi: 10.1287/isre.1100.0322.

Young, K. S. (1998), 'Internet addiction: The emergence of a new clinical disorder', *CyberPsychology and Behavior*, 1(3): 237–244, doi: 10.1089/cpb.1998.1.237.

Young, K. S. and de Abreu, C. N. (eds) (2010), *Internet addiction: A handbook and guide to evaluation and treatment*, London: John Wiley and Sons.

Yu, D. and Hang, C. C. (2010), 'A reflective review of disruptive innovation theory', *International Journal of Management Reviews*, 12(4): 435–452, doi: 10.1111/j.1468-2370.2009.00272.x.

Yu, Z. and Alex, R. (2014), 'A share learning framework for innovation education: Improving creative thinking capability from daily life', *Procedia Computer Science*, 31: 359–368, doi: 10.1016/j.procs.2014.05.279.

Yuan, Y., Xiansong, L. and Chenxia, S. (2018), 'Cost-effective heuristics for workflow scheduling in grid computing economy', *IEEE Xplore*, p. 322.

Zalewski, K. (2014), 'Low is more? User-oriented innovation in low-tech architecture', *SGEM 2014 Scientific SubConference on Arts, Performing Arts, Architecture and Design*, doi: 10.5593/sgemsocial2014/b41/s15.095.

Zeitz, G. (1980), 'Interorganizational dialectics', *Administrative Science Quarterly*, 25(1), doi: 10.2307/2392227.

Zhao, S., Grasmuck, S. and Martin, J. (2008), 'Identity construction on Facebook: Digital empowerment in anchored relationships', *Computers in Human Behavior*, 24(5): 1816–1836.

Zhao, X. and Lindley, S. E. (2014), 'Curation through use: Understanding the personal value of social media', *Proceedings of the 32nd Annual ACM Conference on Human Factors in Computing Systems – CHI '14*, doi: 10.1145/2556288.2557291.

Zhao, Y. (2012), *World class learners: Educating creative and entrepreneurial students*, Thousand Oaks, CA: Corwin Press.

Zilczer, J. (1987), '"Color music": Synaesthesia and nineteenth-century sources for abstract art', *Artibus et Historiae*, 8(16), doi: 10.2307/1483303.

Zimmer, M. (2010), '"But the data is already public": on the ethics of research in Facebook', *Ethics and Information Technology*, 12(4): 313–325, doi: 10.1007/s10676-010-9227-5.

Zittrain, J. (2009), 'How to end the copyright wars', *Nature*, 457(7227): 264–265, doi: 10.1038/457264a.

Zott, C., Amit, R. and Massa, L. (2011), 'The business model: Recent developments and future research', *Journal of Management*, 37(4): 1019–1042, doi: 10.1177/0149206311406265.

Zwick, D. and Knott, D. J. (2009), 'Manufacturing customers: The database as new means of production', *Journal of Consumer Culture*, 9(2): 221–247, doi: 10.1177/1469540509104375.

Zwick, D., Bonsu, S. K. and Darmody, A. (2008), 'Putting consumers to work: "Co-creation" and new marketing governmentality', *Journal of Consumer Culture*, 8(2): 163–196, doi: 10.1177/1469540508090089.

Index

Page numbers in *italics* denote tables, those in **bold** denote figures.